Sunset

PRUNING

BY SUSAN LANG AND THE EDITORS OF SUNSET BOOKS

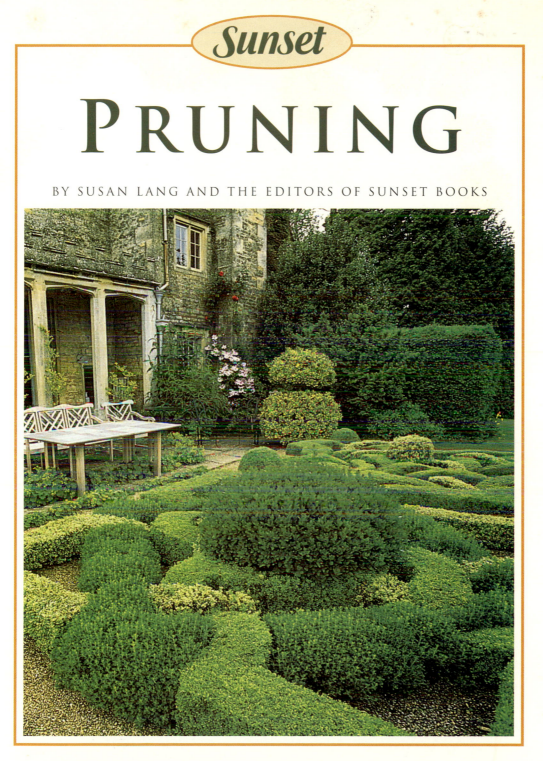

SUNSET BOOKS INC. • MENLO PARK, CALIFORNIA

CUTTING WITH CONFIDENCE

Pruning can be an enjoyable task carried out with confidence rather than a daunting, plant-mangling one, if you apply the basic information furnished in this book. You'll find that we've stressed principles throughout—in fact, the entire opening chapter and the first part of each of the subsequent chapters on trees, shrubs and hedges, vines, and edible-crop plants are devoted to them. There's a good reason for this emphasis on fundamentals: once you understand the whys and wherefores of pruning, you can figure out how to prune just about any plant, even if you lack specific pruning directions for it.

However, chances are good that you'll find explicit pruning information about most of your garden's woody plants here: the plant-by-plant guides at the end of the chapters dedicated to the various plant types contain nearly 200 listings. If your plant isn't among those cataloged, don't despair—just apply the basic principles you've learned and cut with confidence.

For their assistance in preparing this book we gratefully acknowledge the following people: Robert Kourik and Lance Walheim for reviewing the manuscript, and Philip Edinger for being on call to discuss principles and plants.

SUNSET BOOKS INC.

Director, Sales and Marketing: Richard A. Smeby
Editorial Director: Bob Doyle
Production Director: Lory Day
Art Director: Vasken Guiragossian

Staff for this book:

Managing Editor: Susan Bryant Caron
Sunset Books Senior Editor, Gardening: Suzanne Normand Eyre
Copy Editor and Indexer: Pamela A. Evans
Photo Researcher: Tishana Peebles
Production Coordinator: Patricia S. Williams
Proofreader: Claudia Blaine

Art Director: Alice Rogers
Page Layouts: Susan Bryant Caron
Illustrator: Catherine M. Watters
Additional Illustrators: Lois Lovejoy, Mimi Osborne, Wendy Smith-Griswold
Computer Production: Fog Press

Cover: Wisteria vines are rampant growers that need regular pruning to restrain them. Each dormant season cut back to several buds the lateral shoots (inner photograph) that will produce the abundant blossoms (outer photograph) in spring. Photography by Saxon Holt.

First Printing January 1998
Copyright © 1998 Sunset Books Inc., Menlo Park, CA 94025. Fourth edition. All rights reserved, including the right of reproduction in whole or in part in any form. Library of Congress Catalog Card Number: 97-80060. ISBN 0-376-03606-0.

Printed in the United States.

PHOTOGRAPHERS:

Bill Aaron: 66 right; **Marion Brenner:** 34 right, 42 center, 52 left, 101 center and right; **David Cavagnaro:** 3 left bottom, 35 left, 38 right, 41 right, 84 left, 101 left, 102, 104, 105, 120 top left, 121 top and middle right; **Peter Christiansen:** 32 top and middle left, 90 top left; **Crandall & Crandall:** 113 top and bottom; **Claire Curran:** 38 center, 74 center; **R. Todd Davis Photography, Inc.:** 46 right; **Arnaud Descat/Photo M.A.P.:** 81; **William B. Dewey:** 95 center; **Derek Fell:** 3 top right, 6 left, 7 top left and top and bottom right, 20 right and bottom, 22, 31 left and right, 35 right, 36 left, 39 left, 44 center, 47 left and top center, 51 left, 55 left and right, 56, 57, 63 third from left, 70 center, 73 right, 90 bottom left, 95 left, 96 left and right, 97 right, 98 left, 99 top left, 100 left, 111 bottom right, 112 top left and right, 114 bottom left, 115 all, 116, 118 bottom left and right, 123 second and third from top right; **Andy Freeberg:** 8 far left; **Saxon Holt:** 2, 3 left middle, 8 top right, 15 top right, 16 left and right, 18, 19, 29 left, 30 left, 37 center and right, 39 right, 40 left and top right, 42 left, 43 right, 44 right, 48, 51 top, middle, and bottom right, 54 top, 59 top left, 60, 61 top, 63 second and fourth from left, 66 left, 68 left, 71 right, 75 left, 77 left, 80, 89 left, 90 top right, 93 top, 100 center, 106, 114 top left and right, 117, 119 left and bottom right, 122 center and right, back cover bottom left; **Horticultural Photography:** 8 bottom left and right, 110 top and bottom left, 118 top left, 119 top and middle right, 123 first and fourth from top, 125 all; **Arthur Lee Jacobson/Photo Garden:** 24 left, 29 bottom right, 32 bottom left, 34 center, 36 center, 37 left, 39 center, 40 bottom right, 42 right, 45 left and right, 47 right and bottom center; **Kirsten Leitner, Friends of the Urban Forest photo file:** 33 left and right; **Allan Mandell:** 68 right, 78 center; **Charles Mann:** 14 bottom, 36 top and bottom right, 43 left, 46 left, 53 bottom right, 64 top, 69 right, 71 left, 75 center, 83 left, 85 right, 94 center, 95 right, 98 right, 99 right; **Jim McCausland:** 51 bottom center; **David McDonald/Photo Garden:** 24 right, 38 left, 54 bottom; **Jack McDowell:** 59 right, 67 center, 118 top right; **N. and P. Mioulane/Photo M.A.P.:** 91; **Allan Mitchell:** 52 right; **Don Normark:** 10 right; **Jerry Pavia:** 1, 8 top left, 14 top, 50 top left, 53 top right, 54 middle, 59 bottom left, 63 first from left, 65 right, 72 left, 76 right, 77 center, 78 left, 79 right, 82 left, 83 right, 84 right, 88, 93 bottom, 96 center, 97 center, 110 right, back cover right; **Norman A. Plate:** 32 bottom left, 70 left, 98 center, 109 all, 111 top right; **Susan A. Roth:** 3 right middle, 13, 29 top right, 41 left and center, 50 bottom left, 61 bottom, 64 bottom, 69 center, 74 left, 77 right, 86, 122 left, back cover top left; **Chad Slattery:** 53 top left; **Michael S. Thompson:** 3 top left, 4, 7 bottom left, 10 left, 12, 15 bottom right, 20 top left, 21, 25 bottom, 28, 30 right, 32 top right, 35 center, 50 top right, 65 center, 66 center, 67 left, 68 center, 71 center, 73 left, 76 left, 79 left, 82 right, 85 left, 89 right, 94 right, 99 bottom left, 111 left, 112 bottom left and right, 114 bottom right, 120 bottom left and right, 121 left, 123 top and bottom left; **Darrow M. Watt:** 25 top; **Russ Widstrand:** 108 all; **Martha Woodward:** 92 left and right; **Tom Woodward:** 72 right; **Cynthia Woodyard:** 15 bottom left, 44 left, 46 center; **Tom Wyatt:** 121 bottom right, **Linda Younker:** 6 right

CONTENTS

THE ABCs OF
PRUNING

If you've ever cringed at the sight of a butchered tree or gaped at a yardful of shrubby "gumdrops," you know the value of a garden filled with attractive, well-shaped, and healthy plants. Such a landscape will provide untold pleasure and can even increase the actual worth of your property. By pruning wisely and carefully, you can enjoy these benefits.

Though the prospect of pruning can be intimidating, it won't be if you come properly equipped—not only with shears and saw, but also with some basic knowledge about the whys, wheres, whens, and hows of pruning. The more you know, the more confident you will be when you prune—and the greater your chances of success.

Use the information in this book to guide yourself through the pruning process. In this chapter you'll learn the reasons for pruning, how pruning affects plants, the best times to prune, the various types of cuts, how to tackle a plant, and the equipment you'll need. There are even tips on hiring skilled professionals for certain jobs best left to experts, such as removing high tree limbs.

The subsequent chapters provide additional information about pruning the various categories of woody plants: ornamental trees, shrubs and hedges, vines, and plants grown for their fruit. Each chapter also contains instructions for pruning a selection of specific plants within that category.

Healthy, well-shaped plants set off a house beautifully.

Climbing roses, like these trained on an arbor, must be pruned regularly to yield a spectacular flower display.

REASONS TO PRUNE

Perhaps the best definition of good pruning is "removing plant parts for a beneficial purpose." Usually pruning benefits the plant by improving its health. Sometimes it benefits people, too—for example, by saving them from being smacked in the face by a thorny branch or allowing them to sit under what was previously a low-branching tree.

Although you may prune frequently, pruning isn't a routine gardening task. You don't cut back shrubs and trees simply because it's "the pruning season." You don't even trim them all periodically, in the same way that you might water or feed them on a regular basis. How much and how often you prune (or whether you prune at all) depends on each plant and its individual needs. Some plants require heavy pruning annually if they are to produce good flowers or fruit. Others need occasional light shaping. Still others do well with little or no pruning.

If you want to know the proper way to prune but aren't keen on making pruning a full-time occupation, you must ascertain a plant's growth habits before you invite it into your garden. Choose plants with few demands, allow them to assume their natural forms, and step back to enjoy them. If, on the other hand, you discover that you can't get enough of pruning, you'll be happy tending high-maintenance plantings such as an orchard or a rose garden.

Whether you will prune just a little or a lot, you'll need some technical information to do the job right. But before delving into the specifics of how, where, and when to cut, consider the most basic point: the *why* of pruning. The following are among the many sound motives for pruning.

TO DIRECT GROWTH. Every time you make a pruning cut or pinch off the tip of a stem, you stop growth in one direction and encourage it in another. (To learn why this happens, see page 9.) This principle is especially important to consider when training young trees to develop a strong branching structure or when encouraging any plant to assume a desirable shape.

TO REMOVE UNDESIRABLE GROWTH. Suckers are a common type of objectionable growth, and water sprouts can be, as well; see page 15 for more about these vigorous shoots. Other unwelcome kinds of growth are wayward shoots—that is, unruly or misdirected growth—and leafy branches that revert back to green on a shrub with variegated foliage.

TO INFLUENCE FLOWER AND FRUIT PRODUCTION. By pruning in certain ways, you can induce plants to yield better flowers or fruit—and sometimes more of them as well. For example, plants that bloom and bear fruit on new wood will produce a better-quality harvest if they are pruned just before the start of the growing season.

TO EMPHASIZE AN ATTRACTIVE FEATURE. Excess leafy or twiggy growth can hide handsome bark; to reveal it, remove some lower limbs and thin out crowded branches. Thinning a crown will also accentuate a picturesque branching pattern. On plants that produce brightly colored winter bark, notably red- and yellow-stemmed dogwoods *(Cornus)* and willows *(Salix)*,

This Japanese maple *(Acer palmatum)* is pruned only to emphasize its wonderfully gnarled habit.

the youngest growth is usually the most vivid. Severely cutting back these plants each year will produce new shoots and ensure a good show.

TO PROMOTE PLANT HEALTH. Your plants will be healthier when rid of deleterious growth—dead, damaged, rubbing, diseased, and pest-ridden branches. If overly dense growth is blocking sunlight and air to a plant's inner and lower leaves, you can remedy the situation by thinning out the branches. Some plants grow vigorous stems for just a few years and then weaken. To keep these plants robust, you must frequently remove older stems to direct energy toward new growth.

TO PREVENT OR REPAIR DAMAGE. Strong winds, lightning, snow, and ice can all damage trees and shrubs. Thin out growth on susceptible plants—those with brittle wood, for example—to lessen the chance of weather damage. If branches do break on shrubs or small trees, you can prune them to remove the broken parts. If large trees are involved, be sure to leave this aspect of pruning to a professional (see page 21).

TO MAINTAIN SAFETY. Split or broken branches can come crashing down on the house, low-hanging limbs can impede traffic, and spiny branches protruding into a walkway can scratch passersby. Such growth should be removed before it has a chance to inflict harm.

TOP: Older stems of tatarian dogwood *(Cornus alba)* should be cut to the ground yearly to encourage new shoots, which show the brightest color.

BOTTOM: Most fruit trees need regular pruning to produce bumper crops of high-quality, good-size fruit.

A portal has been incorporated into a European beech *(Fagus sylvatica)* hedge.

TO ACHIEVE AN ARTIFICIAL FORM. Plants may sometimes be sculpted into shapes that are foreign to their nature but that nevertheless can be pleasing to the human eye. Formal hedges are one familiar example of this kind of pruning. Other artificial but decorative pruning forms include the arts of bonsai (page 30), espalier (pages 116–117), and topiary (page 55).

TO ALTER OR REJUVENATE. Pruning may allow you to rescue neglected plants. One way to alter an overgrown shrub, for instance, is to remove the lower limbs, transforming it into a multitrunked small tree. You can sometimes rejuvenate old or stagnating plants by cutting them back to a framework of limbs or, in certain cases, by lopping them to within a few inches of the ground. Typically this shock treatment either kills the plant or causes it to grow vigorously.

Picking this lilac *(Syringa)* bouquet is a form of pruning.

TO OBTAIN DECORATIVE MATERIAL. You may not think you're pruning, but that's what you're doing every time you cut branches of flowers, fruit, or foliage for bouquets, wreaths, or holiday decorations—or when you snip budded branches to force their bloom indoors. At such times it's important to follow pruning guidelines about where and how to cut.

TO SERVE A SPECIAL NEED. Perhaps you want to remove some of a tree's lower limbs to accommodate other plants or a seating area. Or your goal may be to reduce the amount of shade in your garden by thinning the branches in a shrub border. Just be sure that you don't sacrifice a plant's health or beauty in fulfilling your needs.

EXPERTS REVISE THE RULES

Experts used to recommend trimming the mass of foliage on a tree or shrub when transplanting, to compensate for the inevitable loss of roots during that procedure. This is no longer considered good practice, because removing top growth actually slows down root regeneration. Prune the foliage, if you have reason to do so, only after the plant is well rooted and has produced new top growth. When transplanting remove only dead, diseased, rubbing, or broken branches.

Choosing appropriate plants lessens the need to prune. Tight boxwood *(Buxus)* hedges flanking a narrow path (top left) are confining, but complement a wider walk (top right). A large rhododendron variety obscures the window (bottom left), whereas a smaller variety makes an ideal foundation planting (bottom right).

WHAT ABOUT PRUNING TO LIMIT SIZE?

There are times when you'll use your shears or pruning saw to restrain a plant—most notably, in cutting back many types of fruit trees to keep them at a convenient size for harvesting and to prevent them from sending up too much top growth that will shade lower branches. Generally, though, it shouldn't be necessary to curtail plants to make them fit the space allocated to them. If you have to force a tree or shrub to mind its place, you have the wrong plant in the spot. Repeated cutting back only destroys the plant's natural form—and makes more work for you.

You can reduce the amount of pruning required simply by choosing an appropriate plant for the location. If you inherit someone else's mistake, consider whether replacing the plant will suit you better in the long run than having to clip constantly. If you decide to live with the ever-increasing plant, don't fertilize it—additional nutrients will only spur its growth.

Before deciding on a plant, find out what size you'll be dealing with in 5, 10, or 15 years. Ask at the nursery how much space to allot—the typical height and width the plant will attain in your area. Those cute little plants in their nursery pots can deceive! If you're told that you can always prune the plant if it gets too big, you should probably shop elsewhere, or at least deal with a more knowledgeable person at that nursery.

Knowing the mature shape of a plant is equally important, because young nursery specimens often give no hint of their adult appearance. If you want a screening plant for a narrow space, make sure you get one with an upright habit and not one that spreads widely in maturity. Pruning to force a plant to accommodate a spot is like trying to fit a square peg into a round hole.

Poorly chosen foundation specimens are probably the most glaring example of the wrong plant in the wrong place. Who hasn't seen overgrown foundation plants billowing out into walkways, obscuring windows, and hitting the eaves? Put a low-growing or dwarf shrub under a window and enjoy a view other than foliage pressing against glass.

WHAT HAPPENS WHEN YOU PRUNE?

It may seem like a simple matter: a shoot sticks out too far, so you snip it off at a point level with the top of the plant. But you didn't solve the problem, because soon there's a candelabra of shoots sticking out even farther. No, nothing went wrong—in fact, the plant's reaction to that cut was predictable. To prune effectively (and avoid such unwelcome outcomes), you must absorb a few basic facts about how plants grow and how they respond to pruning cuts.

Think of a plant's stems (usually called the trunk, branches, shoots, and twigs on a woody plant) as a network of conveying tubes. These tubes carry water and dissolved minerals up from the roots to the growing points (buds, leaves, and flowers); they also transport sugars manufactured by the leaves down to the roots.

The effect of cutting off a stem is to stop growth in that direction and divert the flow of materials to other conveying tubes. Removing many stems actually invigorates a plant (unless you remove more than a particular plant can handle), because the root system is now serving a smaller superstructure.

Where the diverted flow of materials (and any resulting new growth) goes depends on where you make the cut. If you have ever pruned without really knowing what you were doing, you know there are plenty of choices. You can cut off a whole branch or just part of it, either randomly or at some definable point such as a leaf.

Once you know the effect of cutting at various points, you'll be able to prune more confidently and with a greater sense of purpose. With your pruning tools you can guide the shape or productivity of a plant by intentionally shutting down growth in certain directions and encouraging it in others.

GROWTH BUDS

To know where to cut, you have to learn about growth buds—because when you prune, you are really manipulating those buds. Following are the growth buds to be aware of as you work. It will take some practice, but you will learn to distinguish them from flower buds, which tend to be fatter.

The *terminal bud* grows at the tip of a shoot, causing that shoot to grow in length. Actively growing terminal buds produce hormones that move down the stem and inhibit the growth of other buds on that shoot. This phenomenon is called apical dominance (see page 10). Each year when a terminal bud begins to grow, it leaves a bud scale scar, a group of concentric lines around the branch. (You can count these groups of scars to determine how old the branch is.)

Lateral buds grow along the sides of the shoot at leaf attachment points, or nodes: one to three buds may appear at each node. These buds produce the sideways growth that makes a plant bushy. But a lateral bud doesn't form a branch right away. It remains dormant until the growing tip has grown far enough from it for apical dominance to diminish—or until the terminal bud is removed, accidentally or by pruning.

Two other types of buds may develop and grow into shoots under certain circumstances. *Latent buds* lie persistently dormant beneath the bark of many plants. If a branch breaks or is cut off near a latent bud, that bud may develop into a new shoot. Buds that develop where none previously existed—not even in dormancy—are called *adventitious buds*. They may grow after a branch is wounded or pruned improperly, leaving a stub, or section of branch, too far from a growing point. Unlike growth resulting from other buds, growth from these buds is weakly attached and may snap off in a storm.

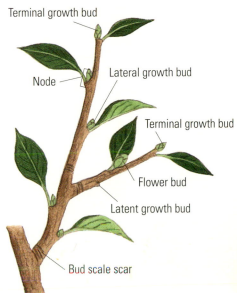

Terminal growth bud

Node

Lateral growth bud

Terminal growth bud

Flower bud

Latent growth bud

Bud scale scar

DIRECTING GROWTH

On a young branched stem, pinch off the side shoots to direct growth upward (left), or pinch off the terminal growth to cause side shoots to lengthen (right).

On an unbranched stem or shoot, remove terminal growth (left) to stimulate buds below the cut to grow (right).

APICAL DOMINANCE

The degree of apical dominance—the suppression of lateral growth brought about by a hormone in the terminal bud—varies among different types of plants. The strongest hormonal control is evident in naturally tall, narrow plants with a single upright leader and few or short side branches, such as fir *(Abies)* and spruce *(Picea)* trees. In other, less markedly vertical plants such as elms *(Ulmus)* and willows, the inhibition is weaker, resulting in a fuller, more densely branched habit.

Columnar aspen
(Populus)

Your life will be easier if you respect a plant's natural inclination. For example, a wide-canopied tree will never have the cone shape of a fir tree, no matter how much you try to shape it. On the other hand, you can cause a fir tree to branch more widely by removing its growth tip and releasing lateral buds from their inhibition—but you'll also ruin the shape of the plant. If the top is accidentally lopped off while the tree is young, you may be able to train another upright shoot to take over the role of leader and reestablish strong apical control.

The dominance of the terminal bud is evident not only in the leader but also in branches throughout a plant (though again, the relative strength or weakness of control depends on the plant species). Terminal buds on upright shoots exert the most influence; their power diminishes as branch angles become increasingly horizontal. You can even "break" apical dominance by moving an erect branch into a horizontal position. In fact, this forcing of horizontal growth is sometimes used on fruit espaliers, because branches gradually moved into that position are more likely to develop flower buds (and thus fruit).

When you remove the terminal bud by cutting back to a lateral bud (or a node), you are "breaking" apical dominance. The result is a flush of new growth from buds just beneath that point. When you cut back to another branch, you are removing all the buds that might have grown. The plant's energy is thus directed to the remaining branches. As explained below, you use this knowledge when you opt for a thinning cut instead of a heading cut, for example.

THE FOUR BASIC PRUNING CUTS

Most pruning involves four basic techniques: thinning, heading, shearing, and pinching. What sets them apart from each other is where you cut in relation to growth buds and side branches. As explained in the following descriptions, each cut has a specific goal, though you will sometimes use more than one technique in pruning a plant. Always keep in mind that, except for shearing, cuts should be made just above a growing point.

THINNING

To thin, you remove an entire stem or branch, either back to its point of origin or to its junction with another branch. You might cut a branch back to the trunk, to the parent branch from which it arose, or—in the case of plants that send up stems directly from the roots—all the way to the ground. If you cut back to a smaller branch at a branch junction, be sure that the branch is at least one-third in diameter of the one you're removing; otherwise, it will be too small to assume the terminal role, and the effect will be more like a heading cut (see following discussion).

When you remove a branch, you're also removing the buds on that branch. Thinning cuts can cause bud growth elsewhere on the plant, but you are much less likely to stimulate clusters of unwanted shoots than you are when you make heading cuts. Thinning therefore lets you reduce the bulk of a plant with minimal regrowth.

The majority of cuts you make on woody plants should be thinning cuts. Use this technique to direct growth, eliminate competing stems, reduce overall size (see "Crown Reduction" on pages 32–33), remove old and unproductive stems, or open up a plant so that more sunlight and air can reach its interior.

This graceful flowering cherry *(Prunus serrulata)* receives only periodic thinning, but the low hedges and topiary are sheared at least twice during the growing season.

HEADING

In heading, you remove just part of a stem or branch—not all of it, as you do in thinning. A heading cut can be back to a bud, or it can be to a twig or a branch too small to take over the terminal role (less than one-third in diameter of the one you're removing). This type of cut stimulates buds just below the cut to grow. Shearing and pinching (see discussions below) are other forms of heading.

Heading is a less desirable technique than thinning for maintenance pruning of most woody plants. The immediate result of heading is a smaller, more compact plant—but it does not stay that way for long. Once headed, the plant will put out vigorous new growth. If you head instead of thin a wayward shoot, you can expect a candelabra of shoots to grow in its place. Continual heading ruins the natural shape of most woody plants, and it can create such crowded branching that the interior of the plant dies out.

Heading is useful, however, in certain cases when you want vigorous growth beneath the cut. These instances include forcing shoots to branch at desired locations, stimulating new shoots to fill a hole in a tree's crown, training young fruit trees, pruning rosebushes for flower production, and rejuvenating old or neglected shrubs.

SHEARING

Shearing is an indiscriminate form of heading. Ignoring all advice about cutting just above a growing point, you clip the outer foliage of the plant to create an even surface. However, because the plants best suited to shearing have buds and branches close together on their stems, actually every cut is made near a growing point. Shearing locks you into high maintenance, as it promotes new growth that spoils the uniformity unless it is clipped again.

This technique should be used sparingly, mainly for pruning formal hedges and topiary. As shearing mangles large leaves, it's best to confine it to small-leaved plants. You may also want to shear the tops of some small shrubs that become woody and floppy with age, such as lavender *(Lavandula)* and santolina, to encourage compact new growth. Some people routinely shear all their landscape plants in the mistaken belief that it is the correct way to prune. The result is a landscape filled with look-alike, lollipopped plants that need regular haircuts.

PINCHING

This is the simplest, most basic pruning technique. Using your thumb and forefinger, or your hand shears, you nip off the tips of new growth. Removing the terminal bud stops the shoot from growing longer and thus stimulates branching. Pinching is done mostly to annuals and perennials to make them bushy and encourage more flowers, but some shrubs and vines also benefit from pinching.

TYPES OF PRUNING CUTS

THINNING

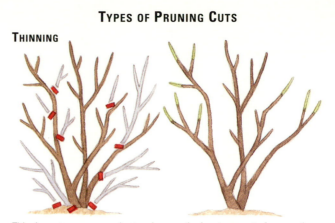

Thinning cuts open up a plant and cause the least amount of regrowth.

HEADING

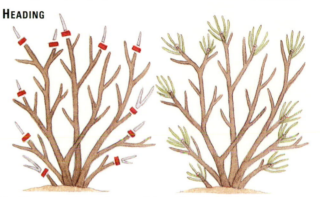

Heading cuts produce a clusters of shoots from buds below the cuts.

SHEARING

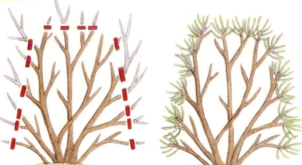

Shearing, which is really random heading, produces an outer layer of dense, twiggy growth from buds below the cuts.

Shown here are three types of pruning cuts: pinching removes the terminal growth; heading removes part of the shoot; and thinning eliminates the entire shoot.

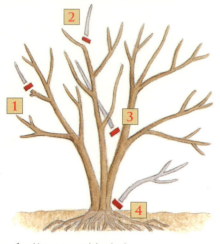

1 Above a promising bud

2 Above a promising side branch

3 To a main branch or the trunk

4 To the ground (on plants that send up
stems from the roots)

CUTTING ABOVE A BUD

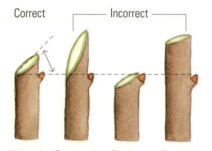

Correct — Incorrect —

45° angle   Too angular   Too low   Too high

POSITIONING PRUNING SHEARS

Blade

Cutting edge

Hook

To make a proper close pruning cut, hold the
pruning shears with the blade closer to the
growth that will remain on the plant. A stub
results when you reverse the position and
place the hook closer to the plant.

MAKING THE CUT

Proper pruning calls for cutting back to a part that will continue to grow—to the trunk,
to another branch, to a bud, or even to the ground, in the case of shrubs that send up
new stems from the roots. At these points of active growth, callus tissue will start to grow
inward from cells at the end of the cut; in time the wound will seal off.

Because clean cuts callus over faster than ragged
ones do, always use an appropriate, well-sharpened
pruning tool (see the section beginning on page 16).
Never force a tool to cut a bigger branch than it is
designed to handle. And remember, you can use your
fingers to pinch tip growth, but never to snap or
break off twigs or small branches.

The placement of a cut is crucial. If you cut too
close to a bud, or make a flush cut at a branch base,
you can cause injury. If you cut too far away from a
bud, you leave a stub. No longer part of the plant's
active metabolism, the stub withers and dies, though
still attached to the plant. In time it will decay and
drop off, leaving an open patch of dead tissue where
it was attached.

Pruning stubs and damaged bark won't
callus over properly.

When using hand shears or loppers with a
hook-and-blade design, be careful how you position
them to cut. The blade should be next to the stem or branch that will remain on the
plant. If the hook is next to it, you'll leave a small stub. You may have to turn the pruners
upside down to position them correctly.

When cutting back to a bud, look for a healthy specimen pointing in the direction
you want the new shoot to grow. A proper cut will be about ¼ inch above the bud, slop-
ing away at approximately a 45° angle. The lowest point of the cut should be opposite the
bud and even with it; the cut should slant upward in the direction the bud is pointing.

When removing a branch, avoid making a flush cut. Position your shears or saw
just outside the branch collar (the wrinkled area or bulge at the base of a branch where
it meets another branch or the trunk). Also refrain from cutting into the branch bark
ridge (the raised bark in the branch crotch). Leaving these areas intact keeps decay to a
minimum; see page 26 for more information.

WHEN TO PRUNE

Rather than prune all your plants at one time convenient for you, do it when it's best for
each plant species. You might think that certain types of plants, such as fruit trees or
evergreen shrubs, would all be pruned on the same schedule, but that's not the case. In
fact, you can't assume that all species within a genus (a related group of species) have
the same recommended pruning time. The various clematis, hydrangea, and spiraea
species, for example, are pruned differently according to when they bloom.

Still, some generalizations about timing hold true. These will make sense once you
know a little about plant metabolism. When you snip off a leafy branch, you're removing
part of the plant's food-making capacity. Plants have the unique ability to take in carbon
dioxide and water and, in the presence of sunlight, convert them into sugars to fuel their
own growth. This process, called photosynthesis, takes place in leaves and other green
parts of plants. A plant produces food most actively in summer. Sugars are stored in the
leaves by the end of summer; in winter, they move into the woody stems and roots,
where they remain until needed to fuel spring growth.

WHAT ABOUT THE WOUND?

Just as your own skin forms a protective scab when cut, a plant responds to a wound by callusing over—forming a thickened tissue that seals off the wound. If the cut is made too far from a growing point, the stub that is left usually dies back first, delaying the callusing process.

As you would expect, smaller wounds seal more quickly than bigger ones do. The U.S. Forest Service therefore offers this valuable advice: Think twice about removing branches larger than approximately 2 inches in diameter, and have a really good reason for removing anything bigger than about 4 inches across.

When pruning off a branch, be careful not to cut into the branch bark ridge or branch collar (see page 26); these areas contain tissue from adjoining limbs, so cutting there creates a more widespread wound and leaves more of the plant open to infection.

Applying a wound paint used to be standard practice, but experts now say there is no need to treat the wound. Just make a good pruning cut and leave the rest to the plant. If you want to paint a wound for strictly cosmetic reasons, use only a thin coat of a water-based material. Products with an oil or asphalt base actually slow callusing and can promote decay.

You must be careful not to deplete a plant of either the foliage it needs to produce the sugars or the stored sugars themselves. Generally, the worst time to prune is right after the flush of spring growth. You're removing the new foliage, which has been fueled by stored sugars, before the plant has a chance to manufacture more sugars. The result is a weakened or stunted plant.

For most plants, pruning just before the start of the growing season encourages vigorous new growth. A significant amount of the stored sugars have moved into the root system and will be unaffected by pruning. This is definitely the right time to prune plants that bloom on growth formed in the current growing sea-

Prune 'Winter King' green hawthorn *(Crataegus viridis)* late in the dormant season, after its fruit display ends.

son. On the other hand, it's the wrong time to prune plants that form flower buds on the prior season's wood for bloom in spring—you'd be cutting off the buds before they blossomed.

Pruning in summer, when growth has slowed, can be beneficial if the plants to be pruned are healthy and the climate suitable. This is a good time to thin out excess growth on plants; thinning fruit trees then will expose the developing fruits to more sunlight and improve their color. Vigorous shoots, such as suckers and water sprouts, are less likely to regrow if removed in summer. It doesn't follow that you can control the overall growth of vigorous plants just by pruning in summer; however, pruning both in summer and again in the dormant season will curb most plants. In cold-winter areas, don't wait too late in summer (quit pruning within a month of the first fall frost date) nor prune too heavily. (For more on summer pruning, see page 109.)

A little minor pruning at the wrong time won't harm a plant, but habitual cutting in the wrong season can cause serious injury. Be especially aware of timing when tackling major pruning. A propitious time to prune is while the plant is dormant (not actively growing) and has a good supply of stored sugars, but when temperatures are not too cold and the danger of heavy freezes has diminished.

Generally, deciduous plants native to temperate regions drop their leaves and become dormant from late fall to late winter or early spring. The duration of dormancy varies according to species; some drop their leaves earlier than others, and some leaf out later. (Note that deciduous plants from subtropical and tropical regions may become dormant at times other than winter.) Although evergreen plants keep their leaves, they typically slow down growth to a level approaching dormancy during the coldest time of year (again, species native to mild or tropical regions may do so at other times). How a semievergreen plant behaves depends on where it is grown; it tends to be evergreen in mild winters and deciduous in colder ones. Close, year-round observation of your plants is your best guide to their individual periods of dormancy.

For a good flower show, prune according to when the plant blooms. The majority of woody plants produce flowers early in the growing season on the prior year's wood; they should be pruned after they bloom (or within a month after the show ends). A smaller number bear their blossoms later in the growing season on the current season's growth; prune them before spring growth begins. Observe your plants to see whether they bloom on old or new wood—note that older branches are usually darker, less pliable, and woodier looking than the new growth.

Here are examples of both types of plants.

PRUNE AFTER FLOWERING

Buddleia alternifolia (Fountain butterfly bush)

Chaenomeles (Flowering quince)

Spiraea prunifolia

Clematis montana (Anemone clematis)

Deutzia

Exochorda (Pearl bush)

Forsythia

Gelsemium sempervirens (Carolina jessamine)

Hamamelis (Witch hazel)

Hydrangea macrophylla (Bigleaf hydrangea)

Jasminum (Jasmine)

Kalmia latifolia (Mountain laurel)

Kerria japonica (Japanese kerria)

Laburnum (Goldenchain tree)

Magnolia × soulangiana (Saucer magnolia)

Philadelphus (Mock orange)

Rosa (Spring-blooming climbing roses)

Spiraea (Bridal wreath spiraeas)

Syringa (Lilac, most species)

Weigela

PRUNE BEFORE SPRING GROWTH BEGINS

Buddleia davidii (Common butterfly bush)

Callicarpa (Beautyberry)

Spiraea × bumalda 'Goldflame'

Clematis × jackmanii (Jackman clematis)

Hibiscus syriacus (Rose of Sharon)

Hydrangea anomala petiolaris (Climbing hydrangea)

Lagerstroemia (Crape myrtle)

Rosa (Hybrid tea, grandiflora, and floribunda roses)

Spiraea (Shrubby spiraeas)

Syringa villosa (Late lilac)

Vitex (Chaste tree)

You'll appreciate two advantages to doing a major overhaul of a deciduous plant during dormancy: the structure is easy to see, and there will be less material to clean up.

Other factors may affect your pruning schedule. If an insect pest or plant disease is a problem in your area at a particular time of year, avoid pruning susceptible plants then. Too, always prune during dry weather; this is especially important in fall and spring, when many plant diseases are easily transmitted by splashing water.

For more information on when to prune the various types of woody plants, see the subsequent chapters of this book.

HOW TO BEGIN

First, be sure you have a solid reason to prune before you proceed; see page 6. Once you're sure that pruning is the right action, formulate a plan. Study the plant from all sides to estimate how much and what kind of pruning it needs before you make any cuts. You'll find it helpful to have read the relevant chapter in this book to obtain some general pruning information for that plant category; also see if your plant is listed in the encyclopedia section of that chapter.

REMOVING THE THREE DS

Begin any pruning job by getting rid of the three Ds—dead, damaged, and dysfunctional growth. Here, a broken limb, a hanging branch, crossing branches, and water sprouts are being removed. That is all the pruning required in this case.

It's always better to underprune than overprune. With that in mind, start by removing "the three Ds"—dead, damaged, and dysfunctional growth. If you're not sure whether a stem or branch is dead, lightly scrape the bark to check for a thin green layer of cambium cells just beneath it—if you see green, the stem's alive. Damaged growth includes stems that are broken, gouged, and seriously pest ridden or diseased. Dysfunctional stems are those that impair the plant's appearance or growth: wayward branches, stems that crowd or cross through the plant's center, weak branches that hang down, suckers, and water sprouts. In many cases, this is all the pruning you'll have to do.

When more pruning is required, remember to work cautiously. For example, in thinning a plant, trace the growth you want to remove down to its base before cutting. If you just reach in and grab the branch, you may choose the wrong one. Step back often to reassess what you're doing. It's easy to get carried away, and to fail to foresee the effect on the whole plant while you're focused on one section.

HOW MUCH TO REMOVE

There's no formula—such as "remove 20 percent of the growth yearly" or "prune off 30 percent of the branches every other year"—that applies to all plants. The amount that you remove depends on the plant, your purpose in pruning, and the time of year.

Plants differ in their pruning needs—for example, rosebushes demand extensive annual pruning, whereas cotoneasters need little attention if given the room to develop naturally. Once their branching structure is established, many ornamental trees require little intervention. On the other hand, most fruit trees won't bear well unless their wood is constantly renewed through pruning.

If your goal is to rejuvenate a neglected shrub, obviously you will remove more growth than if you're maintaining a youthful, well-shaped specimen. Rejuvenation usually calls for removing a third of the old stems over 3 years. However, some plants—including forsythia, hydrangea, and privet (Ligustrum)—will rebound even after being cut to within a few inches of the ground late in the dormant season. Done during the growing season, though, such severe pruning can seriously harm or even kill plants.

Some evergreen plants—including camellia, heather (Erica), juniper, and lavender—should not be cut back to leafless wood, because they seldom resprout. Depending on your goal, you may end up removing a lot of growth from these plants, but your cuts should always be to a point where leaves are growing.

Remove any vertical growth that detracts from the graceful, layered habit of doublefile viburnum (Viburnum plicatum tomentosum).

WHAT ARE SUCKERS AND WATER SPROUTS?

Suckers and water sprouts are vigorous shoots that grow faster than other parts of the plant. Though the two are often referred to interchangeably, they are actually quite different.

Suckers are stems arising from the base of the plant or its roots. In grafted plants, such as many rosebushes and fruit trees, sucker growth comes from the understock. Because it is a different variety than the top growth, the understock will produce different flowers and fruit than the desirable plant grafted onto it. If allowed to grow unchecked, suckers can come to dominate a plant or, in the case of thicket-forming plants, colonize large patches of ground. Suckers are less likely to grow back if they are pulled off rather than cut. If the sucker originates under ground, dig the soil away from it until you expose its base; then grasp it firmly to pull it off.

Sucker

Water sprouts

Water sprouts are extravigorous, upright shoots growing higher up—on branches or along the trunk. They may be weakly attached—especially those arising after a branch is cut to a stub. Eliminate poorly placed or weak-looking water sprouts by pulling them off while they are small and flexible (they'll be less likely to come back if removed this way), or by cutting them off at their base. You can leave a well-placed water sprout to fill a hole in the crown; on a flowering or fruiting tree, you can train the young shoot to be productive by bending it away from the vertical.

REMOVING DISEASED GROWTH

Occasionally you may need to remove diseased branches to prevent the disease from spreading. Depending on where you live and the plants you grow, you may encounter anthracnose, canker and rots, fireblight, or twig blight.

Some diseases can be transferred if a pruning tool's blade touches a diseased branch and then is used to cut healthy stems. To prevent this kind of transfer, remove the diseased stem at least 12 inches below obviously infected tissue; be sure to cut into healthy living tissue (look for the green cambium layer). Disinfect your shears or saw after each cut by immersing the blade in rubbing alcohol or a solution of 1 part household bleach to 9 parts water. Afterward, rinse all bleach from the blade to keep it from corroding the metal. Dispose of all the diseased prunings immediately.

Fireblight on an apple tree

DEALING WITH FREEZE DAMAGE

Freeze damage may be either obvious (blackened growth) or subtle (healthy-looking but slow-to-sprout wood). If you know your plant has sustained freeze damage, take the following steps.

First, examine the limbs for live growth buds. Withered, brown buds are dead. If you don't see live buds, choose a branch and scrape through the bark with your fingernail or a knife. If the cambium layer just under the bark is brown instead of green, that section of the branch is dead.

On a plant that's partly alive, wait until growth starts and the danger of frost is past. Then cut away all dead and damaged growth. Cut back each damaged limb until you see the green cambium layer. Be patient: some freeze-damaged plants need several months to start growing again. Even if all their top growth is killed, some plants will send up new stems from near or below the ground.

Freeze-damaged conifers drop their needles or scales. A plant that loses one-third or less should recover; remove bare twigs later when it's clear which ones are dead. A conifer that drops two-thirds or more of its needles may not live.

Tools

You don't need a big collection of pruning tools to handle every conceivable task. It's more important to have a few quality tools that you will use regularly. Most home gardeners can get along with just three basic implements: hand shears, loppers, and a pruning saw. Add hedge shears (manual or power) if you have formal hedges. If you have a lot of small trees, a pole pruner will be useful.

The rule of thumb to follow when purchasing any kind of gardening tool is to buy the best you can afford. When properly maintained, high-quality tools will work better and last longer than cheaper ones of poorer grade. Before buying, grip the tool; it should feel comfortable to handle. If you plan to sharpen hand shears or lopper blades yourself, be sure the tool is easy to take apart and reassemble.

HAND SHEARS

One-handed pruning shears are designed to remove finger-size or smaller branches (approximately ½ to ¾ inch in diameter). The two main types are hook-and-blade (bypass) pruners, which cut like scissors, and anvil pruners, which make a snap cut by pressing a straight blade against an anvil. The hook-and-blade design makes cleaner, closer cuts and is less likely to crush stems than the anvil type.

Manufacturers offer such refinements as models for left-handed people, models for smaller hands, blades with a nonstick coating, replaceable stainless steel blades, self-lubricating bearings, sap grooves (said to keep blades cleaner), ergonomic handles and grips, and one-hand-operable catches. Some pruners have a ratchet that adjusts the cutting power of the blade—when you meet resistance, a light release of pressure on the grip shifts it out another notch, giving you more leverage for the cut. These are especially useful for people of limited strength.

Because shears are easily mislaid in shrubbery or ground cover, carry them in a leather scabbard or sheath attached to your belt or pocket. You can store them in the same case.

Anvil pruners

GLOSSARY OF PRUNING TERMS

Here are some terms you'll encounter in this book.

APICAL DOMINANCE. Phenomenon in which the terminal bud (at the apex, or end, of a shoot) inhibits the growth of lateral buds on the same shoot.

ARBORIST. Specialist in pruning and other aspects of tree care. A certified arborist is an accredited member of an association such as the International Society of Arboriculture (ISA), the National Arborist Association (NAA), or the American Society of Consulting Arborists (ASCA).

BRANCH BARK RIDGE. Area of a crotch in which the growth of two adjoining limbs pushes up the bark to form a ridge.

BRANCH COLLAR. Bulge created by overlapping tissue, where a branch joins another branch or the trunk.

BROAD-LEAFED. Plants with wide leaves. Usually used in reference to broad-leafed evergreens, to distinguish them from needled evergreens, or conifers.

CALLUS. Scar tissue that forms over pruning cuts and other wounds.

CAMBIUM. Thin green layer of growth cells between a plant's wood and bark.

CROTCH. Angle formed by the junction of two branches or of a branch and the trunk.

CROWN. Upper part of a tree, including the branches and leaves. Can also refer to the point at which a plant's upper structure and roots meet.

DECIDUOUS. Any plant that sheds all its leaves annually.

DORMANCY. Period when a plant is not actively growing.

ESPALIER. Tree or shrub trained so its branches grow in a flat pattern against a wall or fence, on a trellis, or along wires.

EVERGREEN. Any plant that has leaves throughout the year.

HEADING. Removing only part of a branch by cutting back to a bud or to a branch too small in diameter to assume the terminal role, causing vigorous growth just below the cut.

INCLUDED BARK. Bark that is pushed inside a developing crotch, causing weak branch attachment.

LEADER. The primary, upward-growing stem in some woody plants.

NODE. Leaf attachment area, where lateral buds form.

PINCHING. Using thumb and forefinger to nip off shoot tips, thus forcing side growth and making the plant more compact and dense.

SCAFFOLD BRANCHES. Main branches growing from the trunk and forming the framework of a tree.

SEMIEVERGREEN. Any plant that tends to be evergreen in mild-winter areas but deciduous in colder ones.

SHEARING. Clipping the outer foliage of a plant to a uniform length to create an even surface, as in a formal hedge.

SPUR. Specialized stubby twig, found mainly on some fruit trees, where flowers and fruit form.

STUB. Tissue left when a cut is made too far beyond the proper cutting point.

SUCKER. Upright shoot arising from the roots or underground stem of a woody plant. On grafted plants, rootstock growth emerging below the graft union and bearing different flowers and fruit than the desirable plant grafted above.

THINNING. Removing an entire branch or stem to its point of origin, or to its junction with another branch that is thick enough to assume the terminal role.

TOPIARY. Tree or shrub trained and pruned into a geometric shape or whimsical figure.

TOPPING. Undesirable practice of reducing the height of a mature tree by indiscriminately cutting back the top and leaving long stubs.

WATER SPROUT. Vigorous, upright, unproductive, usually weakly attached shoot on a branch or along the trunk.

Labels: Crown, Leader, Stub, Scaffold branches, Crotch, Lateral branches, Water sprouts, Sucker

MAINTAINING YOUR TOOLS

After using shears or a saw, wipe the blade clean. Use a solvent (kerosene, for example) to clean off any sticky sap. If residue is stubborn, or is encrusted from previous neglect, remove it with steel wool. Once the cutting surface is clean, apply a thin coat of light machine oil (even baby oil or mineral oil will do) to prevent rust. Keep an oily cloth handy so that you remember to treat the blade. Unvarnished and unpainted wooden handles will remain in good condition if you rub them periodically with mineral oil. Store your pruning tools in a dry place, such as a garage or shed.

You can sharpen the blades of shears and loppers with a sharpening stone; most suppliers provide instructions along with the stone. When you buy a tool, find out whether both edges or just a single edge should be sharpened. If you'd rather not hone your own blades, take them to a professional sharpener. Sharpening saws is beyond the capability of most home gardeners—you're better off leaving it to an expert.

LOPPERS

Loppers use the same cutting action as do hand shears, but their long handles, gripped in each hand, provide added leverage. Models are available with handle lengths from about 15 inches to 3 feet. The shortest ones have little more cutting power than hand shears, but the longest ones (marketed to professionals) can slice through branches 2 inches or more in diameter. An in-between handle length—about 25 inches—is easily managed by most home gardeners yet still cuts diameters of about 1½ inches.

You face the same basic design choices with loppers as with hand shears: hook-and-blade or anvil. With the former, the hook helps hold a branch in place while the blade cuts through it. Rachet-action models are also available. Handles are made of wood, metal, or fiberglass (the last two have molded hand grips).

Hook-and-blade loppers

HEDGE SHEARS

These are two-handled shears with flat, scissorlike blades about 8 inches long, designed to cut small twigs and foliage. Hedge shears are useful for maintaining formal hedges and topiary, but generally shouldn't be used to prune other kinds of woody plants.

Handles, available in wood or metal (with hand grips), are typically 10 to 12 inches long; shears with extralong handles of 20 to 22 inches allow you to trim tall hedges while standing on the ground. Better-quality hedge shears have neoprene, rubber, or metal-spring shock absorbers to ease the strain on your hands and arms. Some models have one serrated blade that prevents branches from sliding out as you cut. Many kinds also have a limb notch that lets you cut the occasional thick branch.

For power hedge trimmers, see page 20.

AN ASSORTMENT OF PRUNING TOOLS

Hook-and-blade shears

Anvil shears

Hedge shears

Hook-and-blade loppers

Anvil loppers

PRUNING SAWS

A pruning saw is essential for cutting through branches too big for hand shears or loppers—usually this means branches of 1½ inches or more in diameter.

Curved saw

Don't force a carpenter's saw to do garden duty. Pruning saws are designed to cut easily through green, wet wood, whereas carpenter's saws are meant to handle dry wood. Many pruning saws cut on the backward, or pull, stroke instead of on the push stroke, as most carpenter's saws do. Because gravity helps you apply pressure, pull-stroke saws can make cutting overhead branches much easier.

For many years, pruning saw designs were pretty standard. Curved saws come in various sizes, some with D-shaped handles or pistol grips; these cut on the pull stroke and are good for getting into tight spots. Small folding models, held rigid by a wing nut, are convenient for carrying in a pocket, though they can unexpectedly fold while in use. Large-toothed straight saws, many of which cut on the push stroke, are designed for heavy pruning work; their big teeth make a quick but coarse cut. Both curved and straight saws come in raker models, whose teeth contain slots through which sawdust can fall, speeding the sawing. A bow-frame saw cuts quickly, on both push and pull strokes; its triangular shape makes it impractical to use among crowded branches, however.

A new type of pruning saw has fairly small teeth but cuts rapidly and can get into tight quarters. Because its teeth tend to be straight, rather than bent to the left and right as on older saws, its cuts are thinner. It is often referred to as a Japanese saw (as many models come from Japan), frictionless saw, or turbo saw. Folding models usually lock in place as a safety measure, because the blade is so sharp.

Two types of saws that you would be wise to avoid are a two-edge saw and a rope saw. In the case of the two-edge model, which has small teeth on one edge and large teeth on the other, it's difficult to saw a branch without nicking nearby limbs with the top of the blade. The rope saw uses a toothed section in the middle of a rope to cut high branches. You throw the rope over the branch and pull back and forth on the rope ends until the teeth cut all the way through. Unless you're cutting a very small branch, the severed limb usually tears a strip of bark from the parent branch as it falls.

POLE PRUNING TOOLS

Pole-mounted tools give you extra reach for cutting high branches; however, their cuts are not always clean or precise, because you're working from a distance. You can get just shears (hook-and-blade or anvil) or just a saw, or both together, mounted on a pole.

To make the shears work, you pull a cord or press a lever to draw the blade through the branch. Many models feature a beaklike hook that holds the branch in position as you cut. Most

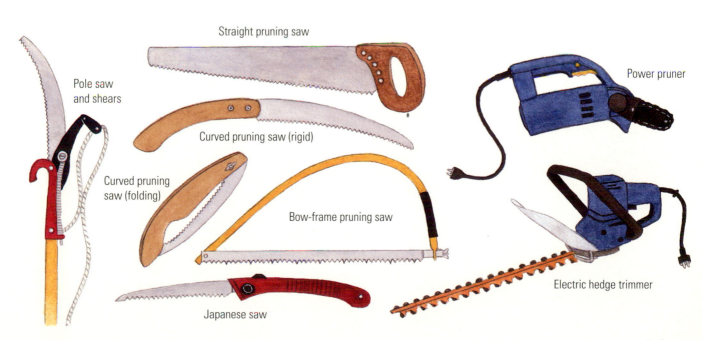

Pole saw and shears

Straight pruning saw

Curved pruning saw (rigid)

Curved pruning saw (folding)

Bow-frame pruning saw

Japanese saw

Power pruner

Electric hedge trimmer

Pole saw and shears

TOOL TIPS

❧ **Choose a suitable tool for the task. Forcing a tool to cut beyond its capability may damage both plant and tool.**

❧ **Make sure that cutting surfaces are sharp. A sharp tool is easier to operate and makes cleaner cuts than a dull one. But wear gloves: it's surprisingly easy to slash yourself with well-sharpened pruning tools.**

❧ **Be very careful when using power tools: wear protective goggles, gloves, snug-fitting clothes, and sturdy shoes or boots. Follow the manufacturer's directions when operating the tool.**

❧ **Keep electric tools away from water or wet foliage. Keep the cord behind you as you work. Plug into an outlet or adapter with a circuit breaker or ground fault circuit interrupter (GFCI) to protect you if you accidentally cut through the cord.**

Three-legged orchard ladder

pole shears will slice through limbs up to about an inch thick. Types marketed as lightweight are usually designed to cut stems about ¾ inch in diameter. The saw is usually a standard pull-cut, curved pruning saw.

Poles come in various lengths: some are telescoping, and others fit together in sections. Their materials include wood, fiberglass, and aluminum. Choose wood or fiberglass if there is any risk of making contact with utility wires, even low-voltage ones, when you prune.

POWER PRUNING TOOLS

Some home gardeners find power tools indispensable for certain pruning jobs; many others do nicely without them. You'll choose from three power options: electric, battery-operated, and gas-powered models. Electric tools are limited by the length of the extension cord. To avoid the limitations of the cord (and the danger of accidentally cutting through it), choose a battery-operated model, though it may not be as powerful as the other options and must be recharged regularly. Gas-powered tools have no cords, but they are the noisiest, heaviest option, and they can be hard to start.

HEDGE TRIMMERS. If you have an extensive hedge that you shear more than once each growing season, you'll appreciate how fast you can get the job done with a power trimmer. Models come in all three power options. Some gardeners use this type of power tool to cut the major planes of the hedge, but use manual hedge shears for careful work on corners.

Electric hedge trimmer

STANDARD CHAIN SAWS. Used by professionals to cut large tree branches, chain saws (available in all three power options) can be very hazardous when used by unskilled home gardeners. If you have a limb too big to remove with a hand saw, or if the limb is high in the tree, you're better off leaving the cut to a pro. Standard chain saws can be useful for clearing large lots, but avoid using them above chest level or climbing with them.

POWER PRUNERS. Those who want quick cutting power but are afraid to use a traditional chain saw can opt for a new category of power tool. Relatively small, lightweight power pruners are available in electric or battery-operated models. Some are tiny chain saws: one type has a 3-inch bar, capable of cutting branches up to 3 inches thick; another has a 4½-inch bar that can slice through corresponding diameters. Others are reciprocating saws, whose cutting ability is similar to that of the little chain saws. Both types also come in pole-mounted versions.

LADDERS

There are two schools of thought about pruning from a ladder. One school is in favor of it so long as caution is used; the other advises always pruning with your feet planted firmly on the ground. If you are at all unsteady on a ladder, join the second school. Otherwise, use a sturdy ladder when you need to, but set it securely on a hard, level surface and never stand above the rung recommended by the manufacturer. If you simply have no level ground, self-leveling models are available.

Most well-constructed aluminum ladders will last a lifetime, whereas wood will deteriorate in time if exposed to weather. On the other hand, though easier to carry around, aluminum's light weight makes it less stable than wood. For the very steadiest freestanding ladder, you may want to invest in a three-legged orchard ladder, available in either aluminum or wood.

HIRING A PROFESSIONAL

Even the most experienced home gardeners don't take on every pruning job themselves. Licensed, insured, professional tree care experts are best trained and equipped to handle situations such as pruning large trees, repairing major storm damage, and pruning around power lines.

Highly skilled specialists exist in most communities—as, unfortunately, do incompetent people who claim to be professional pruners. It's important to know with whom you're dealing before letting that person work on your valuable trees and shrubs. Here are some things to keep in mind when choosing a professional—and remember, hasty or uninformed decisions can be costly in the long run.

This professional pruner is secured by ropes and harness.

Be wary of people who go door to door offering bargain rates. People who claim to be expert pruners may call on you, especially after a storm. Be aware that reputable tree services seldom solicit business that way.

Look at professional pruning work done for friends or neighbors. If you like what you see (and make that judgment only after you've absorbed the basic principles of pruning), get the name of the pruner.

Consider members of a professional organization. Membership in the International Society of Arboriculture (ISA), the National Arborist Association (NAA), or the American Society of Consulting Arborists (ASCA) indicates a certain level of expertise in tree care. Nonmembers may also be qualified to do your job well, but you'll have to do more legwork to check their qualifications.

Consult other resources. The horticulture department of a local college may be able to recommend a professional pruner. If not, try the ads in the Yellow Pages (pruners are often listed under "Tree Services").

Check references when hiring someone whose work you don't know. Don't just talk to the homeowner on the telephone, but actually visit the site and look at the pruned plants.

Ask for proof of insurance. Reputable tree care specialists will have personal and property damage insurance as well as workers' compensation insurance. If it should turn out they lack coverage, you might be held responsible for any damages or injuries. Call the insurance carrier if you want to make sure the coverage is still in force.

Ask the professional how he or she intends to proceed. Be aware of bad practices, such as topping trees (recommended only in rare cases, when a tree has been severely damaged) or using climbing spikes on trees that are not being removed.

Get more than one estimate, and don't base your decision on price alone. A slapdash job will probably cost less than one properly done. Also be aware that two equally skilled services may charge different amounts simply because one has higher overhead costs.

Get it in writing. Make sure that the elements of the job and the total price are specified in writing. An hourly rate for any additional work and responsibility for cleanup should also be specified. If the job start and completion dates are important to you, have them spelled out as well.

Expect to pay only after the job is done to your satisfaction. No reputable professional pruner will ask for payment in advance.

T REES

Ornamental trees are the largest, most visible, and longest-lived plants in the landscape. They have monetary value, as your insurance company may recognize, but their greater worth resides in the beauty they confer upon their setting and in the emotions they inspire. The least we can do in return is to nurture the trees in our care by training and pruning them properly.

Early training will get trees off to a good start and help them avoid future problems. This chapter explains how to develop a sturdy structure that will serve the tree well throughout its life. Though ornamental trees don't require the routine pruning that most fruit trees do, well-informed technique is vital when there is a need to prune. For example, what once was standard practice in tree pruning—cutting flush—is no longer accepted. In this chapter you'll learn about the importance of the branch collar and the branch bark ridge and how they can guide your cuts. You'll also learn why topping trees is a bad practice, and what can be done instead to reduce height. Check the encyclopedia at the end of the chapter for specifics on pruning selected trees.

But first, a caveat about tree pruning: be especially cognizant of safety when dealing with these big, heavy-limbed plants. And remember, no matter how adept at pruning you may become, there probably will be times when you should call in a professional—for example, to remove high limbs.

Arborists have propped and cabled the endangered limbs of this valuable old oak *(Quercus)*.

TYPES OF TREES

The distinction between a tree and a large shrub is sometimes blurred, but trees typically are tall plants with one dominant trunk (though some kinds grow naturally on several) topped by a crown of foliage. Among the many tree species, silhouettes vary greatly from narrowly upright to widely spreading to weeping. Trees live the longest of all landscape plants, most thriving for many decades and some for centuries. New growth springs annually from a framework of established branches to form a gradually enlarging structure.

Two categories of trees are closely related: *deciduous* and *broad-leafed evergreen*. Most deciduous trees start their growth cycle in spring, with a burst of new leaves or flowers, and continue through summer fully clothed in foliage. The leaves often change color in fall before dropping to reveal the structure of bare limbs. Dormancy lasts until new growth begins in spring.

Obviously, though most deciduous trees also have broad leaves, the term *broad-leafed* is usually reserved for broad-leafed evergreens, to distinguish them from needle-leafed evergreens, or conifers. But all evergreens differ from their deciduous counterparts in bearing foliage year-round. Older leaves may fall intermittently or mainly in one season, but there

LEFT: Trees may alter shape as they age. This canoe or paper birch *(Betula papyrifera)*, a large deciduous tree, is pyramidal in youth but often round headed in maturity.

BELOW: Flowering dogwood *(Cornus florida)* is a small deciduous tree with a horizontally layered habit.

is always enough foliage to give the plants complete cover. Nearly all broad-leafed evergreen trees are restricted to regions with fairly mild winters.

Conifers make up the third category of trees. Their leaves are needles or tiny scales. Most of these trees—including the many species of pine *(Pinus)*, spruce *(Picea)*, fir *(Abies)*, and cedar *(Cedrus)*—are evergreen. In fact, in cold-winter climates these plants are usually what is meant by "evergreen" because they're the only evergreen trees around. The few deciduous conifers include larch *(Larix)*, bald cypress *(Taxodium distichum)*, and dawn redwood *(Metasequoia glyptostroboides)*. All conifers produce cones, though on some species the seed-bearing structures look more like berries than they do the more typical scaly cones.

COMMON TREE SHAPES

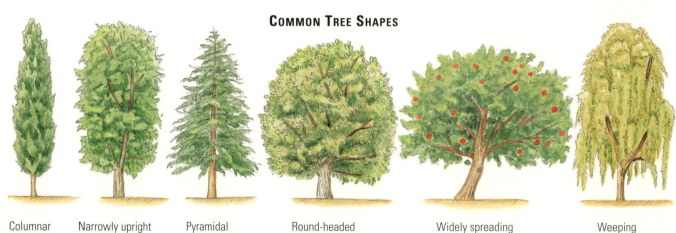

Columnar   Narrowly upright   Pyramidal   Round-headed   Widely spreading   Weeping

Obviously, you should choose a tree well adapted to your climate and growing conditions—but also make sure it won't exceed a suitable size and shape, so that you (or future owners) won't have to prune regularly to keep it in bounds. Ascertain not only how tall the tree typically grows in your area, but also how wide—and keep in mind that a tree's root system usually extends one and a half times (in clay soil) to three times (in sandy soil) the diameter of the crown. Decide which particular shape will best serve your needs—for example, an upright crown to fit a confined area or a spreading canopy for shade.

In a region with regular high winds or consistent annual snowfall, avoid trees described as having weak or brittle wood, such as silver maple *(Acer saccharinum)*, Siberian elm *(Ulmus pumila)*, willow *(Salix)*, ash *(Fraxinus)*, tulip tree *(Liriodendron tulipifera)*, and yellow wood *(Cladrastis lutea)*. Not only can such trees pose a hazard to people and property, but key limbs shorn off may ruin the tree's beauty—and removal may be expensive if you have to call in a professional.

Landscape trees are typically sold as branched specimens 2 and 3 years old. You can also buy larger, more expensive trees, but there are good reasons to choose young trees: they will establish more easily and you'll be able to shape them as desired.

Training a tree is easier when you start out with good material. Nurseries usually stock at least several examples of each species or variety they sell. Try to find one with branches originating at different heights on the trunk and radiating in different directions. Look for good wide-angled branch attachments; among the naturally narrow-angled species, choose the tree with the best angles. A tapered trunk is also desirable. Forgo any tree with a forked leader near the ground or with large circling roots visible at its base.

When choosing your tree, also watch for signs of poor pruning. Some growers top young trees and allow multiple leaders to grow from a cluster of buds just under the cut; these branches look like splayed fingers on a hand. With its small crown atop a young trunk, such a tree may appealingly resemble a miniature version of a mature specimen, but its branching structure is weak. Don't buy any trees with recent large pruning wounds. Also pass up any with obvious flush cuts; sometimes a nursery will remove branch collars (see more about the importance of these on page 26) to give the trunk a "nice, smooth" appearance.

This choice sycamore *(Platanus),* at center, has a sturdy, straight trunk and well-spaced limbs—unlike its companions on either side.

TREE PRUNING PRINCIPLES

Until fairly recently, both flush cutting—making a close cut parallel to the trunk or parent branch—and wound painting were considered sound pruning practices benefiting a tree's health. More than two decades of research by Dr. Alex Shigo during his tenure as a plant pathologist for the U.S. Forest Service altered those views. Shigo pruned thousands of branches on many types of trees; he later felled the trees, cut lengthwise through their trunks, and studied the aftermath of his pruning.

Shigo's research demonstrated that pruning wounds don't heal, in the sense of regenerating new tissue. When a limb is properly removed (by a pruner or by natural shedding), the tissue from the pruned limb rots back to its point of origin. There the decay is halted by a protective biological barrier, and the wound calluses over. Thus the tree compartmentalizes, or walls off, the damage. Your goal in pruning is to cut in a way that doesn't interfere with this natural process.

A proper cut outside the branch collar and branch bark ridge results in even callusing all around the wound.

Shigo also found that some trees—such as bigleaf maple *(Acer macrophyllum)*, alder *(Alnus)*, willow, poplar, tulip tree, and elm—don't compartmentalize very well and so should be pruned as little as possible. (They make up for this weakness by growing rapidly and reproducing prolifically.)

The key sites in proper pruning, Shigo concluded, are the branch collar and the branch bark ridge. Learn to recognize them and use them as your guides when removing any tree limb.

ESTIMATING WHERE TO CUT

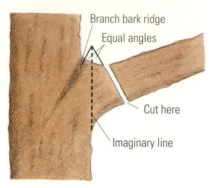

Branch bark ridge

Equal angles

Cut here

Imaginary line

On some trees you may not be able to distinguish the branch collar, but you can estimate its location. Draw an imaginary line from the bottom of the branch, where it joins the trunk or another limb, upward through the branch (dotted line). Gauge the angle between the branch bark ridge and the imaginary line; then cut the branch at a mirror-image angle to that one.

PRUNING A FORKED STEM

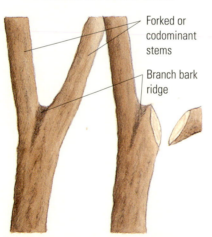

Forked or codominant stems

Branch bark ridge

Because forked stems don't have branch collars, you must use the branch bark ridge as your guide in removing one of the stems. Start the cut just outside the top of the ridge and finish across from its bottom. (If the bark is included and no ridge is visible, you'll have to guess at where to cut. You'll probably have to cut upward, because the space between the forks may be too tight to accommodate a saw.)

THE BRANCH COLLAR

Branches are joined to other branches or to the trunk through branch collars, identifiable as the bulge or wrinkle at the base of a limb. The branch collar contains the protective barrier or chemical zone that impedes the spread of decay into the adjoining limb or trunk. When you make a flush cut, you cut away the collar and thus the barrier. The proper place to cut is just outside of the collar, so that you don't disturb it.

Branch collars differ—they are prominent on some species (though the size can vary on a single tree) but barely discernible on others. They tend to be flat on conifers and sloped to varying degrees on deciduous and broad-leafed evergreen trees. If the collar is very prominent, you may think you're leaving a stub when you cut just beyond it, but you're pruning correctly. If you can't discern the branch collar, you can estimate its location (see the illustration at left).

THE BRANCH BARK RIDGE

This is the point at which tissue from adjoining limbs or from a branch and the trunk meet and are pushed up into a noticeable ridge. Because the ridge denotes the separation between limbs, if you cut into it you are actually cutting into both limbs, not just the one you're removing—and hence you're opening both to decay.

Sometimes you won't see a branch bark ridge, because the bark has become compressed or "included"—forced to grow down into the crotch. Very narrow-angled branches, those arising from points too near each other, and forked branches growing close together often develop included bark. This embedded bark weakens the branch collar—and, as the branch grows, its weight can cause it to split off from the tree. Remove branches with included bark as early as possible, before they cause damage.

INCLUDED BARK

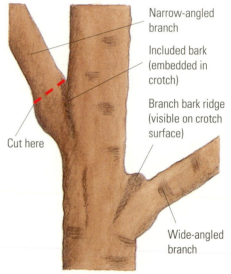

Narrow-angled branch

Included bark (embedded in crotch)

Branch bark ridge (visible on crotch surface)

Cut here

Wide-angled branch

Narrow-angled branches often develop included bark—that is, the bark becomes embedded in the crotch rather than forming a ridge as it does on wider-angled branches. Branches with included bark are weak and should be removed. As shown here, cut upward from the bottom of the branch, just outside of the branch collar.

REMOVING LIMBS

Cut so as to preserve both the branch bark ridge and the branch collar: place your shears or saw beside the ridge and cut downward just outside of the collar. The angle at which you cut depends on the tree—if the collar is nearly flat, make your cut nearly flat; if it's angled out at, say, 40°, cut accordingly. To remove a branch with included bark, begin the cut at the bottom of the branch, just outside of the collar (see above).

You won't be able to use the branch collar as a guide in removing a forked stem, because there is no collar. The two stems of the fork are not separate structures, as true branches are; rather, each is connected to half of the parent stem below. Remove such a stem carefully: without a branch collar, it has no built-in defenses against rot. Use the branch bark ridge as your guide—start the cut just outside the top of the ridge and end up across from its bottom. See the illustration at left.

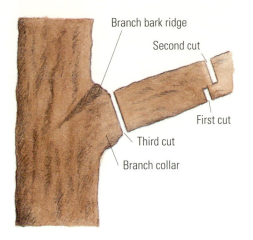

Branch bark ridge

Second cut

First cut

Third cut

Branch collar

REMOVING A BRANCH

When removing larger branches, avoid ripping the bark by shortening the branch to a stub before cutting it off at the branch collar. Using a sharp pruning saw, make three cuts as described below:

1. About a foot from the branch base, make a cut from the underside approximately a third of the way through.

2. About an inch farther out on the branch, cut through the top until the branch rips off. The branch should split cleanly between the two cuts.

3. Make the final cut by placing your saw beside the branch bark ridge and cutting downward just outside of the branch collar. (If the crotch is very narrow, cut upward from the bottom to avoid cutting into the branch collar.)

When removing all but the smallest branches (basically, any that are too big to support in one hand while sawing with the other), make the cut in three steps to avoid ripping the bark and tearing the tissue around the branch collar. Refer to the illustration above.

Wound painting was once an automatic follow-up to branch removal but has since been found to be of little value. It may slow down the spread of decay, but it can't stop it—and, in some instances, it can even harm the tree. If you want to paint a wound for cosmetic reasons, apply only a thin coat of a water-based substance.

TRAINING YOUNG TREES

The intent of early training is to encourage a tree to develop a sturdy trunk (or several trunks, in some cases) from which radiate strong, well-placed main limbs known as scaffold branches. A good solid framework established early in the tree's life makes it less likely to develop major structural problems in later years.

Conifers seldom need training unless they develop more than a single leader where just one should be. If that occurs, remove the weaker of the two stems. If whorls on a whorl-branching conifer (see page 29) are spaced too far apart, induce more branching by pinching or cutting back the leader halfway right after the new growth has lengthened in spring and while it is still soft and flexible. You can also pinch or cut back new lateral growth to make a bushier tree.

With deciduous and broad-leafed evergreen trees, you will spend the first several years guiding the developing structure. Don't rush to establish the tree's final shape, though. A newly planted tree should be pruned as little as possible: just remove dead, broken, or rubbing branches and the weaker limb of a double leader. Wait a full year, until the roots have knitted into the soil and top growth is evident, before doing more. Prune the tree gradually over the next 3 to 5 years, but don't remove too

much wood in any single year—only do what is necessary to enhance the tree's strength and form. Generally, make most cuts during the dormant season or just before spring growth begins; you can remove especially vigorous growth in summer.

No matter where you eventually want the branching to start, temporarily leave on any lower limbs. A leafy lower trunk may look a little messy (some growers refer to it as a "trashy trunk"), but the temporary limbs serve two important functions: they not only nourish the trunk, speeding its increase in girth, but also shade the young bark from sunburn in hot climates. Pinch or head back any of these temporary branches in summer if they become overly long or vigorous. Wait until the tree has been in the ground for 2 or 3 years and the trunk is at least 2 inches in diameter before you begin to remove unwanted lower branches; do it gradually over several years.

FORMING A STRONG TREE TRUNK

A young tree develops a strong trunk faster if its lower branches are left on for the first few years the tree is in the ground. During this time, shorten them if they become too long or vigorous. Once the trunk is at least 2 inches thick, you can begin removing them gradually.

Leave the bottom branches of deodar cedar *(Cedrus deodara)* intact. The nodding tip is characteristic.

growth, producing scaffold branches all the way up and growing lateral branches from the scaffolds. Others lose apical dominance and begin developing multiple leaders rather quickly; from this framework of several main limbs, the tree will produce lateral branches.

Whenever possible, favor wide-angled branches forming U-shaped crotches over narrow-angled ones forming V-shaped crotches. On naturally narrow-angled species, choose shoots with the best angles to become the major limbs. Where the angle is very narrow, the bark may become included or compressed. Such branches are weak and may be torn off by strong gusts or by children climbing on them. In cold-winter climates, snow or ice can get trapped in a narrow crotch, causing the branch to split off.

Keeping the ultimate natural shape of the tree in mind, remove badly placed and superfluous branches before they gain in size; cut back any overly vigorous branches that unbalance the tree's shape, and any that threaten to overwhelm the leader or main branches. Remove lateral branches growing toward the center of the tree. Also eliminate any suckers or water sprouts at their base (but retain water sprouts whose removal would leave gaping holes in the tree's canopy).

Leave on the lower limbs of spruces, firs, and other strongly pyramidal conifers with symmetrical branching all the way to the ground. They look unbalanced without their bottom branches. To make mowing around these trees easier, remove a ring of turf all the way around and mulch the bare soil.

For permanent scaffold limbs, select shoots at fairly evenly spaced intervals, both up the trunk and spiraling around it. Some trees are naturally upright and will continue their vertical

WHAT'S AT STAKE?

A young tree develops a sturdier, more tapered trunk when it grows unsupported and is allowed to sway in the breeze. Stake it only if the location is extremely windy or if the main stem is too weak to stay upright on its own.

Low stakes, rising about a foot above ground, are sufficient anchorage for a windswept site. To determine how high up to stake a weak stem, run your hand up it and stop when the top of the stem no longer flops over—that's where you'll tie the trunk to the stakes. Here's how to do the staking:

∽ Drive two 2-by-2 stakes at least 18 inches into the ground on either side of the newly planted tree, just outside of the tree's root mass.

∽ Position the stakes at right angles to the strongest wind. For added stability you can connect the stakes with a crossbar near the bottom, but don't let the trunk rub against it.

∽ Join the stakes to the trunk (either a foot above ground or where the stem no longer flops) with wide strips of canvas, rubber, or other material that won't bind or cut into the bark; fasten each tie in a figure 8. The tree should be able to move at least 1 inch in either direction.

∽ Cut off the stakes an inch or so above the ties.

∽ Staking is temporary and should be removed after about a year. While the tree is staked, remember to monitor the ties to make sure they aren't cutting into the bark.

SUPPORTING
A WEAK STEM

ANCHORING
THE ROOTS

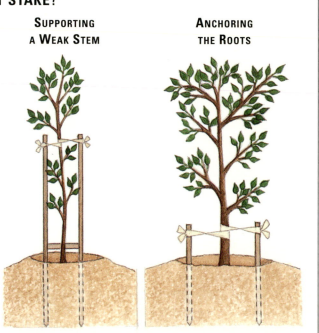

To figure out where to attach ties to a weak stem, run your hand up the stem and find the point where the top no longer flops over. Cut off the stakes an inch or so above the ties. Stakes to anchor a young tree in a windswept site need be only a foot above ground level. In both cases, sink stakes at right angles to the prevailing wind. Remove them after about a year.

PRUNING MATURE TREES

Generally, mature ornamental trees should be pruned just enough to maintain their structure, health, and aesthetic appearance—and often that amounts to minimal or only occasional pruning. Routine annual trimming is neither necessary nor advisable.

Even though relatively little pruning may be needed, you may not be able to handle all of it on your own. Don't risk harming yourself or a valuable tree by tackling limbs that are too big or too high up. See page 21 for tips on hiring a qualified professional.

The basic rules of pruning described in the first chapter apply to ornamental trees. Most cuts should be thinning cuts—removing a branch at its point of origin or at its juncture with another branch. Above all, don't injure the branch collar or the branch bark ridge when cutting (see page 26).

Keep in mind the U.S. Forest Service's advice about not making too many large wounds: think twice about removing branches more than about 2 inches across, and think even longer about cutting off those more than about 4 inches in diameter.

DECIDUOUS TREES

Pruning is usually done during the dormant season, while the tree is leafless and the structure is easy to see. In mild-winter regions, where one growing season blends into another, midwinter is usually the best time to prune. In cold-winter areas, late winter to early spring is the standard pruning period. Some trees—mainly birch *(Betula)*, dogwood, elm, maple, and yellow wood—exude sap from cuts made during late dormancy. The sap doesn't harm the tree, but as it can be unsightly you may want to prune these "bleeders" in summer or early fall. You can prune until the end of January in regions where temperatures remain below freezing.

When pruning a flowering tree be mindful of when the flower buds are formed, so that you don't inadvertently remove them. Trees bearing blossoms early in the season, on the prior year's growth, should be pruned right after they bloom; those flowering later, on the current year's stems, should be pruned before spring growth begins.

BROAD-LEAFED EVERGREEN TREES

These trees typically need very little pruning. You can prune at any time, but avoid doing so during or right after the spring growth flush. Also refrain from cutting at a time that would make the tree more prone to disease or insect attack in your area. For flowering trees, again, prune at a time that will preserve flower buds—after bloom for trees flowering on last season's growth, and before new spring growth begins for trees flowering on new growth.

Cut back new spring growth to control the size and shape of whorl-branching conifers such as this pine tree.

CONIFEROUS TREES

How you prune a conifer (rather, *if* you do, because most are best left alone) depends on its branching habit. Some conifers' branches radiate out from the trunk in whorls; those of others grow randomly along the trunk.

WHORL-BRANCHING CONIFERS. On these conifers—including pine, spruce, fir, and larch—buds appear at the tips of new spring growth as well as along their lengths and at their bases. This is all the growth that occurs for the year. On pines these new growths are usually called candles, because that's what they look like until the needles open out.

TOP: Some deciduous trees, including birch, bleed sap when pruned in the late dormant season.

BOTTOM: Broad-leafed evergreen trees can usually be pruned at any time. However, only prune eucalyptus trees from late fall into spring in areas where the eucalyptus longhorn beetle is a problem.

If a pyramidal conifer develops a double leader, prune out the weaker of the two stems. If the leader breaks, train a new one by tying a nearby branch to a splint or brace; remove the support when the replacement leader has stiffened and remains upright on its own.

PRUNING A DOUBLE LEADER

Weaker stem

TRAINING A NEW LEADER

Replacement leader

Splint

You can pinch or cut anywhere along the new growth (do so before the shoots harden) to induce branching. You can nip back the pliant new growth of the leader and all side branches to make a denser, bushier tree, but this is practical only when the tree is fairly small. If you cut into an older stem—even though it may bear foliage—it won't sprout new growth.

Many whorl-branching conifers have ramrod-straight central leaders. If a double leader develops, remove the weaker of the two limbs. If the leader breaks near the top, train a replacement leader by securing one of the branches from the whorl immediately below into an upright position with a splint or brace.

RANDOM-BRANCHING CONIFERS. These plants—including cypress *(Cupressus)*, cedar, redwood *(Sequoia sempervirens)*, giant sequoia *(Sequoiadendron giganteum)*, dawn redwood, bald cypress, and hemlock *(Tsuga)*—grow in spurts throughout the growing season rather than just in spring. They can be pruned much as deciduous and broad-leafed evergreen trees are. New growth will sprout from branches below your pruning cuts, as long as the remaining branch bears some foliage. Most won't develop new growth from bare branches (hemlock is an exception). There is generally more leeway in the timing of pruning these conifers compared with whorl-branching types, though right before spring growth is usually optimal.

Should the leader of a pyramidal tree break, train a new leader, as described for whorl-branching conifers. Select a new one from the branches nearest the old leader.

The branches of dawn redwood grow randomly along its trunk.

CREATING SPECIAL EFFECTS

Many trees can be trained to assume an unnatural form—a lilliputian version of the real thing, a flat framework, an arbor with a braided-branch roof, or a knobby-limbed dome—and then pruned to remain that way. You may want to try some of these techniques strictly for artistic reasons or for more practical purposes, such as fitting a tree into a tiny yard by espaliering it.

Atlas cedar *(Cedrus atlantica)* makes a good bonsai subject.

BONSAI

This ancient art consists of creating a miniature tree in a shallow container, in scale with its larger counterparts growing in nature. Often bonsai trees take on the appearance of very old, gnarled larger specimens. In fact, they can live hundreds of years, though they look old from a fairly early age. To get the desired effect, bonsai experts meticulously wire and prune branches and trim roots, using small specialized tools.

Small-leafed, slow-growing plants make the best subjects. Start with a young nursery plant or propagate the desired species from seeds or cuttings. Select major scaffolds and secondary branches; the fewer the limbs, the more artistic the effect. Wire the plant if you want it to curve or assume a particular shape. Generally, you control size by pinching out new growth above a bud every few days during the growing season and removing some roots each year. Bonsai artisans will often add to the tree's character by creating cavities that callus over and by exposing some roots.

ESPALIER

Some landscape trees can be espaliered, or grown in a two-dimensional plane, though the technique is more typically applied to fruit trees and some ornamental shrubs. You might espalier an ornamental tree to decorate a bare wall or simply to save space. The training is basically the same as for espaliering a fruit tree; see pages 116–117 for more information.

Small trees with flexible limbs are best adapted to espalier forms. Among the premier candidates are Japanese maple *(Acer palmatum)*, vine maple *(Acer circinatum)*, eastern redbud *(Cercis canadensis)*, goldenchain tree *(Laburnum)*, crabapple *(Malus)*, Korean stewartia *(Stewartia koreana)*, evergreen pear *(Pyrus kawakamii)*, and southern magnolia *(Magnolia grandiflora)*.

PLEACHING

The interweaving or plaiting of branches on adjacent trees can occur naturally when trees are planted close together, or it can be achieved by training and pruning. A single row of pleached trees can form a hedge on stilts; a double row, a long leafy pergola; and a small grouping, a natural gazebo.

Space the desired number of trees (all of the same species or variety) 5 to 10 feet apart. Decide how high up you want the foliage to begin, and keep the lowest branches above that height. Prune the limbs of adjacent trees so that they grow toward one another. When branches from one tree reach those of another, weave them by temporarily tying them together. In time they may form natural grafts. Prune yearly to remove any growth that detracts from the look.

Trees with strong, supple branches adapt well to pleaching. Among the most promising candidates are apple, peach, pear, hornbeam *(Carpinus)*, beech *(Fagus)*, sycamore or plane tree *(Platanus)*, and linden *(Tilia)*.

Pleached hornbeam trees form a long allée, or lined walkway.

POLLARDING

A pollarded tree is one in which all new growth is cut back annually to the point from which it grew. The tree's crown remains about the same size year after year, but the branch stubs from which the stems grow become greatly enlarged and gnarled. Pollarding is used to achieve a formal look or to control the size of street trees—but only a few, such as London plane tree *(Platanus × acerifolia)*, will bear such severe pruning.

PRUNING PALM TREES

Palms are grassy plants rather than woody ones, needing grooming more than pruning. In fact you should never head back palms, because they have only a single growth bud at the top of each trunk.

Many palms retain their dead fronds, which may detract from their beauty. The oldest, lowest fronds die continually rather than seasonally, which often prompts periodic grooming sessions during the year. Occasionally you may also need to remove fronds that have been damaged by frost, storms, or pests. Cut off old or damaged fronds as close to the trunk as possible, leaving only the leaf bases. If the palm doesn't shed its old leaf bases naturally, you can cut them off the following year when you remove more dead fronds. Take care not to wound the trunk, because palms don't callus over. For this reason, professionals groom tall palms from a lift-bucket or cherry-picker rather than damage the trunk by trying to climb it.

Most palms grow as a single trunk topped by a tuft of leaves, but some grow naturally in clumps. If a clump-forming palm has too many stems, you can cut the extra ones to the ground. Some of the single-trunked palms produce basal sprouts; cut these off.

To pollard a tree, give it the standard early training until it has several scaffold branches that are well placed and about wrist thick. Then cut back each limb to 2 to 5 feet long and head back the leader. The branch outline should be dome or mushroom shaped. Each spring the permanent limbs will send out long, slender branches that will form the tree's leafy crown. Each dormant season you will cut these shoots back to their knobby bases.

The limbs of these pollarded London plane trees are pruned back to gnarly stubs each year.

PRUNING TO CORRECT PROBLEMS

Sometimes a tree poses a problem. Perhaps its lower branches impede foot traffic or prevent you from sitting under it. Or maybe a dense canopy casts too much shade on your garden, or the tree has become too large for its location. Careful pruning can often solve these and other problems. Some of the pruning you can handle yourself, but hire a professional to tend to limbs high up or close to power lines.

CROWN LIFTING. The technique of removing the lower limbs of a tree is also called crown raising, limbing up, and skirting up. You may decide to employ it when the branches become a hazard—or to provide clearance for people or cars, make room for planting underneath, or open up a view. Wait until the tree is well established before removing limbs; then do so gradually over several years. When you're through, the crown should constitute at least two-thirds of the tree's height.

The bottom branches of this tulip tree were removed to accommodate traffic.

CROWN THINNING. Here you are opening up the canopy by selectively removing branches. Your motivation may be to let more light reach the ground, to help prevent wind or snow damage, to emphasize an attractive branching pattern, or to reveal glimpses of a view beyond. Don't remove more than a quarter of the crown's wood in any one year. Begin by removing crossing, rubbing, and crowded branches; then selectively thin out other branches so that you end up with an even distribution of limbs throughout the canopy. Favor branches with strong, wide angles of attachment and eliminate those with very narrow crotches.

CROWN REDUCTION. This procedure reduces the size of the canopy—usually to keep branches away from power lines or to uncover a view—without topping the tree. It is often called drop crotching, for good reason: basically, you're thinning groups of branches throughout the tree down to a lower crotch. To reduce the crown's width, thin to crotches closer in, toward the center of the tree. The remaining canopy should constitute at least two-thirds of the tree's height. But don't try this on a pyramid-shaped tree with a central leader, because it will destroy the tree's form.

As shown at top, hawthorn (Crataegus) trees tend to develop a dense, twiggy crown that requires occasional thinning. The improved tree, with its airier crown, is shown after pruning (middle) and after leaf-out (bottom).

WHAT'S WRONG WITH TOPPING?

There's a lot wrong with topping, or reducing the height of a mature tree by sawing off its top limbs. For one thing, it's the quickest way to ruin a tree's appearance forever. For another, it doesn't even reduce the tree's height for very long.

This poor pruning practice may even cut short the life of the tree. Not only does it expose the resultant large wounds to decay and insect attack, but it removes much of the leafy growth needed to manufacture sugars. Moreover, the weak growth stimulated by this practice is always more subject to breakage.

Some topped trees can eventually recover their form, but it may take decades. A good professional arborist will not top a tree that has grown too large for its space, but instead will gradually scale it back by making thinning cuts to lower branches (see "Crown Reduction" on the facing page and below). Thinning cuts will preserve the tree's natural shape and won't produce a lot of vigorous regrowth.

Unlike a bushy hedge that soon sprouts new growth after being severely sheared, a tree does not grow back in a natural-looking way when its upper limbs are pruned to stubs. Instead, the tree sends out scores of shoots from the cutoff points; the effect is one of many brooms, bristle end up, atop the tree. These shoots also tend to be taller, coarser, denser, and more weakly attached than the natural top was.

CROWN LIFTING

CROWN THINNING

CROWN REDUCTION

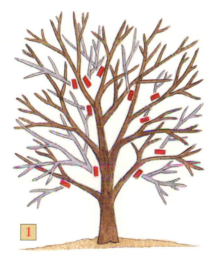

THREE PROBLEM-SOLVING PROCEDURES

LEFT: Crown lifting consists of removing lower branches to allow for activities, traffic, or plantings beneath them.

MIDDLE: Crown thinning opens up a crowded canopy, allowing more sunlight and air to penetrate and more wind to pass through.

RIGHT: Crown reduction lets you decrease the size of a tree without topping it and destroying its natural form.

TREES
A PRUNING GUIDE

The following pages contain instructions for pruning many popular trees. Plants are listed alphabetically by their botanical names. (If you know your plant only by a common name, check to see if it's listed, with a cross-reference to the botanical name, in the index at the back of this book.)

Below the botanical name you'll find any widely used common names, the type of tree (for example, "deciduous" or "coniferous evergreen"), and a symbol (✂) preceding the best time of year to prune it. Remember that even if an entry doesn't specify summer pruning, generally that's a good time to thin unwanted branches and remove suckers and water sprouts, because you'll get less regrowth than if you prune in the dormant season. Of course, you can remove broken, diseased, or dead limbs at any time.

Beneath these "at-a-glance" details comes information on pruning young as well as established trees. Unless otherwise stated, give newly planted trees the routine training described on pages 27–28.

Abies nordmanniana

ABIES
FIR
CONIFEROUS EVERGREEN
✂ SPRING

Firs are big, symmetrical, cone-shaped trees with a whorl-branching habit. Give them ample growing room at planting, because trying to restrict their size later on by pruning will only ruin their natural shape.

You can pinch the elongating new spring growth of young firs to make them bushier, but pruning mature firs is rarely necessary. The trees are more attractive if their branches are left on all the way to the ground. If a branch has been damaged, cut it back to the trunk or closest branch behind the damaged spot. Don't cut back into bare branches, because no new growth will form. If the leader is broken, cut it off and tie a branch from the topmost whorl into an upright position; it will become the new leader.

ACER
MAPLE
DECIDUOUS
✂ DEPENDS ON CLIMATE; SEE BELOW

The many maple species include medium to large shade trees on (usually) a single trunk and small, ornamental, often multi-trunked trees grown for their beautiful foliage or branching pattern. To minimize sap bleed, prune in summer or early fall in mild-winter areas, or from summer until the end of January where temperatures remain below freezing.

MEDIUM TO LARGE TREES. Species include trident maple (*A. buergeranum*), coliseum maple (*A. cappadocicum*), David's maple (*A. davidii*), paperbark maple (*A. griseum*), bigleaf maple (*A. macrophyllum*), box elder (*A. negundo*), Norway maple (*A. platanoides*), sycamore maple (*A. pseudoplatanus*), red maple (*A. rubrum*), silver maple (*A. saccharinum*), sugar maple (*A. saccharum*), and Shantung maple (*A. truncatum*).

Established trees need little pruning; simply remove wood that is dead, broken, weak, or badly placed and interfering with other good limbs. Prune bigleaf maple only when absolutely necessary, as the tree doesn't compartmentalize the damage very well (see "Tree Pruning Principles" on page 25). Silver maple and box elder grow so rapidly that they are weak wooded and their limbs easily damaged; avoid planting these trees in areas of high winds or heavy snows.

SMALL TREES. Species include hedge maple (*A. campestre*), *A. capillipes*, vine maple (*A. circinatum*), Amur maple (*A. ginnala*), fullmoon maple (*A. japonicum*), and Japanese maple (*A. palmatum*). These occasionally grow as single-trunked specimens, but more often have multiple trunks or branches very low to the ground. Plants tend to determine their own unique shapes.

Prune only to accentuate the natural shape, removing any growth that obscures or detracts from it. Thinning out entire limbs usually produces a better effect

Acer palmatum 'Sango Kaku'

than heading back. As its name implies, hedge maple withstands severe pruning and can be clipped into a tall hedge. The flexible limbs of Japanese maple and vine maple make them good informal espalier candidates.

AESCULUS
HORSECHESTNUT, BUCKEYE
DECIDUOUS
➤ DORMANT SEASON OR AFTER BLOOM

Tree types need routine early training for a strong single trunk. Suckering, shrubby species can be transformed into trees by removing excess branches arising from the ground. On established horsechestnuts, prune only to eliminate dead or damaged wood and any awkward-looking limbs.

Alnus cordata

ALNUS
ALDER
DECIDUOUS
➤ DORMANT SEASON

Most alders tend to be pyramidal, with a single trunk and well-spaced branches; the lower limbs can be left intact or gradually removed. Some alders develop several trunks and are attractive grown that way; if you want a single-trunked tree, however, select the strongest stem and remove competitors.

Mature alders need little pruning except to remove suckers, crossing branches, and dead wood—and, in fact, the trees should be pruned as little as possible because they don't compartmentalize well (see "Tree Pruning Principles" on page 25).

AMELANCHIER
SHADBLOW, SHADBUSH, SERVICEBERRY
DECIDUOUS
➤ AFTER BLOOM

The most widely grown of these spring-blooming small trees or large shrubs are naturally multitrunked. For a single-trunked tree, choose the strongest stem and remove all others. Established plants need little pruning, except occasionally to remove crossing, crowded, diseased, or dead branches.

BETULA
BIRCH
DECIDUOUS
➤ DEPENDS ON CLIMATE; SEE BELOW

Birch trees tend to be pyramidal in youth, but their crowns often spread wider with age. When growing birches as individual trees, provide routine training. To grow them in clumps, plant several trees in one large hole, tilting each trunk slightly outward. Alternatively, choose a young tree that has grown in your garden for at least a year and cut it to the ground. When new stems sprout from the base, select the most vigorous and well placed to become the new trunks of the clump.

Young birches often produce two branches of equal size from the same point; removing one of them will create a stronger framework. On established trees, just remove weak, damaged, or dead growth. Don't make unnecessary or large cuts, to avoid providing entry points for the various pests and diseases to which birches are prone. If birch borers are present in your area, don't prune

Betula papyrifera

while the insects are active (check with your local Cooperative Extension office). To minimize sap bleed, prune in summer or early fall in mild-winter areas, or until the end of January where temperatures remain below freezing.

Carpinus betulus

CARPINUS
HORNBEAM
DECIDUOUS
➤ LATE DORMANT SEASON

These small to medium, round-headed shade trees may need some training in youth but seldom require attention in maturity except to remove crossing, broken, or dead branches. Plants tolerate heavy pruning, though, as witnessed by the fact that European hornbeam (*C. betulus*) is sometimes clipped into a tall hedge. Because of their pliant branches, hornbeams are also candidates for pleaching (see page 31).

CATALPA
DECIDUOUS
➤ LATE DORMANT SEASON OR AFTER BLOOM

Medium to large trees that bloom in late spring or early summer, catalpas will seldom develop a dominant leader. As the trees mature they tend to form an open, irregular crown. On established specimens, head back or thin out any branches that look radically out of balance.

Cedrus libani

CEDRUS
CEDAR
CONIFEROUS EVERGREEN

✁ ANYTIME, BUT ESPECIALLY BEFORE
SPRING GROWTH FLUSH

True cedars—Atlas cedar *(C. atlantica)*, deodar cedar *(C. deodara)*, and cedar of Lebanon *(C. libani)*—are very large, random-branching trees that are pyramidal in youth, often becoming flat topped with age. They need little pruning; usually you just remove dead and broken branches. As described below, two of the species may require some special care.

Young Atlas cedars may look awkward, but give them time to grow and they often become quite pleasing. If necessary, pinch back tips of branches that seem too long and heavy. On older trees, remove branches that crowd the structure of the tree.

Note that the tip of a deodar cedar droops naturally (see photo on page 28) and should not be forced upright and tied in place. This species looks best when given lots of room to grow, but it can also be contained. To control the spread and shape of a young deodar cedar, cut back the new growth of side branches halfway in late spring. To make the tree grow low, cut back the new growth of the leader yearly at the same time. This plant will even stand shearing into a large formal hedge.

CERCIDIPHYLLUM
japonicum
KATSURA TREE
DECIDUOUS

✁ DORMANT SEASON

This plant is naturally inclined to be multitrunked; to train it as a single-trunked tree, choose the strongest stem and eliminate competitors. Pyramidal in youth, a katsura tree may either retain its upright habit or develop a spreading crown. Even young specimens are dense and full, so you'll have to thin out crossing and rubbing branches during the formative years. Removal of weak, broken, or dead limbs is usually the only pruning needed on mature trees.

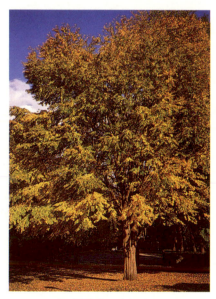

Cercidiphyllum japonicum

CERCIDIUM
PALO VERDE
DECIDUOUS

✁ ANYTIME, EXCEPT IN EXTREME HEAT

These small shade trees native to the California and Arizona deserts are usually multitrunked with a wide-spreading crown. Shade is cast by the twiggy crown rather than the tiny leaves. Prune these trees only to enhance their form by removing crossing, wayward, or excessively low branches. Beware of the sharp spines

as you work. Hold off on pruning when temperatures rise above 100°F (38°C).

Cercidium

CERCIS
REDBUD
DECIDUOUS

✁ DORMANT SEASON OR AFTER BLOOM

Most of these spring bloomers grow as medium to tall shrubs. Types most often trained as multitrunked or single-trunked small trees are eastern redbud *(C. canadensis)* and Judas tree *(C. siliquastrum)*. Mature specimens need little pruning, though you may want to thin some limbs of eastern redbud to reveal the horizontally tiered branches it tends to develop as it matures. You can also train eastern redbud as an informal espalier. Shrubby western redbud *(C. occidentalis)* has a suckering habit; to grow it as a tree, prune off the lower limbs, pull out suckers when they appear, and periodically thin the crown.

Cercis canadensis

CLADRASTIS lutea
YELLOW WOOD
DECIDUOUS

DEPENDS ON CLIMATE; SEE BELOW

Yellow wood is a medium-size, round-headed, usually low-branching tree with brittle wood. When training young trees, be especially careful to select well-angled branches and to remove narrow-angled ones, which tend to crack or split off in storms. Sometimes the lateral limbs of young plants grow overly long, creating spread at the expense of height. To

Cladrastis lutea

encourage the growth of the leader, thin back these limbs to side branches.

Established trees need only occasional attention: eliminate crossing or crowding limbs and remove any broken or dead branches. To avoid bleeding sap, wait until leaves are fully developed in summer before pruning. You can continue pruning until early fall in mild-winter areas, or until the end of January where temperatures remain below freezing.

CORNUS
DOGWOOD
DECIDUOUS (C. CAPITATA IS EVERGREEN)

DEPENDS ON CLIMATE; SEE BELOW

Dogwoods include treelike shrubs and full-fledged trees; for thicket-forming

Cornus florida 'Welchii'

shrubs, see page 69. Cuts callus over slowly, leaving large wounds open to infection. Therefore, try to confine pruning to small branches and make thinning rather than heading cuts. You can prune in summer after blooms have faded, or later if you wish—but not too late, or sap will bleed. You can prune up to early fall in mild-winter areas or until the end of January where temperatures remain below freezing.

SHRUB-TREES. Cornelian cherry (*C. mas*), evergreen dogwood (*C. capitata*), pagoda dogwood (*C. alternifolia*), and kousa dogwood (*C. kousa*) will grow as tall as small trees, retaining branches and foliage to the ground. You can remove lower limbs to convert shrubs into trees (usually with several trunks); or you can train a young plant into tree form from the start. Note that cornelian cherry usually looks best when allowed to grow naturally. Also, select either an upright or a vase-shaped young kousa dogwood, depending on how you want the mature plant to look.

On established specimens, emphasize the usually horizontal branching pattern by thinning superfluous branches. Also remove any broken or dead limbs.

TREE TYPES. These dogwoods are the most widely planted for blooms: the small flowering or eastern dogwood (*C. florida*) and its hybrids, and the much larger giant dogwood (*C. controversa*) and Pacific or western dogwood (*C. nuttallii*). Usually you grow them as single-

trunked trees, but you can choose young plants with several trunks. Flowering dogwood has a tiered branching pattern, typically with dense lower branches that, on older trees, touch the ground.

Prune these trees as little as possible, as they tend to form naturally attractive shapes. Remove dead, broken, or diseased limbs as well as branches that detract from the desired outline.

CRATAEGUS
HAWTHORN
DECIDUOUS

LATE DORMANT SEASON

Most hawthorns are naturally dense and twiggy small trees that can be grown on a single trunk or several trunks. When training them to a single stem, select only three to five main branches to prevent overcrowding later.

On established trees, thin out weak and crowded branches occasionally to open up the crown and let wind pass through easily. Remove suckers and water sprouts.

In some areas fireblight infects hawthorns, blackening its growth. Cankers may also develop on large branches, which they can eventually girdle and kill. Cut out blighted and cankered branches well below the diseased parts, disinfecting your pruning shears after each cut (see page 16).

Crataegus laevigata

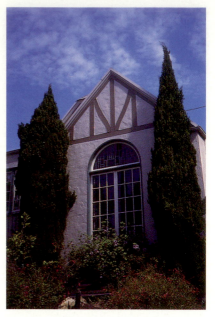

Cupressus sempervirens

CUPRESSUS
CYPRESS
CONIFEROUS EVERGREEN
 ANYTIME, BUT ESPECIALLY BEFORE SPRING GROWTH FLUSH

These random-branching plants range from tall, pencil-thin accent plants to large, picturesque trees that start out pyramidal and may become wider spreading with age. They can be planted as individual trees or in rows for tall screens or windbreaks. They need little pruning; in general, just remove dead or diseased branches.

The best-known columnar kinds are varieties of Italian cypress *(C. sempervirens)*. At times their branches may pull away from the narrow column, spoiling their impeccable vertical form. Don't tie a straying branch back into place: instead, cut it off just inside the point where it grows away from the column. This will force side growth to fill in and restore symmetry.

The pyramidal Arizona cypress *(C. glabra)* often grows too fast for its root system to support it in strong winds. To slow its growth, water infrequently. In gusty areas, selectively thin out branches to let wind pass through.

ERYTHRINA
CORAL TREE
DECIDUOUS AND NEARLY EVERGREEN
VARIES BY SPECIES

In mild-winter regions, *E. bidwillii* and cockspur coral tree *(E. crista-galli)* can be grown either as small trees trained to one or more trunks or as shrubs. Both bear flowers on new wood and thus should be pruned before spring growth begins. These plants can be cut back severely; *E. bidwillii* can even be lopped to the ground. To develop treelike plants, however, prune only for shape and to eliminate any badly placed branches. After each wave of bloom, cut off old flower shoots and dead branch ends to encourage more blossoms.

In the colder part of their range, these two plants are perennials—each winter the top dies, but in spring a new flowering shrub grows from the roots.

Erythrina falcata

The other familiar kinds of coral tree are more recognizably trees. Most have to form some woody branch structure before they will flower. Typically, trees have wide-spreading umbrella shapes with several stout branches growing low on the trunk or from the ground. *(E. falcata,* however, is upright.) Generally, prune only to shape, removing branches that are too low; thin out twiggy, broken, or dead branches. Naked coral tree *(E. coralloides)* usually produces so many interlacing twisted limbs that you must occasionally thin it heavily to enhance its unusual beauty. Prune these plants in midwinter, when they are most dormant.

EUCALYPTUS
EVERGREEN
ANYTIME, EXCEPT AS NOTED

Eucalyptus trees are vigorous growers, putting out new growth from even a bare stump. If you delay training a young tree and find that it has become tall and top-heavy, you can cut it low to the ground and allow new shoots to form. Remove the weakest, leaving one or several stems to train.

Once established, most trees need little or no pruning. The most common reasons for pruning are to control the size of an overlarge plant and to remove broken limbs. If the tree's flowers are a significant feature, wait to prune until blooming is finished. Where the eucalyptus longhorn beetle is a problem, prune during its inactive period (December through March), because freshly cut wood attracts the pest. Remove dead branches immediately and dispose of them.

Occasional deep or prolonged freezes may kill even large trees. Do not be too hasty about removing them, however; they may sprout new growth from the trunk or large branches, though heavy freeze damage often alters the tree's appearance. Delay removal or heavy pruning until summer (or until December through March where the eucalyptus longhorn beetle is present).

Eucalyptus

Fagus grandifolia

FAGUS
BEECH
DECIDUOUS

🦥 DORMANT SEASON

Typically, an unpruned beech will become a tall, broadly pyramidal tree with low branches that sweep the ground. During training be sure to remove branches with weak, V-shaped crotches. Because beech wood is brittle, such narrow crotches are likely to split in storms or simply from the weight of foliage.

As your tree grows, remove its lower limbs if you want to expose the trunk or to sit or walk under it. (Note, however, that it's best to avoid too much foot traffic under beeches; they grow best in uncompacted soil.) In later years, just remove weak, crowding, dead, and broken branches. The only pruning that the narrow columnar varieties need is the removal of irregular branches that stick out too far.

The flexible limbs of beech trees are ideal for pleaching (see page 31); beeches also tolerate being sheared into hedges (see page 71).

FRANKLINIA alatamaha
(Gordonia alatamaha)
DECIDUOUS

🦥 LATE DORMANT SEASON

In milder regions of the South and West, franklinia will become a 20- to 30-foot tree with upright, spreading branches. Where winters are cold, growth is slower, and the plant makes only a medium to large shrub.

Once trained as a single- or multi-trunked tree, franklinia needs little pruning. If a vigorous branch grows too long, cut it back to a strong lateral. If limbs are damaged by winter freezes, cut back to healthy wood in spring.

Fraxinus angustifolia 'Flame'

FRAXINUS
ASH
DECIDUOUS (*F. UHDEI* IS NEARLY EVERGREEN)

🦥 DORMANT SEASON

Ashes are fast-growing trees with rather brittle wood. Young trees are often topped in nurseries (you'll recognize them by a cluster of branches emanating from near the same point). Avoid these specimens, because they will need much corrective pruning. Start off with an untopped tree and give it careful early training to develop as sturdy a framework as possible and minimize the chance of major branches breaking in later years. Ashes tend to grow with a lot of weak, V-shaped crotches where their branches join the trunk, so select shoots with the best angles for scaffold limbs. If the limbs are too long and vigorous, head them back to stimulate branching.

Some species—notably *F. uhdei, F. velutina,* and their varieties—form two pairs of buds at each node. The upper, primary bud is the one that would normally grow into a branch—but it would be narrow angled because of its location. You'll get a wider-angled branch if you force the lower, secondary bud to grow; do this by rubbing or snipping off the upper bud. Secondary buds remain alive for a few years, so if a branch has already developed from a primary bud you can still cut it off after one or two seasons and stimulate the secondary bud to grow.

As the tree develops, prune out any vertical branches and cut back overlong branches that spoil the crown's symmetry. Once the tree's shape is well established, you'll only need to remove occasional broken or dead branches.

GINKGO biloba
MAIDENHAIR TREE
DECIDUOUS

🦥 LATE DORMANT SEASON

Young trees may grow asymmetrically; if this occurs, cut back awkward branches to well-placed laterals. Also cut off any vertical shoots that grow parallel to the central leader. Older trees need little pruning; just remove weak, broken, or dead branches.

KOELREUTERIA
DECIDUOUS

🦥 LATE DORMANT SEASON

These small to medium trees are grown for their summer or fall flowers followed by lanternlike fruit. Once trained to a single trunk or several trunks, they need

Koelreuteria paniculata

little pruning. Cut off any broken or dead branches, thin out any crowded or crossing branches, and remove any water sprouts that form along the trunk. Vigorous clumps of new shoots sprout from beneath any cut; rub off these shoots unless you need to save one as a new branch. Trees often branch irregularly; to keep the shape balanced, cut back any overvigorous branches to laterals.

LABURNUM
GOLDENCHAIN TREE
DECIDUOUS
✂ AFTER BLOOM

Usually trained as a small, single-trunked tree, goldenchain tree grows into a slender vase shape and produces yellow, wisterialike blooms in spring. If possible, cut off the developing seedpods that follow: they are both poisonous and messy. At the same time cut out dead or crowding branches in the tree's center. Avoid making large cuts, because wounds callus over slowly. Because of its flexible branches, goldenchain tree can be trained as a formal or informal espalier.

Lagerstroemia

LAGERSTROEMIA
CRAPE MYRTLE
DECIDUOUS
✂ LATE DORMANT SEASON

The ultimate size of a crape myrtle depends on both the variety and your climate. Most varieties grow as single- or multitrunked trees in mild-winter areas of the South, Southwest, and West. Nurs-

eries also offer some special dwarf shrubby varieties that will never attain tree size. Crape myrtles grow as shrubs or root-hardy perennials in the colder part of their range. There, a plant may freeze back partially or to the ground.

Many crape myrtle varieties develop beautiful mottled bark; gradually remove lower branches to reveal it. Plants bloom in summer on new shoots produced in spring; to promote better flowering, each year cut back terminal growth by 12 to 18 inches. Also remove dead or broken limbs and any twiggy, crowding, or crossing branches. Cut back any overlong limbs to good laterals.

In regions where the plant is partly damaged by frost, wait until new growth starts before cutting away dead limbs. Where plants freeze to the ground, remove dead material before new growth starts in spring.

LARIX
LARCH
DECIDUOUS CONIFER
✂ LATE DORMANT SEASON OR SUMMER

Normally these trees grow tall and straight, with a dominant central leader and a whorl-branching habit. They need no routine pruning. Cut out any broken branches and gradually remove the lower limbs if you want a tree you can walk under. If a tree forms a secondary leader parallel to the main trunk, cut it off at its point of origin.

LIQUIDAMBAR
SWEET GUM
DECIDUOUS
✂ DORMANT SEASON

American sweet gum (*L. styraciflua*) is a tall, narrow tree in youth, but it broadens with age. Chinese sweet gum (*L. formosana*) is more irregular in shape. Oriental sweet gum (*L. orientalis*) is shorter with a broader, rounded crown.

When training sweet gums, pay special attention to developing a strong cen-

Liquidambar styraciflua

tral leader—do this by pinching back side branches. You can gradually remove all of the lower branches, though trees look beautiful with limbs all the way to the ground.

You may need to thin a young tree's crown to encourage it to develop a well-spaced framework of branches. Usually the only pruning necessary for a mature tree is the removal of an occasional broken limb.

LIRIODENDRON tulipifera
TULIP TREE
DECIDUOUS
✂ LATE DORMANT SEASON

Tulip tree naturally grows tall and straight. During the tree's early years, remove any upright stems that compete with the central leader. Established trees

Liriodendron tulipifera

need no routine pruning. If a branch grows too long, pinch it back (if its wood is still soft) or cut it back to a lateral to forestall the need for later pruning. This tree compartmentalizes poorly (see "Tree Pruning Principles" on page 25), so avoid making large cuts whenever possible. However, because the brittle wood is subject to breakage from storms or ice, some large cuts to remove damaged limbs may be unavoidable.

Magnolia × soulangiana

MAGNOLIA

DECIDUOUS AND EVERGREEN

AFTER BLOOM FOR DECIDUOUS TYPES; BEFORE SPRING GROWTH FLUSH FOR EVERGREEN TYPES

Be especially careful when pruning magnolias: cuts made on them are slow to callus over, and large wounds invite disease. Make all cuts back to laterals or main branches, paying special attention to leaving the branch collar and branch bark ridge intact (see page 26). Be sure to remove any dead, diseased, or storm-damaged wood. Pull out suckers, especially those arising from the rootstock of a grafted variety.

The tree magnolias need early training. In windy areas, stake them to anchor their thick, fleshy, sensitive roots. Though southern magnolia or bull bay *(M. grandiflora)* is usually grown as a tree, you can train it as an espalier; as such, it will

grow in climates where it would not survive if planted in the open.

Prune young shrub-tree magnolias, including saucer magnolia *(M. × soulangiana)* and star magnolia *(M. stellata),* only enough to encourage the development of a good branch framework. Remove interfering branches and thin out crowded and weak branches from the plant's center.

Generally, the best pruning for established magnolias is preventive. If you see new growth (especially suckers) where you don't want it, cut it off before it hardens. Pinch back tips of shoots that grow too long. Rather than prune deciduous types after bloom, you can cut when flower buds are plump and bring the budded branches indoors to open.

MALUS

CRABAPPLE

DECIDUOUS

LATE DORMANT SEASON OR AFTER BLOOM

The many crabapple varieties are small trees ranging in shape from narrow and upright to broad and spreading to weeping. Allow the tree to assume its natural form: for example, don't try to make a narrow, upright tree out of one that is naturally spreading. Many varieties lend themselves equally to formal or informal espaliers.

Prune young trees to build a good framework. Because growth tends to be dense and twiggy, you'll have to remove

Malus 'Dorothea'

awkward and crossing branches. Prune established trees when necessary rather than routinely every year. Remove crowded growth as well as any dead or damaged wood. Fireblight bacterial disease can be troublesome during wet springs; prune off blackened growth according to the directions on page 16. Many crabapple varieties are grafted, so be ready to pull out suckers whenever they appear.

Metasequoia glyptostroboides

METASEQUOIA
glyptostroboides
DAWN REDWOOD

DECIDUOUS CONIFER

ANYTIME, BUT ESPECIALLY BEFORE SPRING GROWTH FLUSH

Dawn redwood is a random-branching conifer that naturally grows tall and straight. Occasionally a limb may grow too long, marring the tree's neat conical shape; cut it back to a lateral. The tree is handsome with branches all the way to the ground, but you can gradually remove the lower limbs if you want a tree to walk under. The lower branches of trees planted in groves will eventually be shaded by higher ones; when the bottom branches stop growing vigorously and decline, cut them off.

NYSSA sylvatica
SOUR GUM, TUPELO, PEPPERIDGE
DECIDUOUS
✂ DORMANT SEASON

This medium to large native tree is pyramidal when young, becoming more spreading and irregular in maturity. Part of the tree's charm lies in its crooked branches, which will provide your garden with intriguing patterns in the dormant season. You'll need to pay special attention to early training. Limit the tree to just one leader and cut out spindly, twiggy stems and crossing branches.

Once you've succeeded in encouraging a young tree to develop a good framework, you'll have little pruning to do. Remove dead wood, broken branches, any vertical shoots, and vigorous irregular branches that mar the plant's basic form or that cross other branches.

Nyssa sylvatica

PICEA
SPRUCE
CONIFEROUS EVERGREEN
✂ SPRING

Spruces are symmetrical, whorl-branching trees that need little or no pruning—in fact, indiscriminate pruning can permanently damage their form. Nevertheless, situations do arise that call for selective attention.

Picea pungens

If a plant develops a double leader, cut out the weaker of the two stems. Occasionally a branch will grow out too far; cut it back to a well-placed side branch. To make a tree denser or limit its growth, you can cut back the new growth by half. Don't make indiscriminate cuts into older branches and don't cut back into bare wood. Spruces look best with their branches retained to the ground.

PINUS
PINE
CONIFEROUS EVERGREEN
✂ SPRING

Pines are whorl-branching conifers that tend to be pyramidal in youth but more open or round topped in maturity. You can shape all types to some extent by pruning, but you must do it carefully. The best time to prune them is in spring, when needles start to emerge from the spires of new growth (usually referred to as candles). Cutting back partway into these candles will promote bushiness and allow some overall increase in tree size; cutting out candles entirely will limit size without distorting the natural shape.

In time, the lower limbs of most pines will die naturally. When this happens, cut them off. Remove any other dead branches when you notice them. You can cut out any unwanted limbs to shape a pine or to accent its branching pattern. But remember that once a branch is removed, a new one won't sprout to take its place. If you leave a gaping hole in the canopy, the best you can hope for is that new growth on nearby branches will cover the blank spot.

To shape a pine in the oriental manner requires some skill but is not inordinately difficult. Cut out any branches that interfere with the desired effect, shorten others, and create an upswept look by removing all twigs that grow downward. Cutting the main vertical trunk back to a well-placed side branch will induce side growth. Wiring or weighting branches will produce a cascade effect.

Pinus strobus

PLATANUS
PLANE TREE, SYCAMORE
DECIDUOUS
✂ DORMANT SEASON

Allow plenty of room, as all of these are large trees with heavy trunks and a sculptural branch pattern. American sycamore (*P. occidentalis*) is usually single trunked, with an irregular form and contorted branches. Occasionally it grows with multiple or leaning trunks. California sycamore (*P. racemosa*) is likely to have several trunks with one or more leaning at interesting angles, though it can be trained to a single, upright stem. London plane tree (*P. × acerifolia*) tends to start out pyramidal, developing an open, wide-spreading crown in maturity.

To make them fit smaller spaces, these trees—especially London plane tree—are sometimes pollarded (see page 31). Branches of pollarded trees must be cut back yearly from an early age, but trees allowed to grow naturally need only occasional pruning after their early training. Cut out any dead, diseased, or broken wood, making all cuts back to another branch or to the trunk. You may want to thin out smaller branches to reveal more of the tree's rugged branching and patchy bark.

POPULUS

POPLAR, COTTONWOOD, ASPEN
DECIDUOUS
✂ DEPENDS ON CLIMATE; SEE BELOW

The big poplars and cottonwoods are not often planted in gardens, because of their great size and invasive, suckering roots. If you do plant one, give it routine early training to establish a sturdy, upright trunk. In later years, cut out dead and broken branches.

Columnar accent trees include Lombardy poplar (*P. nigra* 'Italica' and *P. n. thevestina*) and Bolleana poplar (*P. alba* 'Pyramidalis'). These will grow tall and straight without any assistance, but do remove dead branches and suckers.

Quaking aspen *(P. tremuloides)* has a lightweight grace, even though it may become quite tall. It's most attractive

Populus tremuloides

when planted in groves of several to many trees. You can try to train it, but it grows without assistance into a handsome curving or angular shape that training would discourage. Cut off lower limbs to reveal the trunk's beauty, and remove any dead wood.

Prune all species as little as possible, because they don't wall off the damage very well (see "Tree Pruning Principles" on page 25). Most species will bleed sap if pruned during much of the dormant season; to minimize the problem, prune in summer or early fall in mild-winter areas, or from summer until the end of January where temperatures remain below freezing. Summer is the best time to prune species that are susceptible to canker or that sucker profusely.

PRUNUS

FLOWERING FRUIT TREES
DECIDUOUS
✂ AFTER BLOOM

These trees are grown for their spring flower display (though some also bear fruit as a bonus); they are therefore pruned somewhat differently from their crop-producing cousins. Prune right after blossoms fade (after harvest if you want fruit on bearing types). Alternatively, you can prune just before buds open (bring the budded branches indoors for bloom) or while plants are in flower (again, use the pruned branches in bouquets). Be sure to pull out rootstock suckers on grafted varieties.

FLOWERING ALMOND. *P. triloba* is the species commonly trained as a small tree, though it can also be grown as a large shrub. Either way, it needs little pruning. Open the plant's center by removing twiggy, crowding branches.

FLOWERING CHERRY. After you've established the tree's basic framework, prune as little as possible. Remove lower limbs, as needed, to raise the crown high enough to walk under. Remove awkward or crossing branches and any dead or

diseased growth. Pinch back the occasional overvigorous shoot to encourage branching. Cut out any upright shoots that may develop on a weeping variety.

Flowering cherry

FLOWERING PEACH AND NECTARINE. These trees produce the best flower display when most of the crown consists of 1-year-old shoots. Train a young tree as you would a fruiting peach or nectarine tree (see page 115).

Once the basic framework is established and the tree is about the size you want it to remain, begin regular annual pruning. Severe pruning—cutting stems that flowered to about 6 inches and then thinning out the resulting new growth—will produce an almost overwhelming number of flowers, but on a lollipop-shaped crown. For a more moderate approach and a more attractive tree, thin the crown annually and cut back new growth by about a third.

FLOWERING PLUM. Train a young plum tree as you would other landscape trees. As the crown develops, cut out crossing or inward-growing branches and extravigorous vertical branches. Because these trees branch densely, you'll want to thin their centers frequently. Avoid heading back branches to limit the size of a tree; this usually causes the tree to sprout profusely. You may need to do some additional thinning in summer, as stems become heavy and droop from the weight of growing foliage.

PYRUS
ORNAMENTAL PEAR
DECIDUOUS AND EVERGREEN

DORMANT SEASON

The deciduous pears include *P. callery-ana,* sand pear *(P. pyrifolia),* and willow-leafed pear *(P. salicifolia).* Regular early training will produce a single-trunked tree with a strong branch framework. After that, prune as needed to thin out the crown. Remove crowding branches (especially upright ones) as well as weak, broken, or dead limbs. Cut back any overvigorous branches to well-placed laterals. Remove suckers and water sprouts.

Without support, evergreen pear *(P. kawakamii)* is a broad, sprawling shrub or, in time, a multitrunked small tree. To train it as an upright tree, stake the trunk (leaving stakes in place until the trunk is self-supporting) and shorten side growth. Cut overlong, drooping branches back to upward-facing growth buds or branchlets. Established, well-shaped plants need little pruning.

Its fast growth and limber branches make evergreen pear easy to train as a formal or informal espalier. To encourage more bloom on an espalier, cut off two-thirds of the previous year's growth from each branch after bloom.

All pears are more or less susceptible to fireblight, a disease that results in blackened, scorched-looking leaves and branches. If your tree shows signs of infection, remove affected branches as described on page 16.

Pyrus salicifolia 'Pendula'

Quercus palustris

QUERCUS
OAK
DECIDUOUS AND EVERGREEN

DORMANT SEASON

Young oaks need early training to develop a single trunk. Often they become twiggy at the expense of upward growth; encourage the leader to grow by pinching off the tips of unwanted small side branches. If a forked leader develops, cut off the weaker fork.

Once a young oak has gained height and has begun to establish a framework of branches, it needs less attention. Thin out twiggy interior branches that are not a part of the main framework. Use thinning cuts to remove shoots or branches that grow in unwanted directions or compete with desirable limbs.

Note that the lower branches of pin oak *(Q. palustris)* sweep downward during the tree's youthful pyramidal stage. If you remove those branches to gain walking space beneath the tree, the limbs above will simply bend into the same down-sweeping position. Wait until the tree is mature and has formed a rounded top: the down-sweeping process then stops, and you can remove the lower limbs.

ROBINIA
LOCUST
DECIDUOUS

DEPENDS ON CLIMATE; SEE BELOW

Locusts are upright trees with an open, airy crown. Brittle wooded, they need early training to develop a strong trunk and framework of branches. Once the

plant's basic form is established, though, you'll have little routine pruning to do. Make thinning cuts to remove any broken or dead limbs and to eliminate branches that detract from the tree's overall limb structure. Locusts often spread by suckers; pull out these shoots while they're young. To minimize sap bleed, prune in summer or early fall in mild-winter areas, or from summer until the end of January where temperatures remain below freezing.

Two grafted locusts need special attention: *R. hispida macrophylla* and *R. pseudoacacia* 'Umbraculifera'. These two are usually grafted onto the trunk of another locust species and form dense, rounded crowns of foliage. Thin out the crown, removing weak and twiggy stems, so that wind can pass through.

Salix babylonica

SALIX
WILLOW
DECIDUOUS

DEPENDS ON CLIMATE; SEE BELOW

These weak-wooded, suckering trees include various weeping types such as *S. alba tristis, S. babylonica,* and *S. blanda* as well as upright kinds such as *S. matsudana* and its variety, corkscrew willow *(S. m.* 'Tortuosa'). All of these potentially large trees need routine early training. On weeping kinds, be careful to establish a strong, tall leader by shortening side branches. Your goal is a permanent framework high enough to allow the pendulous branches to drape down fully. Pruning established willow trees consists mainly of removing dead and weak branches as well as suckers and water sprouts. Cuts will bleed the least sap if made in summer or early fall in mild-winter areas, or from summer until the end of January where temperatures remain below freezing.

Sassafras albidum

SASSAFRAS albidum
SASSAFRAS
DECIDUOUS
🪒 DORMANT SEASON

Often shrubby in youth, sassafras matures into a dense, pyramidal tree with a heavy trunk, rather short branches, and suckering roots. Ordinarily it needs no special training to become a straight, single-trunked tree. Just make sure the young plant has one vertical trunk (pull out any suckers that develop); also shorten any side branches that grow at the expense of the leader. Established trees should need little pruning beyond pulling suckers and cutting out the occasional damaged or dead branch.

SCHINUS
PEPPER TREE
EVERGREEN
🪒 BEFORE SPRING GROWTH FLUSH

Brazilian pepper tree (*S. terebinthifolius*) and California pepper tree (*S.*

molle)—both of which produce bright berries in late fall and winter—differ markedly in both appearance and pruning requirements.

California pepper tree develops a thick, gnarled trunk and heavy limbs that support a crown of delicate, drooping branches and leaves. Early training is crucial with this tree. Developing a strong framework during the early years will lessen the need for pruning later—an important consideration, because the tree recovers poorly from pruning wounds. Be sure to establish a tall leader (shorten side branches to encourage upward growth) so that later you will be able to walk beneath the drooping branches.

Brazilian pepper tree forms a broad, dense, umbrella-shaped crown of non-pendulous branches and larger leaves than those of California pepper tree. Either use it as a single-trunked shade tree or grow it with several trunks. Wind, storms, and even the weight of its own leaves can break its brittle branches. Therefore, shorten overlong limbs and thin the crown to let breezes pass through easily.

SEQUOIA sempervirens
COAST REDWOOD
CONIFEROUS EVERGREEN
🪒 ANYTIME, BUT ESPECIALLY BEFORE SPRING GROWTH FLUSH

Some specimens in the wild tower 350 feet, but garden trees may grow to only about 90 feet tall and a third as wide in a gardener's lifetime. Make sure that a young tree develops a single leader by cutting out any that try to compete. Though it has a random branching pattern, this tree grows so symmetrically that it normally needs no shaping. If the occasional branch grows too long, cut it back to a lateral. Trees will generally retain branches down to the ground for many years. To gain space to walk or sit under your coast redwood, remove its lower limbs.

SEQUOIADENDRON giganteum (Sequoia gigantea)
GIANT SEQUOIA, BIG TREE
CONIFEROUS EVERGREEN
🪒 ANYTIME, BUT ESPECIALLY BEFORE SPRING GROWTH FLUSH

In extreme age, this conifer can reach 300 feet tall with a trunk up to 30 feet in diameter. In a gardener's lifetime, it forms a broad cone less than 100 feet tall, making it suitable for larger gardens only. Though random branching, its growth habit is so orderly that pruning is seldom needed. If a second leader develops, cut out the weaker of the two stems. This tree retains branches to the ground for many years. Remove the lower limbs if the tree spreads too much at ground level, or if you want a tree to walk under.

Sequoia sempervirens (left) and *Sequoiadendron giganteum* (right)

SOPHORA japonica
JAPANESE PAGODA TREE, CHINESE SCHOLAR TREE
DECIDUOUS
🪒 AFTER BLOOM

This medium to large tree has a broad, rounded crown in maturity; it blooms in summer or early fall, depending on the climate. You can train it to either a single trunk or several trunks. Thin out weak, crowding, and unwanted branches as the young tree develops. Little pruning is necessary once the tree is established. Ordinarily you would prune a late bloomer just before the spring growth flush, but this plant will bleed sap then, so wait until flowering is over. Where winter temperatures remain below freezing, you can prune until the end of January.

SORBUS
MOUNTAIN ASH
DECIDUOUS
 DORMANT SEASON

Tree forms such as European mountain ash or rowan (*S. aucuparia*) are handsome with either a single trunk or several trunks. During early training, remove any competing leaders and thin out any vertical or crossing branches in the center of the crown. After the main framework is established, prune to remove dead or broken branches. Fireblight may infect mountain ash, blackening growth; immediately cut out blighted growth well below the diseased part, as described on page 16.

You can train the larger shrub species to become shrub-trees by thinning out stems from the ground or limiting their number from the start. Also remove lower branches.

Sorbus aucuparia

Stewartia monadelpha

STEWARTIA
DECIDUOUS
 LATE DORMANT SEASON

Stewartia only needs a little pruning to guide its shape. You can train trees— *S. koreana*, *S. monadelpha*, and *S. pseudocamellia*—to a single trunk, or allow them to grow as low-branching or multistemmed shrubs that eventually become trees. Shrubby *S. malacodendron* and *S. ovata* in time will grow about 15 feet tall; you can let them grow naturally as shrubs, or remove their lower branches to convert them into shrub-trees.

Prune established plants as little as possible. Thin out crowding interior branches and remove any broken or dead limbs.

STYRAX
DECIDUOUS
 AFTER BLOOM

Both Japanese snowbell or Japanese snowdrop tree (*S. japonicus*) and fragrant snowbell (*S. obassia*) tend to grow as shrubby trees, with several main stems branching from the ground or close to it. These spring bloomers differ in shape, however: Japanese snowbell has wide-spreading horizontal branches, whereas fragrant snowbell is much narrower.

These trees need periodic thinning to remove weak and crowding branches from the tree's interior. Prune back to strong laterals any limbs that grow too long for the size of the crown, and cut out any dead or broken branches.

TAXODIUM
DECIDUOUS AND EVERGREEN CONIFERS
 ANYTIME, BUT ESPECIALLY BEFORE SPRING GROWTH FLUSH

Deciduous members of these tall-growing, random-branching conifers include bald cypress (*T. distichum*), the Spanish moss–draped tree of southern swamps, and the similar but somewhat narrower pond cypress (*T. ascendens*). Normally they grow tall, straight, and symmetrically. Montezuma cypress (*T. mucronatum*), evergreen in mild climates, has a strongly weeping habit.

Train all species to a central leader and remove any competing shoots. Established trees require only corrective pruning to remove unwanted branches and dead or diseased wood.

Taxodium distichum

TILIA
LINDEN
DECIDUOUS
 DORMANT SEASON

Young trees need early training to establish a strong trunk and leader. After this, you'll have no routine pruning to do. Thin out any crowding branches that develop, remove any dead or broken branches, and pull out suckers when they appear. Lindens are among the trees that take well to pleaching because of their flexible limbs (see page 31).

TSUGA
HEMLOCK

CONIFEROUS EVERGREEN

ANYTIME, BUT ESPECIALLY BEFORE
SPRING GROWTH FLUSH

Hemlocks are random-branching conifers. They become very large, graceful, pyramidal trees without pruning. (Just make sure no competing leader develops.) With light trimming they make exceptionally handsome background screens. Because plants resprout from bare wood, they can take heavy pruning and be hedged (see page 85).

Tsuga caroliniana

ULMUS
ELM

DECIDUOUS AND SEMIEVERGREEN

DORMANT SEASON

American elm (*U. americana*) and the large European elms need routine early training to encourage a tall, straight leader and a main branch framework that begins high on the trunk. Once this is accomplished, you'll have little pruning to do. Cut out dead, broken, diseased, or infested wood as it appears. On young trees, head back any wayward limbs to strong laterals. Pull out suckers.

Semievergreen Chinese elm (*U. parvifolia*) and deciduous Siberian elm (*U. pumila*) need more work, as their branches tend to be brittle and form a dense crown. To lessen wind resistance and reduce the weight of branches, thin out the crown on both young and estab-

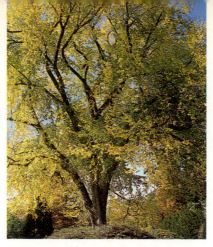

Ulmus americana

lished trees. Cut out weak, spindly, crowding branches and cut back long, wispy ones to strong laterals for a stronger, more compact framework. Pull out suckers and remove broken limbs whenever they occur. You'll need to cut back Chinese elm's pendulous lower branches to maintain clearance beneath the tree.

Elms generally are poor at walling off damage (see "Tree Pruning Principles" on page 25), so don't prune unnecessarily.

VITEX
CHASTE TREE

DECIDUOUS AND EVERGREEN

LATE DORMANT SEASON

Where there are no hard freezes, the deciduous *V. agnus-castus* and *V. negundo* can be trained as single- or multitrunked small trees about 25 feet tall with a broad, spreading habit. You must periodically thin out their crowns. Prune before the spring growth flush begins, as the plants bloom in summer on the season's new shoots.

Vitex agnus-castus

In colder regions, the plants are either shrubs 8 to 10 feet tall or shrubby perennials 3 to 5 feet tall. If they die back only partially, cut them back to live shoots in the late dormant season; the larger the surviving framework, the larger the shrub will be. In regions where the plants die to the ground yearly, you can cut them back in fall as you would other perennials.

Evergreen New Zealand chaste tree (*V. lucens*) needs little attention beyond early training as either a single- or multitrunked tree that will eventually reach 60 feet. It, too, blooms in summer on new shoots, so do any pruning before spring growth starts.

Zelkova serrata

ZELKOVA serrata
SAWLEAF ZELKOVA

DECIDUOUS

LATE DORMANT SEASON

In its natural state, sawleaf zelkova grows as a vase-shaped tree with multiple leaders rising from a short trunk. If you want this form, all you need to do is thin out developing branches as necessary to relieve crowding.

To get a taller tree with a single straight leader, on the other hand, you'll need to be conscientious about maintaining one dominant leader and cutting out all competitors.

After your tree's permanent structure is established, prune only to thin crowding growth and remove dead or broken branches.

Shrubs are the permanent plants that give substance and character to a garden. They define spaces, soften edges, provide a backdrop for smaller plants, and can keep you well supplied with flowers, fruit, and foliage for bouquets. Depending on the role you want your shrubs to play, you can

SHRUBS
AND
HEDGES

grow them individually as specimens or mass them, either in clusters or in rows as hedges or screens.

How you prune a shrub depends largely on the plant type (deciduous, broad-leafed evergreen, or coniferous) and its growth habit. In most cases, you'll prune in accordance with the shrub's natural shape, preserving its innate beauty and character and giving your garden plenty of variety. Sometimes—mainly when growing formal hedges or creating topiary figures—you'll disregard a plant's branching pattern and shear or closely clip it to a uniform surface.

Shaping hedges and creating topiary are among the specialized applications of pruning discussed in this chapter. You'll also learn how to prune to attain specific goals, such as promoting blooms. A problem-solving section addresses cutting overgrown shrubs down to size, rejuvenating old shrubs, and restoring sheared shrubs to their natural shapes. For specifics on pruning selected shrubs, consult the encyclopedia at the end of this chapter.

Sheared boxwood *(Buxus)* hedges enclose a planting of rosebushes.

Although shearing is not recommended as a way of pruning most landscape shrubs, it is essential in developing and maintaining a knot garden. The pattern is nothing more than a series of intertwining low formal hedges.

Shrubs

Typically multistemmed woody plants, shrubs range in size from ankle-high dwarfs to plants the size of small trees. They grow in many profiles, including rounded, vase-shaped, weeping, conical, and columnar—even globular shrubs shaped by Mother Nature rather than pruning shears. Many others are irregular in form, jutting out in all directions.

Types of shrubs

Some shrubs grow in much the same way that trees do, establishing a permanent woody framework in their youth and then building on it for the remainder of their lives. Unlike trees, however, they usually hide that framework in foliage down to the ground. Other shrubs produce shorter-lived woody stems each year from the plant's base, a few to many new stems emerging as the older stems decline in productivity. These plants are sometimes called cane producers.

Some people ignore natural growth habits and routinely prune all their shrubs into "gumdrops," "lollipops," or "meatballs"—epithets conferred by those who don't appreciate the effect. Shearing shrubs or reshaping them are certainly appropriate techniques for topiary figures and formal hedges, or when training a plant to assume an unnatural form such as a standard or an espalier. In those cases, your goal is to make the shrub look like something it's not.

Shearing foundation shrubs into separate boxy shapes usually obliterates their charm—and identity.

But in general, you're better off following the shrub's inclinations if you want to enjoy its natural beauty.

As a category, even natural-form shrubs are pruned more often than landscape trees, perhaps because shrubs are smaller and easier to reach with pruning shears. Many shrubs, however, need little pruning. How much growth you remove—and when—depends on the particular shrub and your purpose in pruning. Whatever cuts are required, remember to execute them properly. Cut back to a point of active growth: to a trunk, to another branch, to a bud, or to the ground. When cutting back to a bud, make the cut as shown on page 12. When removing limbs on large shrubs, cut

Allowed to branch naturally, inherently graceful pieris needs little pruning.

just outside the branch collar and the branch bark ridge, as you would to remove tree limbs; see pages 25–27 for the correct techniques. On smaller shrubs, where these features are difficult to discern, cut close enough so that you don't leave a stub. On the relatively few grafted shrubs, such as modern roses, pull out suckers below the graft union before they have a chance to overtake the desirable variety.

There are three categories of shrubs, just as there are of trees: deciduous, broad-leafed evergreen, and coniferous. Following are some generalizations about pruning each type; for tips on pruning specific shrubs, consult the encyclopedia beginning on page 65.

DECIDUOUS SHRUBS

A deciduous shrub drops all of its leaves at one time each year, typically in fall, and remains dormant until the growth cycle begins anew in spring. Most plants in this category send up new stems, often referred to as canes, directly from the plant's base. These shrubs increase in size and often become overcrowded as more and more shoots emerge. If a plant forms too broad a clump, you can contain its spread by cutting off the outermost roots and stems with a sharp spade.

To keep these cane producers healthy and vigorous, periodically remove the oldest (the darkest and thickest) and the weakest stems at their base. This will expose the whole plant to more sunlight and air. How often you thin out the stems depends on the shrub—you may have to do it every dormant season for robust growers but seldom for less vigorous growers. You can shape the plant as needed by thinning the remaining stems back to side branches or by heading back some to outward-facing buds.

Some deciduous shrubs—primarily the larger ones that can be trained as small trees—form a permanent framework of branches. They include rose of Sharon *(Hibiscus syriacus)*, smoke tree *(Cotinus coggygria)*, winged euonymus *(Euonymus alata)*, witch hazel *(Hamamelis)*, and the deciduous hol-

SHRUB GROWTH HABITS

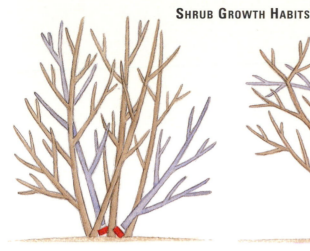

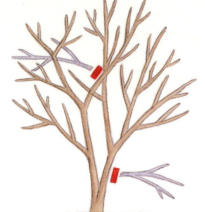

NEW STEMS FROM THE BASE

Most deciduous shrubs and some evergreen ones grow by producing new stems, or canes, from the plant's base. Keep these plants vigorous by periodically removing the oldest and weakest stems.

A FRAMEWORK OF BRANCHES

Most evergreen shrubs and some deciduous ones form a permanent framework of branches. Often, the only pruning required is the removal of dead, damaged, diseased, or unattractively placed branches.

Carolina allspice (*Calycanthus floridus*) produces new stems from its base.

lies (*Ilex*) and viburnums. Generally, prune these plants as you would broad-leafed evergreen shrubs that produce a framework of branches (see below).

Whatever the shrub's growth habit, remember to prune it at the proper time if you want flowers. Most deciduous shrubs bloom in spring on the prior season's growth; prune them right after bloom. A smaller number flower in summer on the current season's growth; prune them before spring growth begins. See the lists on page 53 for examples.

TOP: This cane-producing deciduous shrub has become overcrowded; its stems need thinning out if the plant is to remain vigorous.

MIDDLE: Cut out the oldest and weakest stems at their base. Depending on the plant, you would do this during the dormant season, as shown here, or after flowering or fruiting.

BOTTOM: The thinned shrub is now open to more sunlight and air.

BROAD-LEAFED EVERGREEN SHRUBS

These shrubs retain their foliage all year. They are termed *broad-leafed* because their leaves are broad compared with the narrow needles or scales produced by evergreen conifers. Most broad-leafed evergreen shrubs won't survive very cold temperatures and are thus restricted to mild-winter areas. A small number—including the evergreen hollies, mountain laurel (*Kalmia latifolia*), and the hardiest boxwoods (*Buxus*) and rhododendrons—thrive in cold climates.

The majority of broad-leafed evergreen shrubs produce a framework of branches rather than sending up new stems from the base. Typically these shrubs need little pruning, except to excise dead, damaged, or wayward branches. On some, such as rhododendrons, deadheading (removing spent flowers) is the main pruning you'll do. On those that can become rangy, you may want to pinch the

Most broad-leafed evergreen shrubs, like these rhododendrons, form a framework of branches.

Most coniferous shrubs require little or no pruning when allowed to branch naturally.

TREAT THESE AS PERENNIALS

In the coldest part of their range, some shrubs act as perennials, usually freezing in winter and regrowing from their roots in spring. Such plants include common butterfly bush *(Buddleia davidii)*, blue-beard *(Caryopteris)*, rose of Sharon, and Russian sage *(Perovskia)*. Similarly, some plants that grow as trees in mild-winter areas will survive as smaller shrubby plants in frostier regions; during very cold winters, they may act as perennials. They include cockspur coral tree *(Erythrina crista-galli)*, crape myrtle *(Lagerstroemia)*, and chaste tree *(Vitex agnus-castus)*.

Buddleia davidii

Because all of the plants cited above bloom on new growth, they are able to put on a good flower show as perennials. In areas where they normally die to the ground, cut back the tops in autumn. If any of these plants die back only partially in your climate, leave them unpruned at the end of the growing season and then cut them back to live shoots in early spring.

DEADHEADING

Growth bud

Rhododendron and its relatives are the shrubs most often deadheaded—that is, the faded flowers are removed before they can form seeds. Snap off the spent flower cluster between your index finger and thumb. Don't damage the growth buds just below the cluster.

shoot tips (on fuchsia, for example) or even shear the foliage (on lavender, for example) to make the plants more compact.

Some broad-leafed evergreens—including leucothoe, heavenly bamboo *(Nandina domestica)*, mahonia, and sarcococca—send up new stems from their base, just as most deciduous shrubs do. Thin the oldest stems periodically, as you would do with their deciduous counterparts.

When pruning flowering species, do so at a time that will preserve the flowering wood—after bloom for shrubs blossoming on last season's growth, and before spring growth begins for shrubs blossoming on new shoots (see the facing page for examples).

CONIFEROUS SHRUBS

The shrubby conifers are evergreen, retaining their needles or scales throughout the year. Like coniferous trees, they should be pruned according to their branching habit: whorled or random (see pages 29–30).

One of the most commonly grown whorl-branching shrubs is mugho pine *(Pinus mugo mugo)*, a rock garden plant that grows slowly to about 4 feet high. Another is dwarf Alberta spruce *(Picea glauca 'Conica')*, which reaches 7 feet tall in about 35 years. Neither needs any pruning, though you can pinch the new spring growth if you feel the plant isn't bushy enough.

Random-branching shrubby conifers include arborvitae *(Platycladus* and *Thuja)*, false cypress *(Chamaecyparis)*, juniper, and yew *(Taxus)*. You can cut yew back to leafless branches and still expect regrowth—that's why it makes such a good formal hedge. Though you can shear many of the other random-branching conifers, pruning selectively is often a better choice. This is especially true of plants with a distinctive shape, such as the vase-shaped juniper varieties. When pruning selectively, make thinning cuts well into the shrub so that overlapping growth will conceal the cuts.

PRUNING FOR FLOWERS

You don't necessarily have to prune to get flowers—many shrubs will put on a colorful show without any pruning at all. But other shrubs will produce better-quality or better-distributed blooms if their growth is periodically thinned out or cut back. Whether you prune to encourage blossoms or for some other reason, you should be aware of your shrub's bloom cycle so that you don't accidentally lop off potential flowers.

The majority of flowering shrubs bloom toward the beginning of the growing season, on the previous year's growth. Some of these shrubs—forsythia and camellia, for example—bloom very early, their flowers appearing directly on the old wood. In the case of deciduous plants, the flower display often occurs before the plant leafs out. Other shrubs—mock orange *(Philadelphus)*, for instance—flower a little later, on short lateral shoots produced from the old wood during spring. On both types of plants, do any pruning immediately (no later than a month) after flowers fade; or prune them during bloom as you gather bouquets. This will allow new growth to mature before the

Keep lavender plants compact by shearing them yearly.

next bloom season. If you wait until winter or early spring to prune, you'll cut off potential blossoms in the form of either flower buds or wood that produces the flowering laterals.

A second category produces flowering stems in spring on which blossoms open in the middle or toward the end of the growing season. Any pruning should be done before spring growth begins. The more severely you prune, the fewer but larger the flowers will be. Not pruning at all will result in masses of smaller blossoms.

A few shrubs—the modern roses, including hybrid teas, grandifloras, floribundas, and polyanthas, are notable examples—bloom on both old and new wood. The roses are prolific repeat bloomers, producing blooms from laterals formed on the old wood, from vigorous new canes, and from shoots that have already flowered during the current season. The best time to prune these plants is toward the end of the dormant season, before spring growth starts. Not all roses fall into this category, however—some bloom only once in spring from old wood and should be pruned after flowering. (See pages 81–82 for more information on pruning roses.)

DISBUDDING AND DEADHEADING

Although these special pruning techniques are usually associated with annuals and perennials, they are sometimes used to influence flower production on shrubs.

When you disbud a plant, you remove some of its flower buds by rubbing them off with your fingers. The purpose is to direct more energy into the remaining buds, for fewer but larger flowers. Roses and camellias are the shrubs most often disbudded.

To deadhead is to cut off faded flowers remaining on a plant. Rhododendron and many of its relatives such as mountain laurel, which produce flowers in clusters called trusses, will bloom better the following year if deadheaded after blooming. Break off the whole flower cluster as shown in the illustration on the opposite page. Certain other plants, such as repeat-flowering roses and common butterfly bush, will bloom for a longer period if the spent flowers are pinched or cut off. Because their energy has thus been diverted from seed production, these plants will continue to produce flowering shoots. Heath *(Erica),* heather *(Calluna vulgaris),* lavender, and santolina tend to become rangy; deadheading them by shearing their foliage will stimulate new growth and keep them compact.

WHEN TO PRUNE FOR BLOOM

PRUNE AFTER FLOWERING

The following are among the shrubs that bear blooms on the previous year's wood and thus should be pruned after flowering. This category includes very early bloomers whose flowers appear directly on the older wood, often before it leafs out, as well as plants that flower a little later on short lateral shoots produced by older wood in the spring.

Buddleia alternifolia (Fountain butterfly bush)
Camellia
Ceanothus (Evergreen types)
Chaenomeles (Flowering quince)
Chimonanthus praecox (Wintersweet)
Deutzia
Exochorda (Pearl bush)
Forsythia
Fothergilla
Hamamelis (Witch hazel)
Hydrangea macrophylla (Bigleaf hydrangea)—pictured
Hydrangea quercifolia (Oakleaf hydrangea)
Kalmia latifolia (Mountain laurel)
Kerria japonica (Japanese kerria)
Kolkwitzia amabilis (Beauty bush)
Philadelphus (Mock orange)
Pieris
Rhododendron
Rosa (Non-repeat-flowering shrub and old garden roses)
Spiraea (Bridal wreath types)
Syringa (Lilac, most species)
Weigela

PRUNE BEFORE SPRING GROWTH BEGINS

These are among the shrubs that bear flowers later in the growing season on the current season's shoots. They should be pruned before their spring growth flush.

Buddleia davidii (Common butterfly bush)
Callicarpa (Beautyberry)
Caryopteris (Bluebeard)—pictured
Ceanothus (Deciduous types)
Clethra
Hibiscus syriacus (Rose of Sharon)
Hydrangea arborescens (Smooth hydrangea)
Hydrangea paniculata 'Grandiflora' (Peegee hydrangea)
Rosa (Repeat-flowering roses)
Spiraea (Shrubby spiraeas)
Syringa villosa (Late lilac)

TOP: Bright berries are pyracantha's main appeal, so prune after fruiting is over.

MIDDLE: 'Gilt Edge' elaeagnus leaves are yellow rimmed; remove any branches with all-green foliage.

BOTTOM: The young shoots of redtwig dogwood are the brightest; renew its wood by cutting the oldest stems to the ground yearly.

PRUNING FOR OTHER FEATURES

Certain shrubs have desirable qualities other than flowers that can be enhanced by pruning. You may want to prune, for example, to get a better display of colorful stems, ornamental fruit, or patterned foliage.

VIVID STEMS. Shrubs grown for their brightly hued stems typically show the best color on new growth. To encourage these new shoots, cut the oldest stems to the ground each year, late in the dormant season. The shrubs most commonly grown for this effect are various types of dogwood *(Cornus)*, including tatarian dogwood *(C. alba)*, blood-twig dogwood *(C. sanguinea)*, redtwig dogwood *(C. stolonifera* or *C. sericea)*, and yellowtwig dogwood *(C. s. 'Flaviramea')*.

ORNAMENTAL FRUIT. Some shrubs have showy fruit late in the season; they include beautyberry *(Callicarpa)*, cestrum, holly, barberry *(Berberis)*, mahonia, pyracantha, and cranberry bush viburnum *(Viburnum trilobum)*. Because the fruit develops from flowers, you must take care to safeguard both flower buds and blossoms. Wait until after the fruiting is over to prune.

COLORFUL FOLIAGE. Shrubs with variegated foliage are among those that may need pruning to preserve the effect. Prune out any shoots with leaves that have reverted to green, because they grow faster than the variegated growth and could take over the shrub if allowed to continue.

In a few cases, you may want to prune to get rid of flowers that detract from beautiful foliage. For example, nip off the flower buds of 'Goldflame' spiraea if you'd rather enjoy the chartreuse foliage without the pink blooms.

PROVIDING SPECIAL TRAINING

Instead of letting a shrub assume its natural shape, you may want a different form, such as that of a small tree or an espalier. Other forms requiring training are topiary (see the opposite page) and hedges (see page 59). Once established, all of these contrived shapes need regular pruning to prevent them from reverting to their natural form.

SHRUBS AS SMALL TREES

Some shrubs make attractive small trees. One technique, suitable for large species and varieties, calls for letting the shrub assume its natural growth habit and then "limbing up"

TRANSFORMING A SHRUB INTO A TREE

Select major stems to become trunks, gradually removing the lower branches to form a crown at the desired height.

by removing its lower branches once it reaches a good size. Another method involves training a newly planted shrub as a standard—a plant like a tree rose, with a single upright trunk topped by a head of foliage. Compared with limbed-up shrubs, standards are smaller plants with a more artificial form; they are often used as decorative accents near a front door or in a garden bed.

LIMBING UP. In this gradual process, you remove the lowest branches over a period of several years—but wait until the plant is about 8 feet tall before you begin. The longer the lower branches are left on, the stronger and thicker the trunk or trunks will become. Once those limbs are gone, remove any subsequent growth that forms along the trunk. For a more attractive treelike appearance, thin out the crown if it is very crowded or has a lot of upright branches. Maintain the plant as you would a small tree, pruning only when necessary to maintain its health and attractive shape.

Among the shrubs often limbed up are callistemon, camellia, winged euonymus, holly, lilac *(Syringa)*, oleander *(Nerium oleander)*, osmanthus, common pearl bush *(Exochorda racemosa)*, privet *(Ligustrum)*, wintersweet *(Chimonanthus praecox)*, witch hazel, large rhododendrons, and some viburnums.

TRAINING FOR STANDARDS. You can buy shrubs that have already been trained as standards (they often have a spindly stem taped to a stake), or you can train your own. Tree roses are the most familiar examples of standards, but they're actually three-part plants grafted together—a rootstock, an interstock for the trunk, and a flowering variety budded at the top. You'll have an easier time training an ordinary plant growing on its own roots.

Begin with a young specimen of your chosen plant. At planting

This lantana has been trained as a standard.

TOPIARY: DECORATIVE PRUNNING

An ancient art dating to Roman times, topiary turns plants into living sculpture. It ranges from the whimsical—plants clipped into animal shapes—to strongly geometric—plants sheared into boxes, spheres, and pyramids. Topiary figures have the greatest impact if used sparingly as a special feature or accent in the garden rather than lavishly.

Topiary training forms are available—you place the cage over a plant and shear off any growth that pokes through. However, traditional topiary is a freehand art performed by a patient person with a good eye and a sharp pair of pruning shears. That is how it is done at the famous topiary garden in Pennsylvania's Longwood Gardens. The artists there occasionally bring out a measuring stick or template to adjust a shape, but basically the work is done freehand.

The best candidates for topiary are small-leaved evergreen shrubs with dormant buds all along their stems. Ideal topiary plants—notably boxwood and yew—will produce new growth even from bare wood. The Longwood topiaries comprise several varieties of yew chosen for their cold hardiness, moderate growth rate, and ability to take severe pruning. Other good topiary plants include myrtle *(Myrtus)*, juniper, lavender, rosemary, small-leaved hollies, and some types of false cypress—but note that none of these will resprout from bare wood.

Some larger-leaved plants—including cotoneaster, pittosporum, privet, pyracantha, and sweet bay *(Laurus nobilis)*—are also easy to train, but close clipping will make the leaves look chopped and ragged.

Select a plant whose natural contour roughly matches the shape you intend to create—a bushy, rounded plant for a sphere, a tall, upright plant for a column. You may need to use more than one plant to create a complex figure. For a large topiary elephant, for instance, you might need to set out four plants—one for each leg. As the plants grew, you could prune them as a unit to form the body, head, and trunk.

While you're training the topiary, use pruning shears rather than hedge clippers to make selective cuts that will direct new growth toward the shape you want. In general, you can apply the directions for growing formal hedges (see page 60) to topiary. As with hedges, remember to shape your figure so its bottom will be exposed to enough sunlight to remain leafy. Beyond this, topiary quality depends as much on artistic talent as it does on horticultural skill.

Once your figure gets to the desired size, simply cut back new growth to maintain it. In cold-winter climates, try to keep topiary figures free of snow and ice, which can break branches and mar the shape.

Tiered pyramids and fanciful birds are among the topiary figures on display at the renowned Longwood Gardens.

Because of their open growth habits and pliant branches, the following shrubs are among the best choices to espalier.

Callistemon citrinus (Lemon bottlebrush)

Camellia japonica

Camellia sasanqua

Cestrum

Chaenomeles (Flowering quince)

Cotoneaster

Euonymus

Forsythia

Fuchsia

Gardenia

Hibiscus

Ilex cornuta 'Burfordii' (Burford holly)

Osmanthus fragrans (Sweet olive)

Photinia × fraseri (Redtip)

Poncirus trifoliata (Hardy orange)

Pyracantha

Sarcococca ruscifolia

Viburnum × burkwoodii

This 'Mohave' pyracantha has been formally espaliered.

time, eliminate all stems except the strongest one, which will form the trunk. Retain lateral shoots on it for the first year to nourish the trunk, but shorten them so they won't compete with the leader. Tie the stem to a stake and let it grow until it reaches the desired height. Then head back the stem just above the point where you want the crown to start, and allow buds below that cut to develop into shoots. Pinch the shoot tips to stimulate more branching until a treelike top is formed. To maintain the standard, frequently pinch the shoot tips in the crown and remove any growth along the trunk. You may have to stake the plant permanently if it's still too weak to stay upright on its own.

Good choices for small standards (2 to 4 feet high) are fuchsia, lantana, rosemary, and certain azaleas *(Rhododendron)* such as the Southern Indica hybrids. Larger specimens (4 to 6 feet) include camellia, hibiscus, lilac, pyracantha, and witch hazel.

SHRUBS AS ESPALIERS

Growing plants in a flat plane against a vertical structure or on wires is a technique most commonly associated with fruit trees, but some ornamental shrubs also lend themselves to being espaliered. This centuries-old art form allows you to decorate a bare wall or fence with a tracery of branches, foliage, and flowers—and it may be the only way to grow shrubs in a very narrow side yard.

The shrubs best suited to espaliering are those with a rangy growth habit and branches that are strong enough to be self-supporting yet flexible enough to be guided. If the espalier is informal, the plant is allowed to branch out without any definite pattern. You can use the natural shape of the plant as your guide in developing the espalier; just prune off stems and shoots that grow in the wrong plane or detract from the shape you want. Some shrubs, such as pyracantha, are easily grown in tidy, formal designs. Use the same procedures to establish and maintain a shrub espalier as you would a fruit tree espalier; see pages 116–117.

PRUNING TO CORRECT PROBLEMS

Whether you've inherited a problem or created it yourself, you may be able to prune your way out of the difficulty. Typical shrub problems that home gardeners run into include plants that are too large for their allotted space, though healthy in other respects; shrubs that have become eyesores or unruly messes; and shrubs whose natural form has been ruined by shearing.

The following will explain how to take a shrub down in size, how to salvage an old or messy shrub, and how to restore a sheared shrub to its natural habit.

CUTTING SHRUBS DOWN TO SIZE

If an otherwise well grown, attractive shrub has become too large for its spot and you don't want to replace it with a smaller-growing plant, try cutting it down to size. How you go about this depends on the shrub's growth habit.

If the shrub forms a framework of branches, reduce its size as you would a tree crown—by drop crotching, or thinning groups of branches throughout the shrub down to the next-lower crotch. To make the shrub narrower, thin to a crotch closer to its center. This will reduce height and spread without altering the natural form. See "Crown Reduction" on pages 32 and 33.

As for shrubs that send up new stems from their roots, you can cut the whole plant close to the ground and let it regrow—but only if the species can withstand severe pruning. For details, see "Rejuvenating" on the opposite page. If you're not sure how the shrub will react, follow the safer course of pruning it back over several years, as you would a less tolerant shrub. On these plants, thin out about a third of the stems annually and cut overly tall stems back to well-placed side branches.

SALVAGING OLD SHRUBS

Your garden may be harboring a shrub that's seen better days—perhaps its unpruned limbs have grown into a dense tangle, or it has become very rangy or leggy. What can you do with such a shrub? You could discard it (digging it up could be a big job, though) and plant a new shrub. Or, with judicious pruning, you could try to salvage the plant. Depending on the shrub's growth habit and response to pruning, you may be able to transform the unruly plant into a small tree or rejuvenate it. In either case, if the shrub has some attractive features it's worth a try before giving up on it.

TRANSFORMING. This option is suited to shrubs that have one or several mostly upright stems and a framework of branches. You limb up the plant, creating a small tree with your pruning wizardry (see page 55).

If only one stem is in good shape or well placed, cut all others to the ground and remove the side branches on the remaining stem (now a trunk) to the height where you want branching to begin. If the plant has several good stems, leave them all and remove the side branches on each up to where you want branching. Now thin out any superfluous branches in the crown to make the "tree" more attractive.

REJUVENATING. Sometimes the best way to handle a big, straggling shrub is to cut it back drastically. Then, as it grows back, you can keep it under control.

Some shrubs that send up stems, or canes, from the roots can withstand severe pruning. On such plants (see the list of examples at right), cut all growth close to the ground before new spring growth begins. This approach usually either kills the plant or produces robust new growth. However, even shrubs that respond well may take several growing seasons to recover fully.

On other cane producers, you'll have to spread your pruning over several years. The first year, fertilize and water the plant well to make it as healthy as possible. During the next 3 years, remove about a third of the oldest wood annually. Cane producers are easy to rejuvenate, because you simply cut the oldest stems to the ground each year, taking all the attached top growth on those stems along with them.

Mahonia bealei

REJUVENATING A SHRUB

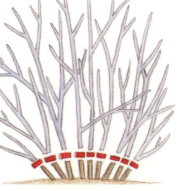

GRADUALLY

DRASTICALLY

GRADUALLY
On shrubs that send up new stems from the base, as shown in the illustrations at left, remove about a third of the oldest growth annually for 3 years. If the shrub forms a framework of branches, severely head back about a third of the oldest branches yearly.

DRASTICALLY
If the shrub withstands severe pruning (see the list of examples above), you can cut back the whole plant to rejuvenate it.

Shrubs that form a framework of branches cannot be treated thus, however. Rather than lop off their stems at the base, you must prune from the top down to rejuvenate them. Over a period of several years, you will have to head back selected branches severely to force new growth. Keep in mind that although some shrubs will sprout new growth from leafless branches, others won't. Know what to expect from your shrub before you cut—check the encyclopedia at the end of this chapter or ask a knowledgeable nursery employee.

Once you have achieved a smaller shrub boasting vigorous young growth, you can thin out any weak, badly placed, or crowding shoots.

RESTORING SHEARED SHRUBS

If you've inherited a shrub that has been shorn of its identity (or if you did it yourself and now regret the appearance or amount of upkeep), you can try to restore the plant's natural shape. In the case of a blooming shrub you'll reap the bonus of a better flower show, because you won't be shearing off the flower buds.

Examine the sheared shrub: you'll find that the outer layer of growth consists of dense clusters of twiggy, candelabralike growth, with less branching toward the middle of the plant. If you recall that heading (and shearing is nothing more than indiscriminate heading) produces clusters of shoots from buds beneath the cut, what you see will make sense. Note how crowded the twiggy clusters are—that's because the shrub has been sheared repeatedly.

Shrubs that send up new stems, or canes, from the plant's base are easier to restore than those that form a framework of branches. That's because you can get rid of a lot of the twiggy top growth by cutting out stems at their base. And if the shrub can withstand severe pruning, restoration is a snap. Follow the same method discussed on the previous page for rejuvenating this type of plant—cut all the stems close to the ground and let the plant grow anew.

For cane growers that are less tolerant of extreme pruning, "unshear" more gradually. Each year, remove up to a third of the oldest and weakest stems and cut back some of the remaining branches to outward-facing buds or side branches. Direct the subsequent new growth so that the shrub gradually takes on a natural shape.

Restoring a shrub with a framework of branches is a little more difficult, because you can't just lop off stems at the base but rather must remove twiggy growth throughout the plant. Spread the job over several years, and don't remove more than about a third of the growth each year. Begin by thinning out clusters of twigs; cut each cluster back to a lateral branch. Do this throughout the crown. Also remove any crossing or weak branches. At first you won't see much difference in the shrub's form. The next year, continue to open up the plant by thinning out more twiggy clusters; also thin any new growth that is poorly placed. By the third year the shrub should start looking more natural. Continue to thin out twiggy and ill-placed growth until you are satisfied with the results.

"UNSHEARING" A SHRUB

To restore a shrub that forms a framework of branches, you must gradually thin out the twiggy clusters that were created by repeated shearing. In the first year, remove some of the densest clusters by cutting them back to lateral branches; also eliminate weak or crossing shoots. In the second year, continue to open up the plant by thinning out additional twiggy growth and excising any weak or wayward growth. In the third year, continue the process—but by now you should start seeing the results of your work. (In the illustrations below the gray shoots represent growth that has been removed, the green shoots new growth that has sprouted since the plant was thinned the previous year.)

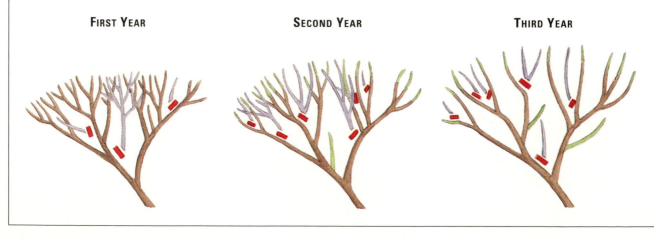

FIRST YEAR · SECOND YEAR · THIRD YEAR

TOP: Formally sheared tall hedges needn't be boxy; this one is rounded.
BOTTOM: Sheared boxwood makes a good low edging for parterres.

HEDGES

A hedge is a living fence or wall consisting of a row of evergreen or deciduous plants, usually of one single species or variety. Ideally, hedge plants are dense, carry their foliage to the ground, and have neat growth habits.

Mature hedges vary in size from less than a foot high to well above head level. Low types (lower than 3 feet) are used decoratively or to form low boundaries, such as the edging for a bed or the divisions in a parterre. Medium-size hedges (lower than eye level) are used to define spaces and create backdrops for smaller plants. Tall hedges (above eye level) are for privacy and screening as well as forming backdrops for larger plants. Medium and tall hedges of thorny plants also serve as barriers.

HEDGE STYLES

The style of a hedge can be formal, semiformal, or informal — that is, the plants can be sheared to a flat surface, pruned to a fairly soft contour, or left natural. Some plants can be trained to any hedge style — an example is boxwood, even though it is most often associated with formal sheared hedges. Other plants are best suited to one style or another. For instance, beech *(Fagus)*, ordinarily grown as a tree, makes a good tall formal hedge; pyracantha puts on a better fruit display if grown semiformally or

informally; and roses, forsythia, and other plants grown for their lavish blooms look prettier and produce more blossoms if grown informally.

Read on for more information about the various hedge styles. For examples of plants suited to each, see the chart on pages 62–63. Before deciding on a tall formal or semiformal hedge, consider the difficulty of maintaining it (or the expense, if you have to hire someone). At the least, you'll need to prune it from a ladder, and you may even need scaffolding. The top width of such a hedge shouldn't exceed twice your reach if you are to prune the entire top surface.

FORMAL HEDGES

With this type of hedge, you are not aware of individual plants; instead, you see a single unit with a smooth, sheared top and sides. The shape can be boxy, rounded, or pointy topped; in climates where heavy snow loads can damage hedges, the round or pointed top will help shed snow. The hedge's profile is maintained by regularly cutting back new growth with manual hedge shears or a power hedge trimmer.

The rigid appearance of a formal hedge is suited to highly manicured landscapes, or to very structured ones marked by symmetry and straight or geometric lines. The best plants for formal hedging are rugged, small-leaved types grown for their foliage rather than flowers or fruit. Boxwood *(Buxus)* is among the most widely used plants for formal hedges. Several types of conifers — mainly yew *(Taxus)*, hemlock *(Tsuga)*, and arborvitae *(Platycladus* and *Thuja)* — are also commonly employed.

A formal hedge is shown at bottom, a semiformal one above it.

SEMIFORMAL HEDGES

This style is more structured than an informal hedge, yet not so rigid as a formal one. You see a single unit, as you do with a formal hedge, but the overall effect is softer, looser, and more billowy. Instead of shearing the plants to a smooth surface, you use your pruning shears to selectively cut back any branches that stick out too far beyond the contour you've established.

You would choose this style when you'd like a formal-looking hedge but are growing large-leaved plants that don't lend themselves to shearing or close clipping. For example, shearing English laurel *(Prunus laurocerasus)* disfigures the foliage with an ugly cut surface. If you've chosen plants known for their flowers or fruit, you'll get a better show with a semiformal hedge than you would with a strictly formal one, because you can prune to preserve some of the flower buds.

INFORMAL HEDGES

An informal hedge requires the least amount of work to grow and maintain, because the plants are treated as if they were individual shrubs that just happen to be growing in a row. You let the plants grow in their natural shape, pruning only as required for that species or variety with pruning shears or loppers.

This type of hedge is in keeping with informal or naturalistic landscapes—those with flowing lines and irregular shapes. It is the best choice for flower producers such as abelia or for fruiting plants such as cotoneaster, because you're not constantly cutting off flower buds. An informal hedge also allows you to preserve the attractive growth habit of such shrubs as forsythia, whose arches would be turned into sticks by either shearing or shortening the branches. Plan on an informal hedge if it is to demarcate a property line and you don't have easy access to the other side for maintenance.

INITIAL TRAINING

Depending on the hedge style and the type of plant you're growing, you may have to do a lot of heading back and pinching during the hedge's formative years. In other cases, very little pruning will be required. Here's how to establish your hedge to get a full, dense planting.

FORMAL AND SEMIFORMAL HEDGES

Space the plants closer together than if they were growing naturally—generally, 1 to 3 feet apart (but as close as 6 inches for the smallest dwarf hedges). The exact spacing will depend on how far the plants will spread and, to some extent, on how quickly you want the hedge to fill in. Also allow adequate space for the hedge to grow in depth, especially if it is to border a walkway or a property line. Some species require more room than others even when sheared, so check with your nursery before planting.

In most cases, you must prune at planting time to force branching if you are to end up with a thick hedge whose foliage

In general, flowering hedges are best treated informally, as in this beautiful example of closely planted 'Simplicity' rosebushes. A great deal of the charm and many of the flowers would be lost if the hedge were pruned formally or semiformally.

reaches to the ground. Deciduous shrubs require more severe pruning than do broad-leafed evergreen or coniferous ones. After planting, cut back larger deciduous plants by about a third and smaller ones to within several inches of the ground. Also cut back fast-growing broad-leafed evergreen plants, but less severely than you would deciduous ones. Don't head back slow-growing broad-leafed evergreens or conifers, but rather shorten their lateral branches.

During the rest of the first growing season, don't prune except to cut back overly vigorous shoots. Each year thereafter, cut back new growth by about half to encourage your hedge to branch densely. Remember, shear a formal hedge with manual hedge clippers or a power hedge trimmer, but a semiformal hedge with handheld pruning shears to make selective cuts to a leaf or a branch. Prune during the spring growth flush and repeat as needed later in the growing season; where plants are subject to frost damage, don't prune after midsummer.

To develop the hedge's shape, you may need to use string stretched between stakes or a wooden frame or other template as a guide in pruning. Whatever the chosen shape, be sure to slope the sides so that the bottom is wider than the top. This will allow sunlight to reach the entire hedge surface, stimulating

SLOPING THE SIDES OF A HEDGE

WRONG

RIGHT

Slope the sides of a formal or semiformal hedge so that the bottom is wider than the top, allowing sunlight to reach the entire hedge surface. Without adequate light, the lower leaves and stems will die. In snowy climates, a peaked or rounded top will keep snow from accumulating on the hedge and possibly damaging it.

USING A WOODEN FRAME

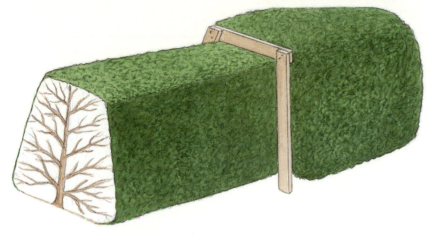

A simple, inexpensive wooden frame consisting of 1-by-2s nailed together serves as a guide for shearing a formal hedge or selectively pruning a semiformal hedge.

growth all over the plant. If the lower branches are shaded, they will grow more slowly and eventually die. Tapering the sides of very low hedges isn't necessary, because they don't get tall enough to block sunlight.

INFORMAL HEDGES

Space the shrubs so that the branches of adjoining plants will extend into each other when the hedge is fully grown. In most cases, this means a spacing that measures slightly less than the mature width of a plant—for example, 4 feet apart for plants that will spread 6 feet wide, and 6 feet apart for ones that will grow 8 feet across.

Don't cut the shrubs back as you would after planting a formal or semiformal hedge. As the plants grow during the first year, however, pinch the branch tips to get full, bushy growth. Even though the hedge is informal, you want to avoid holes and see-through areas.

If branches didn't form low enough on the plants, pinch again in the second year to encourage more branching. Also make sure that one or more plants don't outgrow the others.

MAINTENANCE

Once the hedge has reached the desired proportions, your job isn't over—hereafter, you must prune periodically to maintain its size and fullness.

FORMAL AND SEMIFORMAL HEDGES

Each year, cut back the new growth close to its point of origin, but don't remove it entirely. Do this after the spring growth flush has stopped, to prevent the hedge from growing any bigger. (However, if you need to fill out some bare spots, prune during the growth flush to encourage more branching.) As you prune be sure to maintain tapered sides, so that the bottom is wider than the top.

Some formal hedges need only one shearing per year, but others will send forth new growth after the first trimming and will need to be pruned again. In mild-winter regions, you may find yourself pruning vigorous growers well into autumn. In cold-winter climates, remember to stop pruning at least a month before the first expected fall frost.

Because of their softer contour, semiformal hedges don't require perfectly clean lines. With many plants, you could probably get by with a single pruning in spring—however, give it a few snips here and there with your pruning shears during the growing season to keep the hedge beautiful.

TOP: Use hedge shears or a power hedge trimmer to prune formal hedges like this low boxwood.

BOTTOM: Make selective cuts with pruning shears when pruning a semiformal or informal hedge such as this shrubby hemlock.

HEDGE CANDIDATES

The following are among the many plants that make good hedges, categorized by size. The symbol (∿) indicates the plant type and preferred training styles for each.

LOW HEDGES (TO BE KEPT BELOW 3 FEET)	DECIDUOUS	EVERGREEN	FORMAL	SEMIFORMAL	INFORMAL
Abies koreana 'Prostrata' (Korean fir)		∿			∿
Berberis thunbergii 'Aurea' (Yellow-leafed Japanese barberry)	∿		∿	∿	∿
Buxus (Dwarf varieties of boxwood)		∿	∿	∿	∿
Cotoneaster apiculatus (Cranberry cotoneaster)	∿			∿	∿
Deutzia gracilis (Slender deutzia)	∿			∿	∿
Ilex vomitoria 'Nana' (Dwarf yaupon)		∿	∿	∿	∿
Lavandula (Lavender)		∿			∿
Pittosporum tobira 'Wheeler's Dwarf'		∿			∿
Rosmarinus officinalis (Rosemary)		∿	∿		∿
Salix purpurea 'Gracilis' (Dwarf purple osier)	∿		∿		
Salvia greggii (Autumn sage)		∿	∿	∿	∿
Santolina		∿	∿		∿
Spiraea (Low-growing shrubby types)	∿			∿	∿
Taxus × media 'Brownii' (Yew)		∿	∿		
Thuja occidentalis (Dwarf varieties of American arborvitae)		∿			∿
Viburnum opulus 'Nanum' (Dwarf European cranberry bush)	∿				∿

MEDIUM HEDGES (TO BE KEPT BELOW EYE LEVEL)	DECIDUOUS	EVERGREEN	FORMAL	SEMIFORMAL	INFORMAL
Berberis darwinii (Darwin barberry)		∿		∿	∿
Buxus microphylla japonica (Japanese boxwood)		∿	∿	∿	∿
Chaenomeles (Flowering quince)	∿			∿	∿
Gardenia jasminoides		∿			∿
Ilex crenata 'Convexa' (Japanese holly)		∿	∿	∿	∿
Juniperus chinensis 'Armstrongii' (Armstrong juniper)		∿			∿
Ligustrum obtusifolium (Border privet)	∿		∿	∿	
Myrtus communis (Myrtle)		∿	∿	∿	∿
Prunus laurocerasus (English laurel)		∿		∿	

Berberis thunbergii 'Aurea'   *Berberis* and *Santolina*   *Prunus laurocerasus*   *Tsuga canadensis*

MEDIUM HEDGES (TO BE KEPT BELOW EYE LEVEL)	DECIDUOUS	EVERGREEN	FORMAL	SEMIFORMAL	INFORMAL
Pyracantha 'Apache'		✓		✓	✓
Rhaphiolepis		✓			✓
Rhododendron (Evergreen azaleas)		✓	✓	✓	✓
Rosa (Shrub roses)	✓				✓
Spiraea (Moderate-size bridal wreath types)	✓				✓
Tsuga canadensis (Canada hemlock)		✓	✓		
Weigela 'Variegata'	✓				✓

TALL HEDGES (TO BE KEPT ABOVE EYE LEVEL)	DECIDUOUS	EVERGREEN	FORMAL	SEMIFORMAL	INFORMAL
Camellia		✓			✓
Chamaecyparis lawsoniana (Port Orford cedar)		✓	✓		
Elaeagnus pungens (Silverberry)		✓	✓	✓	
Fagus (Beech)	✓		✓		
Ilex cornuta 'Burfordii' (Burford holly)		✓	✓	✓	✓
Laurus nobilis (Sweet bay)		✓	✓	✓	✓
Nerium oleander (Oleander)		✓			✓
Osmanthus		✓		✓	✓
Photinia × fraseri (Redtip)		✓		✓	✓
Poncirus trifoliata (Hardy orange)	✓			✓	✓
Prunus laurocerasus (English laurel)		✓		✓	✓
Rhamnus frangula 'Columnaris' (Tallhedge buckthorn)	✓		✓	✓	✓
Syringa (Lilac)	✓				✓
Taxus × media 'Hicksii' (Yew)		✓	✓	✓	✓
Tsuga canadensis (Canada hemlock)		✓	✓		
Viburnum dentatum (Arrowwood viburnum)	✓				✓

Prune this informal lilac hedge just as you would if each plant were growing alone.

Sheared hedges can develop bare spots over time, often as a result of shaving off all the new spring growth each year. A good solution is to renew the hedge, either by cutting it to the ground (if it will withstand such treatment) or back to a framework of stems.

INFORMAL HEDGES

Generally, you need only prune informal-hedge plants individually as required for the species or variety you're growing. Yet you must take into account the plants' overall impression as a hedge. For uniformity, make sure that one or more plants don't outgrow the others. To keep all of the plants in balance, you may have to thin out branches on some and head back growth on others to encourage branching. Maintain the vigor of plants that send up stems from the roots by removing some of the oldest and weakest stems each year.

RENOVATION

Over time hedges may become too large or leggy, or may develop holes or bare spots. Rather than pull out the old hedge and replant, try renovating it.

One of the most common problems is a leggy, leafless bottom. The cause is usually a lack of sunlight at the base of the hedge, though it may be improper early training that made the hedge leggy from the start. In either case, cut back the top growth heavily to stimulate branching at the bottom—actually, dormant buds throughout the plant will begin to grow, but you're most interested in the ones near the base. When retraining a formal or semiformal hedge, shape it properly so that it's wider at the bottom than the top.

If your formal or semiformal hedge sports holes or bare spots, you can try "pluck pruning"—cutting into the hedge to let sunlight reach the interior, thus encouraging new growth. The bare spots may have been caused in part by removing the entire flush of new growth each year. Once the spots fill in, help prevent a recurrence by leaving about ¼ inch of new growth when trimming the hedge. Occasionally an old hedge—or one component of it—will have to be replaced if it develops dead areas where no new growth will appear.

If the quick fixes described above don't work or if your problem is an overgrown, rangy, or ratty-looking hedge, the best solution is to renew the hedge in basically the same way that you would rejuvenate individual shrubs (see page 57).

With plants that can tolerate severe pruning (see page 57 for examples), you can cut the whole hedge low to the ground and let it grow back. This treatment is often used on old privet *(Ligustrum)* hedges. If you don't want to lose the screening that your hedge provides, you can try cutting one side of the hedge back severely, close to the main stems if necessary; do the same to the other side the next year. Treat a formal or semiformal hedge as a unit when rejuvenating. With an informal hedge, you can tend to each plant individually, rejuvenating only those that require it or even replacing those that fail to keep up with the others.

You can take the opportunity afforded by renovation to switch from a formal to an easier-to-maintain informal hedge if you want to; just allow the new shoots to grow naturally instead of cutting them back. Be aware, though, that if the space between plants was calculated properly for a formal hedge, you may not have enough room for truly natural branching and may therefore have to compromise with semiformal training. Very tight original spacing, however, may allow you to remove every other plant and have enough room for the remaining plants to branch naturally.

If you have a large-leaved hedge that has been sheared in the past, you can let it grow out a little and then thin out some of the shoots with your pruning shears to end up with a semiformal hedge.

SHRUBS AND HEDGES
A PRUNING GUIDE

The following pages contain instructions for pruning many commonly grown shrubs. Plants are listed alphabetically by their botanical names. (If you know your plant only by a common name, check to see if it's listed, with a cross-reference to the botanical name, in the index at the back of this book.)

Below the botanical name you'll find any widely used common names, the type of shrub (for example, "deciduous" or "evergreen"), and a symbol (✂) preceding the best time of year for routine pruning. Remember that even if an entry doesn't specify summer pruning, generally that's a good time to thin unwanted branches and remove suckers. Typically, the best time to rejuvenate overgrown shrubs is during the late dormant season, before spring growth begins. Of course, you can remove broken, diseased, or dead branches at any time.

Beneath the "at-a-glance" details comes information on pruning that plant. For particulars on training and maintaining hedges (including when to prune), see the section beginning on page 60. To convert a shrub into a small tree, see page 54.

ABELIA
EVERGREEN, SEMIEVERGREEN, AND DECIDUOUS
✂ AFTER BLOOM OR DORMANT SEASON

These gracefully arching shrubs flower on the previous year's growth; where the growing season is long enough, they also bear on the current season's shoots. Cut old twiggy and unproductive stems to the ground—the more that you remove, the more open and arching next year's growth will be. Also cut back any overlong stems to strong laterals. Pinch the tips of new spring growth to make the plant bushier. The best hedge style for abelia is informal, because it preserves the graceful habit and produces the most flowers.

In areas where stems freeze back but roots survive the winter, these plants act as perennials: they bloom late in the season, on new growth only. In fall, cut back all stems to about 4 inches and mulch the plant's crown.

Abelia × grandiflora

ABIES
FIR
CONIFEROUS EVERGREEN
✂ SPRING

Dwarf varieties of these whorl-branching conifers are useful for foundation plantings and informal hedges. They need little or no pruning, though you can pinch the elongating new spring growth to make the plant bushier.

Arctostaphylos uva-ursi 'Emerald Carpet'

ARCTOSTAPHYLOS
MANZANITA
EVERGREEN
✂ AFTER BLOOM OR AFTER FRUITING

The many manzanita species and varieties range from mat-forming ground covers to large shrubs. Many have beautiful irregular branching patterns and smooth, mahogany-colored limbs. Regular pruning is not required for any of the manzanitas.

To make plants more dense and uniformly compact, pinch the tips of new spring growth to force branching. Don't cut back into bare wood; the plant will not send out new growth. Make thinning cuts to remove any lopsided or wayward branches.

Larger species, such as *A. manzanita*, naturally become treelike, usually with several trunks or with branches close to the ground. As a plant grows, its lower limbs die. In nature they break off, leaving a canopy of leaves crowning a framework of handsome, angular limbs. To give nature a hand, cut out all dead wood annually and remove any limbs that detract from the branching habit.

BERBERIS
BARBERRY
DECIDUOUS, SEMIEVERGREEN, AND EVERGREEN
✂ LATE DORMANT SEASON FOR DECIDUOUS TYPES; AFTER BLOOM OR FRUITING FOR EVERGREEN TYPES

The various barberries are dense, thorny plants ranging in size from about 1½ to 10 feet tall. Annually thin out the oldest wood and prune as needed to shape the plant. You can rejuvenate an overgrown, neglected barberry by cutting the whole plant low to the ground before new spring growth begins. Continues >

Berberis thunbergii 'Aurea'

Barberries, particularly the types grown for flowers and fruit, make attractive informal hedges. That is the best way to preserve the colorful crop, which is borne on the previous year's growth. The types grown for vivid foliage can be trained in a formal, semiformal, or informal style.

BUDDLEIA
BUTTERFLY BUSH
DECIDUOUS OR SEMIEVERGREEN
✄ VARIES BY SPECIES

Common butterfly bush *(B. davidii)* flowers in summer on new spring growth; prune it during the dormant season. You can remove the weakest stems entirely and cut back the remaining stems to a third of their length. Alternatively, you can cut all the stems low to the ground. Remove spent flowers to promote summerlong bloom. The plant acts as a perennial in cold climates, freezing to the ground yearly and rebounding in spring.

Fountain butterfly bush *(B. alternifolia)* bears spring flowers on growth made the previous year. Prune it after blossoming is finished. Cut back the oldest, least productive wood completely or to within two growth buds of the ground; strong new stems will emerge. Thin out twiggy and crossing stems. You can convert this plant into a small tree by limbing up; after bloom cut back old, unproductive branches in the crown.

BUXUS
BOXWOOD, BOX
EVERGREEN
✄ SPRING AND SUMMER

Small leafed, with a naturally billowing and dense habit, the various boxwoods range from foot-high shrublets to bulky shrubs the size of small trees. They take well to shearing and are classic topiary and formal hedge plants. Boxwoods are also attractive grown as semiformal and informal hedges.

Prune as needed during the growing season: pinch new shoots for thicker growth, selectively cut back overlong shoots, or shear. To renew boxwood, cut it low to the ground or back to a framework of branches in spring, just as active growth is beginning.

Callicarpa bodinieri 'Profusion'

CALLICARPA
BEAUTYBERRY
DECIDUOUS
✄ LATE DORMANT SEASON

These medium-size shrubs produce summer flowers and subsequently clusters of decorative autumn-into-winter berries on the current season's growth. In cold-winter climates the plants may freeze to the ground, but they come back from the roots; in these regions, treat them as perennials and cut them to the ground yearly at the end of the growing season. In

milder climates, annual pruning should consist of either thinning out about a third of the oldest and weakest stems or lopping the whole plant low to the ground.

Callistemon citrinus

CALLISTEMON
BOTTLEBRUSH
EVERGREEN
✄ AFTER BLOOM OR BEFORE SPRING
　 GROWTH FLUSH

Most of the bottlebrushes offered in nurseries are medium to large shrubs. Some are naturally dense and compact (they make good informal hedges); others are sparse and open (they can be limbed up into small trees). Types with pliant branches, notably lemon bottlebrush *(C. citrinus)*, can be grown as informal espaliers.

Routine pruning mainly entails removing any weak or dead branches. To control shape, cut back selected branches to laterals. Don't cut into leafless wood, because it may not send out any new growth.

CALLUNA vulgaris
SCOTCH HEATHER
EVERGREEN
✄ VARIES ACCORDING TO BLOOM TIME

The many varieties of Scotch heather, all with tiny, scalelike leaves, range in size from 2 inches to 3 feet. Most bloom in mid- to late summer; shear off their

Calluna vulgaris 'Spring Torch'

faded flowers and branch tips after bloom. A few types flower into late fall; delay pruning those until just before the spring growth flush. In both cases, avoid cutting into older wood, because it does not resprout readily.

CALYCANTHUS

DECIDUOUS

LATE DORMANT SEASON

The eastern native Carolina allspice or sweetshrub (*C. floridus*) and the West Coast native spice bush (*C. occidentalis*) are clump-forming shrubs with slightly arching stems. They produce blossoms at the ends of the current season's growth.

For both, annually remove older stems that have produced only twiggy growth; then thin out any crowded and crossing branches. These plants are more attractive if you don't cut back the remaining growth. The western native is sometimes trained into a small multi-trunked tree.

CAMELLIA

EVERGREEN

ANYTIME, BUT ESPECIALLY AFTER BLOOM

These medium to large shrubs can be grown as specimen plants, limbed up into single- or multitrunked small trees, treated as informal hedges, or espaliered.

Camellias don't need routine pruning to stay healthy and attractive, but you may want to do a little pruning now and then for special purposes. The best time to prune is at the end of the bloom period, before active growth begins. However, you can do minor snipping or even remove branches at any time of year.

When young, some camellias grow wider than tall; shorten side branches to encourage upward growth. Some camellias have sparse foliage (notably, some kinds of *C. reticulata*); pinching the shoot tips of young plants will increase bushiness.

Older plants may be so full of leaves and small branches that they bear few or poor-quality flowers. Thinning out weak growth will increase both the quantity and quality of flowers and will improve the plant's form.

Some varieties bear too many flowers. To get the nicest display, disbud the plant in midsummer: from branch-end clusters rub off all but one or two round flower buds (the leaf buds are narrower); from buds along the stems, remove enough to leave a single flower bud every 2 to 4 inches.

Camellia japonica

WHERE TO PRUNE. Where you make your cuts will determine whether the resulting regrowth consists of a single shoot or several shoots. An unbranched shoot will send out several branches if you cut it just above a bud scale scar. These mark the end of one year's growth and the beginning of another: look for a slightly thickened, somewhat rough area where the bark's texture and color change slightly. But if you cut the stem between scars, in the middle of a year's growth,

only one branch will arise from the bud immediately below the cut. Removing a branch's terminal growth bud will stimulate several buds below it to grow.

REJUVENATION. You can cut an old camellia back to a smaller shrub—either in a single step or in two steps spaced a year apart. Do this at the end of the bloom period. (Warning: don't try this with reticulata types, because they may not resprout from the remaining branches.)

In the single-step procedure, you cut back the plant to a completely bare skeleton, as you would a rosebush. The remaining plant will send out new shoots profusely, especially if you fertilize it monthly during the growing season. From among the new shoots, choose those heading in the directions you want; pinch or rub out all others. Pinch the selected shoots' tips to get branching.

For a two-stage operation, cut off all branches along the bottom two-thirds of the main trunk; leave the top third of the plant alone. New growth will sprout from the cuts and will develop into short branches. During the next dormant season, cut the plant down to the height you prefer (somewhere along the bottom two-thirds of the trunk, where new growth has formed). Thin out any crowded branches on the renewed, smaller plant.

CARYOPTERIS

BLUEBEARD

DECIDUOUS

LATE DORMANT SEASON

These woody plants are usually treated as shrubby perennials. In colder areas they freeze back in winter; cut off dead wood after frost danger is past. In milder climates, where plants usually survive intact during winter, cut them nearly to the ground in spring. Blossoms appear in late summer on the current season's growth. Lightly cut back the stems after flowering—another crop of blossoms may come along.

Ceanothus 'Julia Phelps'

CEANOTHUS
WILD LILAC
EVERGREEN AND DECIDUOUS
✂ VARIES BY TYPE

The majority of these plants are spring-blooming evergreens pretty much limited to the West Coast; a couple of deciduous species are summer bloomers native to eastern and central North America. They are pruned according to type.

EVERGREEN TYPES. These range in habit from low and spreading to compact and bushy to upright and angular. The spring flowers come on shoots growing from the previous year's wood, so prune after the blooms have faded. Avoid cutting off branches of more than 1 inch in diameter; they don't callus over well. Control plant growth by frequently pinching the shoot tips during the growing season.

You can train the more rangy, angular growers as informal espaliers. Those that grow to tree size (*C.* 'Ray Hartman', for example) look best with multiple trunks or with branches very close to the ground.

Low-growing types used as ground covers range from nearly flat carpets to plants about 3 feet high. Pinch or cut off the tips of new growth or cut back young shoots to control spread and promote dense foliage. Cut out any branches that grow unattractively upright.

DECIDUOUS TYPES. This group consists of two small shrubby species—New Jersey tea (*C. americanus*) and *C. ovatus*. They flower in late spring or summer on new spring growth, and so should be pruned during the late dormant season. Cut back the main branches to 1½ or 2 feet and shorten the laterals, leaving two to six buds. Remove any weak growth.

CESTRUM
EVERGREEN
✂ SPRING AND SUMMER

Cestrums are vigorous, rangy, but frost-tender plants growing 6 to 12 feet tall. Prune out any cold-damaged wood in spring, as soon as frost danger is past. Prune again, heavily, after flowering or fruiting to control the plant's size.

Night jessamine (*C. nocturnum*) and willow-leafed jessamine (*C. parqui*) are grown for their powerfully fragrant blossoms. Pinch the tips of new growth regularly to produce denser, more compact plants, and thin out older, twiggy growth as needed.

Showy flowers and fruits are features of orange cestrum (*C. aurantiacum*) and red cestrum (*C. elegans;* formerly *C. purpureum*). Both are lax plants, best used as espaliers or shrubby vines.

CHAENOMELES
FLOWERING QUINCE
DECIDUOUS
✂ AFTER BLOOM

These plants are valued for their early blossoms (as early as January in mild-

Chaenomeles

winter climates), which appear on the previous year's growth. Many named varieties are sold; some are tall and upright, others low and spreading. All have attractive branching patterns, usually with many small, angular branches and twigs that result in a dense, thicketlike plant. They can be grown as flowering accent plants, semiformal or informal hedges, or espaliers.

After bloom thin out old and weak wood as well as crossing and tangled branches. Also head back any overly long branches. You can make some of your cuts earlier if you like, snipping budded branches for forced bloom indoors or cutting flowering shoots for bouquets.

Renovate an old, neglected bush by removing a third of the oldest wood each year for 3 years, or by lopping the whole plant low to the ground.

Chamaecyparis obtusa 'Fernspray Gold'

CHAMAECYPARIS
FALSE CYPRESS
CONIFEROUS EVERGREEN
✂ ANYTIME, BUT ESPECIALLY BEFORE SPRING GROWTH FLUSH

These random-branching conifers range from rock garden shrublets to timber trees. Small shrubs and shrublets are grown for their often irregular and picturesque form. Larger types usually grow symmetrically and make good screens and hedges.

To maintain shape and keep height even in row plantings, pinch out or cut back the tips of new growth. Plants take well to shearing into formal hedges; even the large timber tree Port Orford cedar (*C. lawsoniana*) can be sheared into a tall hedge. Don't cut back into old leafless wood, because new shoots will not sprout. Some varieties will take topiary training, usually of the "Ming tree" sort, in which a cluster of foliage perches alone at the end of each selected branch. Many types also make good bonsai subjects.

CHIMONANTHUS praecox
(C. fragrans, Meratia praecox)
WINTERSWEET
DECIDUOUS
✂ AFTER BLOOM

Tall (to 10 to 15 feet) and open growing, usually in a fountain shape, wintersweet bears its blossoms on the previous season's branches, while they are still leafless in the late dormant season. Prune right after bloom to promote the growth of new wood to bear next year's flowers. You can also prune during bloom if you want fragrant flowering stems to bring indoors.

Thin out old, weak, dead, or crowding stems yearly. If you want to keep the plant low, head back the stems to well-placed buds. Wintersweet can become leggy and unattractive with age; rejuvenate it by limbing up into a small tree or by cutting the whole plant to within a foot of the ground.

CLETHRA alnifolia
SUMMERSWEET, SWEET
PEPPERBUSH
DECIDUOUS
✂ LATE DORMANT SEASON

This plant grows strongly upright from 5 to 10 feet tall, with many slender stems that slowly form a broad clump. It can be used as a specimen shrub or as an informal hedge or screen. The flowers appear in summer, on the current season's shoots, so prune before spring growth gets under way. Cut back any overly tall

Clethra alnifolia

stems and periodically remove the oldest wood to make way for new.

CORNUS
DOGWOOD
DECIDUOUS
✂ LATE DORMANT SEASON

The shrubby dogwoods include thicket-forming plants grown for red or yellow winter stems. They comprise the following species and their varieties: bloodtwig dogwood (*C. sanguinea*), redtwig or red-osier dogwood (*C. stolonifera* or *C. sericea*), and tatarian dogwood (*C. alba*).

Because young growth shows the best color, prune yearly to encourage new shoots. Some gardeners even cut the plants low to the ground annually; this produces clumps of upright stems with few branches. For a more moderate approach, thin out about a third of the older stems and shorten the remaining ones. New growth will sprout from the roots and from the curtailed stems, producing a bushier plant than one lopped to the ground. Plants spread by underground stems or by suckers; to keep them from getting too large, dig up any shoots that emerge beyond the desired area.

For dogwood shrub-trees and full-fledged trees, see page 37.

COTINUS coggygria
(Rhus cotinus)
SMOKE TREE
DECIDUOUS
✂ LATE DORMANT SEASON OR
AFTER BLOOM

Smoke tree grows naturally as a multi-stemmed large shrub, though it can be

trained from the start as a small tree or converted from a shrub to a tree by limbing up. Little pruning is needed: cut out dead or broken limbs and remove crowding or awkward branches. You can do this in the late dormant season or wait until after bloom.

Purple-leafed varieties are sometimes treated as perennials: they are cut to the ground yearly in the late dormant season to force vigorous new growth, which will be more colorful than older growth. Because flowering occurs on older wood, such plants will not bloom—but as they're grown for their foliage, it doesn't matter.

Cotinus coggygria

COTONEASTER
DECIDUOUS, SEMIEVERGREEN, AND EVERGREEN
✂ DORMANT SEASON

The many cotoneaster species range in size from low growers to treelike shrubs, and in shape from horizontal to fountain-like to erect. Where these plants have room to branch naturally, they require little pruning. Cut back any shoots that mar the basic form, and occasionally remove the oldest wood to allow new growth to develop. If plants suffer freeze damage, remove dead wood but delay any other pruning until after spring growth has begun and the extent of injury is clear. To renew a neglected shrub, cut back severely—vigorous new growth will sprout from old wood. Continues >

Cotoneaster lacteus

Many types of cotoneaster, especially among the upright kinds, make good hedges. Formal hedging eliminates much of the berry display, so you're better off with a semiformal or informal style. Some of the smaller-leaved species are sometimes used for topiary; these look best when pruned selectively, however. Types with a rangy habit or long, arching branches are occasionally espaliered. Larger shrubs can be converted into multitrunked small trees by limbing up.

Fireblight may infect cotoneaster, blackening growth; cut out the diseased growth as described on page 16.

DAPHNE

EVERGREEN, SEMIEVERGREEN, AND DECIDUOUS

AFTER BLOOM

Though daphnes will respond to heavy pruning, they rarely need anything more than an occasional snip to correct the shape of the plant. Cut back to lateral branches or to just above obvious growth buds. You can cut budded branches of the deciduous species for fragrant forced bloom indoors.

DEUTZIA

DECIDUOUS

AFTER BLOOM

Because the flowers are carried on shoots that grew after the prior year's bloom, you prune after the flower display is over. Actually, new growth begins before the flowers fade, so don't wait until the show is completely finished.

On low-growing or medium-size types, such as slender deutzia (*D. gracilis*) and *D. rosea*, cut some of the oldest stems to the ground every other year. Heavily prune tall-growing types, such as *D. scabra*, by cutting back all wood that has flowered to outward-facing side branches. Don't wait for the bloom period to remove any winter-damaged growth, however; do this as soon as frost danger is past. You can rejuvenate an old, untidy plant by cutting it to within 6 inches of the ground, either after bloom or during the late dormant season.

Slender deutzia is probably the best hedge candidate among the various species: grow it as a semiformal or an informal hedge.

Deutzia gracilis

ELAEAGNUS

DECIDUOUS AND EVERGREEN

LATE SPRING OR EARLY SUMMER

These suckering shrubs typically grow into dense masses that need little pruning if grown naturally—just cut back any overlong branches. On variegated types, cut out any growth that reverts to all green as soon as you notice it.

On old plants that have become sparse and lost vigor, remove the oldest stems and heavily cut back the remaining branches. Plants pruned in this manner will normally send out vigorous new growth from cut branches as well as from the ground.

These shrubs serve mainly as screens and background plants. You can

also train them as formal or semiformal hedges (they tend to look straggly as informal hedges). Evergreen types make good informal espaliers.

ERICA

HEATH

EVERGREEN

AFTER BLOOM

These plants with small, needlelike leaves range from less-than-foot-high ground cover and rock garden candidates to 18-foot-tall specimen shrubs. On all types, refrain from cutting into leafless wood, because new growth may not sprout.

To prune the smaller heaths, shear them, removing spent flowers and the outer layer of foliage. This will stimulate new growth and keep the plants from becoming rangy. When plants get old and die back in the center, dig them out and replace them with new plants.

On the taller kinds, cut off spent blooms just below the flower spikes. You can control a plant's shape by cutting back wayward shoots to side branches or to just above a leaf.

EUONYMUS

DECIDUOUS AND EVERGREEN

LATE DORMANT SEASON

Neither the deciduous nor the evergreen group of euonymus shrubs needs routine pruning.

Among the most commonly grown deciduous types are winged euonymus or burning bush (*E. alata*), a large, dense, twiggy shrub to 15 or 20 feet tall and typically broader, and its variety 'Compacta', which usually grows only 6 to 10 feet high and a little narrower. They make good informal hedges and screens as well as specimen shrubs. Occasionally thin out some of the oldest stems; also cut back to laterals any branches that mar a plant's symmetry. These plants can also be converted into small trees by limbing up.

Euonymus alata

Large evergreen shrubs include varieties of *E. japonica* and *E. kiautschovica* *(E. patens),* used primarily as screens and hedges—either formally sheared or left with a more natural outline. Pruning of individual shrubs consists mainly of removing dead branches and cutting out any weak, twiggy stems in the plant's center. Older plants of *E. japonica* are sometimes limbed up into small trees.

The shrubby varieties of *E. fortunei* make good hedges. Grown as individual shrubs, most kinds will form mounding plants with branches that root where their tips touch moist soil. Pull the tips loose and head back the branches to keep the plant from spreading.

Variegated kinds of *E. japonica* and *E. fortunei* often develop shoots that revert to all-green foliage. Cut these off as soon as you notice them.

EXOCHORDA
PEARL BUSH
DECIDUOUS
✂ AFTER BLOOM

Pearl bush is a multistemmed, upright shrub with arching side branches. For a bushier plant, head back the main stems to promote branching or pinch the tips of new growth. Every year after bloom, remove spent flower spikes and cut out all weak wood in the plant's center.

Every few years, cut the oldest stems to the ground; new shoots will replace them. To restrict height and spread, cut branches back to strong laterals.

Common pearl bush (*E. racemosa*), which will grow 10 to 15 feet tall, is sometimes limbed up into a multitrunked small tree.

FAGUS
BEECH
DECIDUOUS
✂ SPRING AND SUMMER

Normally grown as a tree, beech is sometimes trained as a tall formal hedge about 15 feet high and as narrow as 1½ feet. But a beech hedge can be maintained lower—as low as 6 feet. Shearing twice during the growing season should keep hedges tidy. See page 39 for information on pruning beech trees.

Fagus sylvatica

FATSIA japonica
(Aralia sieboldii, A. japonica)
JAPANESE ARALIA
EVERGREEN
✂ SPRING OR SUMMER

Multistemmed and sparsely branched with bold, fan-shaped leaves at the branch tips, Japanese aralia doesn't need regular pruning, even though it responds well to it. Cut back any stems that become too tall (plants typically grow 5 to 8 feet tall), and thin out growth in the middle of the plant if it is too dense. To control a plant's spread, use a spade to remove unwanted stems springing up at the edges of the clump.

Rejuvenate old, spindly plants by cutting them low to the ground just before the spring growth flush. When new shoots emerge, thin them out if they're crowded.

FORSYTHIA
DECIDUOUS
✂ AFTER BLOOM

These fountain-shaped plants send up many stems from their roots. At the end of the dormant season, they are covered with blooms that appear directly on the previous year's leafless wood.

Don't prune a forsythia for several years after planting. Once the plant reaches the desired size, prune it annually after bloom: cut to the ground a third of the oldest stems and remove any weak, crowded, or dead branches. Pinch the tips of new shoots when they are 1 to 2 feet long to stimulate branching and to increase the next year's flower display. (You can do some of your pruning earlier, by cutting budded branches for forced bloom indoors and harvesting blooming stems for bouquets.)

To renew an old, neglected, and overcrowded plant, cut the whole thing nearly to the ground before it leafs out. As new growth appears, remove weak and crowding shoots.

In addition to being used as specimen shrubs, forsythias can be grown as informal hedges and espaliers.

Forsythia × intermedia

FOTHERGILLA
DECIDUOUS
✂ DORMANT SEASON OR AFTER BLOOM

These graceful shrubs produce twiggy stems from their base; the blossoms appear before, or sometimes with, the new leaves. Plants don't need routine pruning, but every few years you may want to open up the plant by cutting the oldest stems to the ground and removing weak, straggling, or dead branches.

Fuchsia 'Gartenmeister Bohnstedt'

FUCHSIA

EVERGREEN OR DECIDUOUS

✄ DEPENDS ON CLIMATE; SEE BELOW

Fuchsias vary in form from upright and bushy to vinelike. The plants are evergreen in mildest-winter climates; in colder areas, they may lose their leaves or even die to the ground.

The most commonly grown types are upright, frost-tender hybrids, which can be used as garden shrubs in suitable climates and container plants in all regions. Less commonly grown are large, upright, shrubby species such as *F. magellanica*, used as garden shrubs in areas where they are hardy. Vinelike or trailing plants, often called hanging basket fuchsias, look best grown in containers from which their stems and flowers can drape attractively. Both upright and trailing types can be trained as standards and espaliers.

Despite differences among fuchsias, you can follow a basic set of pruning guidelines in caring for all types. Because plants bloom on new growth from summer until frost, the goal is to develop a good framework from which strong new growth will emerge.

CONTAINER PLANTS. Prune severely to keep a plant growing in proper proportion to its container—new growth will hide a framework of short, woody stems. Cut back plants around November

in the mildest-winter climates, during early spring in colder regions. Where plants won't survive winter cold, store them indoors and prune them in spring only after all frost danger is past.

To prune upright fuchsias, first remove crossing and weak growth; then cut back the remaining branches to one or two pairs of buds. With hanging basket fuchsias, begin by cutting all stems up to the container's edge and eliminating upward-growing stems; then proceed as for upright fuchsias. Remove the plant from the pot, shake some soil from the roots, and cut back the root mass to half its size; replant in fresh potting mix.

In all regions, let about three pairs of leaves per shoot develop in spring before pinching the growing tips to promote branching. Continue pinching throughout the growing season for bushier plants and more flowers.

GARDEN PLANTS. Prune severely to keep plants small; prune moderately to allow plants to grow larger. Remove crossing and crowding branches and dead, broken, or weak stems; do this at the same time as you would prune fuchsias in containers. In the colder parts of fuchsia's range, wait until frost danger is past before pruning. To keep the plants from becoming leggy, pinch their new tips frequently during the growing season.

GARDENIA

EVERGREEN

✄ DURING BLOOM

Grow gardenias as either specimen shrubs or informal hedges. Some types are very long blooming, producing flowers from spring to fall. Most need little pruning to maintain a neat appearance. During bloom, thin out any weak branches that are bearing no flowers and that have few or small leaves. At the same time, on leggy plants (especially *G. jasminoides* 'Mystery'), lightly cut back shoots to encourage branching. Remove spent flowers to prolong the bloom period.

To renew an old, rangy plant, prune it before spring growth begins. Thin out twiggy growth and a portion of the unproductive branches. Cut back some of the oldest, weakest branches severely to stimulate new growth from the plant's base. A year later remove more old, weak wood. Continue this process annually until all growth is young and vigorous.

In the coldest part of their range, gardenias have been killed to the ground but have resprouted in spring.

Gardenia jasminoides

HAMAMELIS

WITCH HAZEL

DECIDUOUS

✄ AFTER BLOOM

Witch hazels are medium to large multi-stemmed shrubs, usually with a spreading habit and angular or zigzagging branches; some types are treelike. These plants need little pruning, but if they become too dense you should thin out enough old wood to open up the interior. Also remove any poorly placed, weak, twiggy, broken, or dead branches. To keep the plants from getting too big, cut back overly long shoots to well-placed side branches. On grafted plants, be sure to remove suckers.

Instead of waiting to prune until after blossoms fade, you can thin plants during bloom and use the flowering branches for bouquets.

HIBISCUS

DECIDUOUS AND EVERGREEN

✄ LATE DORMANT SEASON

Because these plants bloom on the current season's growth, they should be pruned—severely, if necessary—before the spring growth flush. The various types make attractive informal hedges; they can also be trained as standards or converted into small trees by limbing up.

DECIDUOUS TYPES. The most commonly grown species are rose of Sharon (*H. syriacus*) and confederate rose (*H. mutabilis*).

In warmer regions, they can become tree size if they're not heavily pruned. Annually thin out the oldest stems as well as any weak, broken, or dead wood. Cut back overlong stems to well-placed side branches or growth buds. Established plants can take almost any amount of pruning. To encourage the formation of large flowers, cut back the previous season's growth to two buds. The plants can also be cut low to the ground to rejuvenate them.

In the colder part of their range, these plants act as perennials, usually freezing to the ground in winter and resprouting from the roots in spring.

EVERGREEN TYPES. The flashy Chinese hibiscus (*H. rosa-sinensis*) grows as a tender shrub or small tree in the warmest parts of the West and South. The many varieties range from about 4 to 15 feet tall.

Young plants seldom need pruning, but pinching back the tips of new growth will increase bushiness and the number of flowering branches. To maintain a mature plant's vigor, prune out about a third of the old wood in early spring, after frost danger is past.

Hibiscus syriacus

To rejuvenate a big, woody, old shrub that produces few flowers, prune it in several stages. Start in spring, cutting back one or two old stems each month through August. By the end of the growing season, you should have pruned out about half of the stems.

HYDRANGEA
DECIDUOUS
VARIES BY SPECIES

Hydrangeas fall into two groups: those you prune after bloom because they flower on the previous season's growth, and those you prune in the late dormant season because they bear on new spring growth.

AFTER BLOOM. Types blooming on the prior year's growth include bigleaf hydrangea (*H. macrophylla*—formerly *H. hortensia, H. opuloides,* and *H. otaksa*) and oakleaf hydrangea (*H. quercifolia*).

On bigleaf hydrangea you cut back the stems or branches that have flowered, leaving a certain number of bud pairs below. Leave two to four pairs on stems that grow from the ground and two pairs on side branches. As the plant matures, begin to thin out the oldest wood. Be sure to remove any crowded, crossing, broken, or dead wood. In cold climates these plants often die to the ground and grow back from the roots in spring; in such cases, they won't flower.

Note: prune 'All Summer Beauty' as you would other bigleaf hydrangea varieties, but do it in the late dormant season, because it blooms on new spring growth. If it is winter killed, it will rebound in spring and bloom that summer.

Oakleaf hydrangea produces many stems from the ground, quickly spreading into a clump. Thin out old, weak, and crowding stems yearly after bloom. In cold climates, the plant dies back in winter and thus produces no flowers. Gardeners who prefer the foliage to the blooms intentionally lop the plant to the ground each year in the late dormant season.

LATE DORMANT SEASON. Plants blooming on new shoots include smooth hydrangea (*H. arborescens*) and peegee hydrangea (*H. paniculata* 'Grandiflora').

If you didn't prune smooth hydrangea or its variety 'Grandiflora', you would have a large shrub with an abundance of small blooms. For a neater plant with larger flower clusters, prune these plants back yearly at least halfway; be sure to cut out any crowding, weak, or dead wood at the same time. To get really big blooms (take care: they may cause the stems to droop) on a smaller plant, some gardeners cut back the previous year's growth to two or three buds, or even cut the entire plant to the ground.

When growing peegee hydrangea as a large shrub (it can be trained as a small tree), make sure that the young plant is either multistemmed or branched low down. If it isn't, cut it back to within two buds of the ground to force branching. Prune it annually, as for smooth hydrangea; how much growth you remove will determine its flower and plant size.

Hypericum 'Hidcote'

HYPERICUM
ST. JOHNSWORT
EVERGREEN, SEMIEVERGREEN, AND DECIDUOUS
DORMANT SEASON

Without attention, these shrubs become twiggy and straggling after several years. Every 2 or 3 years, therefore, thin out crowded growth by cutting out the oldest stems and any weak, twiggy, or dead wood. Cut back the remaining plant by one-third to one-half of its previous size.

The more upright shrubby species can be used as informal hedges.

Aaron's beard or creeping St. Johnswort *(H. calycinum)* is a vigorous ground cover that spreads by underground runners. Mow or cut it to the ground every few years—or more often, as needed. In areas where foliage is freeze damaged, trim the planting to the ground yearly after frost danger is past.

Ilex verticillata

ILEX

HOLLY

EVERGREEN AND DECIDUOUS

DORMANT SEASON

These plants range from low shrubs to full-fledged trees. The smaller shrubby hollies make good foundation and border plants, the larger ones good screens. The small-leaved types can be sheared into formal hedges or topiary figures. Larger-leaved types are better used as semiformal or informal hedges. As a rule, female plants produce berries only when pollinated by a nearby male holly (though a few holly types are self-fruitful).

Most hollies tend to be dense and symmetrical. Prune primarily to shape them, cutting back poorly placed or wayward branches. Also excise all broken or dead branches. The December holiday season is a good time to prune, because clipped branches can be used for indoor decorations. You can restore a holly that has become too open or ragged by severely shortening its branches and allowing new growth to fill in.

JUNIPERUS

JUNIPER

CONIFEROUS EVERGREEN

SPRING OR SUMMER

Junipers are random-branching conifers ranging in size from low ground covers to large trees and varying in shape from symmetrical to twisted or angular. To keep pruning chores to a minimum, be sure to select the juniper most likely to give you the look and size you want for the allotted space.

Prune a juniper to correct its shape, to accent its form (usually its irregularity), to limit its size, or to renovate an overgrown plant.

TO CORRECT SHAPE. A good time to do this is before the spring growth flush, so that new stems will hide pruning scars. However, you won't harm the plants if you wait until summer.

Prune awkward branches that spoil the plant's form. On ground cover junipers, cut back a vertical stem to a branch that grows horizontally. On angular and upright junipers, cut back irregular branches to others that point in the direction you want future growth to go. Don't cut back to a bare stem, because it may not grow again.

You can make a scrawny plant bushier by cutting back new growth about halfway in summer.

TO ACCENT IRREGULARITY. Pruning to accent irregularity is entirely a matter of personal taste. In spring or summer, selectively cut back or remove whole

Juniperus chinensis

limbs to emphasize a twisted or gnarled form, an angular branching pattern, or sprays of foliage held in horizontal planes.

You'll need to look carefully to determine which branches are contributing to the plant's character and which are obscuring it. Remove the latter with thinning cuts.

TO LIMIT SIZE. Prune to limit size only during summer, after new growth has stopped. Cut back new shoots nearly to their point of origin, preferably to small branches that head in the same direction as the growth you are removing. You can shear the new growth of junipers that are upright, conical, or regular in form, but selectively hand-prune any plants with irregular or open growth. Plants that are cut back in this way each year will increase in size very slowly.

TO RENOVATE. You can't cut an old juniper back to leafless wood and expect regrowth. However, you can convert an old, overgrown shrub into an attractive multitrunked small tree by limbing up. Thin out the top a bit to reveal the branching and foliage pattern.

KALMIA latifolia

MOUNTAIN LAUREL, CALICO BUSH

EVERGREEN

AFTER BLOOM

This rhododendron relative is rounded in youth, often reaching 15 feet tall and becoming more irregular with age. It seldom needs pruning, but responds well to it when it is necessary. Do any pruning after bloom, as the plant flowers on the previous year's shoots.

New growth comes from beneath the flower clusters and at the tips of stems that have not bloomed. To maintain the plant's appearance, break off spent flower clusters carefully so that you won't damage growth buds just beneath (see the illustration on page 52). Also cut back any overlong branches to strong laterals. To get branching on shoots that didn't flower, pinch off the tips.

On an old, leggy plant, you can cut the oldest stems to the ground after bloom. You could prune more severely before the spring growth flush, but regrowth might be slow.

KERRIA japonica
DECIDUOUS

✄ AFTER BLOOM

An open, rounded shrub to 6 feet tall, kerria should be given adequate room to display its graceful, arching form. It bears flowers on the previous year's wood and should be pruned heavily after the blooms fade.

Remove any suckers and all dead or weak wood; then cut out all of the stems that flowered. Cut most of them to the ground, but shorten a few to the point where new growth is sprouting low on the stem. Growth from these shortened stems will fill in the lower part of the bush. You can rejuvenate kerria by lopping the whole plant low to the ground, either after bloom or during the late dormant season.

Kerria japonica

KOLKWITZIA AMABILIS
BEAUTY BUSH

DECIDUOUS

✄ AFTER BLOOM OR LATE
DORMANT SEASON

Given ample room, this big shrub with arching branches needs only enough pruning each year to ensure strong new growth. Blossoms appear on the previous

year's wood. Each year after bloom, cut a few of the oldest stems to the ground. You can renew the plant by cutting all stems to the ground, either after bloom or during the late dormant season.

Some gardeners prefer to wait and thin the plant in winter, when it is leafless—by doing so, they're also able to enjoy the ornamental fruits that follow the blossoms.

Lantana

LANTANA
EVERGREEN

✄ BEFORE SPRING GROWTH FLUSH

These plants are evergreen in mild-winter areas; in colder regions, where they may lose their leaves or die out, they are usually treated as summer annuals. Plants bloom on the current season's shoots. They will take almost any amount of pruning and make a vigorous comeback, sprouting from old as well as young wood. Without pruning, the shrubby varieties—used as foundation, container, and hedge plants—become ungainly or ratty looking, and ground cover types often build up a thatch of dead stems.

After frost danger is past, prune shrubby lantanas in the ground by removing crowding, weak, broken, and dead wood; then cut back the remaining growth as lightly or as severely as you want, to control size and shape. Cut back container plants to a small framework of very short branches (the same procedure recommended for potted fuchsias; see page 72). If you have only a few plants to

care for (whether in the ground or in pots), pinch their growing tips frequently to promote branching and compactness.

LAURUS NOBILIS
SWEET BAY, GRECIAN LAUREL

EVERGREEN

✄ SPRING AND SUMMER

This plant's growth habit is dense, compact, and neat. Without pruning, it forms a broad cone of foliage and eventually becomes a tree, usually with multiple trunks. To maintain a natural form, just cut back any awkward branches to strong side branches.

Sweet bay is often sheared into hedges and topiary figures, though the leaves tend to look a little ragged when trimmed so closely—you may want to make individual, selective cuts instead.

LAVANDULA
LAVENDER

EVERGREEN

✄ AFTER BLOOM IN MILD CLIMATES;
BEFORE SPRING GROWTH FLUSH IN
COLDER AREAS

Unpruned lavenders in time become untidy, floppy, or sparse. Cut back plants each year to keep them compact and attractive. Remove all spent flower spikes and at least an inch of leafy shoot below them, either by selectively cutting back each shoot or by shearing the plants. (Avoid cutting into old, leafless wood, however.) Lavenders make good low informal hedges.

Old, neglected, overgrown plants are seldom restored by severe pruning; replace them with young plants instead.

LEUCOTHOE
EVERGREEN AND DECIDUOUS

✄ AFTER BLOOM

These plants form clumps of many-branched stems. Occasionally cut the oldest stems to the ground to make way for strong new growth; also cut back any overly tall or straggling stems to well-placed side branches or growth buds. Lop a neglected plant to the ground to renew it, either after bloom or during the dormant season.

LIGUSTRUM
PRIVET

DECIDUOUS, SEMIEVERGREEN, AND EVERGREEN

✂ SPRING AND SUMMER

The growth habit of these tried-and-true hedge plants is dense and compact. They withstand frequent shearing as formal hedges and topiary figures—though as topiary, privet is best trimmed selectively with hand shears. Even so, it tends to look a little coarse compared with figures fashioned from smaller-leaved plants. Shearing privets sacrifices their flower display, though the blooms are not prized by many gardeners because of their characteristically odd fragrance.

You can also grow privets as specimen shrubs; if you want the flowers, you can wait and prune after bloom. Cut out any crossing, weak, dead, or wayward branches. Pinch back shoots to encourage bushiness. Privets can also be trained as standards or limbed up into small trees.

Ligustrum

MAHONIA
EVERGREEN

✂ AFTER BLOOM OR AFTER FRUITING

Some of these cane-producing shrubs make good sculptural accent plants; others become bulky bushes, and still others grow as ground covers. Each type has different pruning requirements, though all

can be rejuvenated by lopping them to the ground before spring growth begins.

ACCENT PLANTS. Leatherleaf mahonia (*M. bealei*), *M. fortunei,* and *M. lomariifolia* consist of vertical stems, unbranched or sparsely branched, with tufts of large leaves at the branch tips. Their beauty is in their sparse, linear shape; don't try to prune them to become low and dense. If an old stem grows too tall for its space, cut it to the ground; new stems will sprout from the base.

SHRUB TYPES. These include Oregon grape (*M. aquifolium*), *M. fremontii, M. nevinii,* and *M. pinnata.* Pinch back the stems of newly planted shrubs to encourage low branches and new shoots from the base. Do the same to an established plant if it becomes leggy and sparse. You can also cut back any wayward branches severely. When plants become too big and bulky, cut the oldest stems to the ground.

GROUND COVERS. These plants—including *M. aquifolium* 'Compacta', longleaf mahonia (*M. nervosa),* and creeping mahonia (*M. repens)*—spread under ground to form low colonies of upright, somewhat branching stems. Prune only to trim stems that grow above the level of foliage you want to maintain.

MYRTUS communis
MYRTLE

EVERGREEN

✂ ANYTIME

This rounded, dense, and bulky but fine-textured shrub reaches 5 to 6 feet tall (as much as 15 feet in old age), with a greater spread. Allowed to branch naturally as a specimen shrub or in an informal hedge or screen, it needs little or no pruning. However, the plant will withstand the shearing needed for formal hedging and topiary work.

To grow myrtle as a character shrub, thin it selectively to reveal the limb structure. The goal is to see clumps of leaves interspersed with open spaces

along the main limbs, instead of a solid foliage canopy. You can either leave the branches on the plant all the way down or limb it up into a small tree.

Myrtus communis

NANDINA domestica
HEAVENLY BAMBOO, SACRED BAMBOO

EVERGREEN OR SEMIEVERGREEN

✂ BEFORE SPRING GROWTH FLUSH

Each plant forms a clump of vertical stems that may reach 6 to 8 feet tall, with few or no branches. In time, unpruned clumps usually become top-heavy and bare at the base. If new stems keep forming at the base, however, the plants will remain leafy to the ground. Encourage this by cutting the oldest canes to the ground yearly. In mild-winter climates plants produce red or white berries in late fall or winter; if you prune then, you can bring cut branches indoors for decoration.

Rejuvenate plants that are too tall and straggling in two stages. First, cut half the stems to within 6 to 12 inches of the ground. After they have sent out good new growth, cut back the remaining stems as you did the first set.

Dwarf varieties need little work; just cut back any unsightly or wayward stems.

NERIUM oleander
OLEANDER

EVERGREEN

✂ BEFORE SPRING GROWTH FLUSH

Oleander grows naturally as a many-stemmed, bulky shrub. It blooms on the current season's growth; the peak bloom period is summer, though some flowers are evident nearly year-round. Routine pruning isn't necessary, but sooner or later you may need to prune to solve problems.

To limit size and help renew plants, cut the oldest stems to the ground. You can shorten the remaining stems if the plant is getting too tall for your purposes. Stimulate new growth low on the plant by severely cutting back the stems on the outer edge of the clump. During the growing season, snip off stem tips to encourage branching. You can take more drastic action with an old, unattractive, leggy plant—just lop the whole plant low to the ground.

Oleander makes a good informal flowering hedge or screen. Plants are often limbed up into single- or multi-trunked small trees; new shoots sprout freely from the base, so you will have to remove them to maintain the tree form.

All parts of the plant are extremely poisonous if ingested: be careful to keep prunings away from children and animals. Never burn the prunings, because smoke from the wood is severely irritating. Even the sap can be caustic in contact with skin.

Nerium oleander

OSMANTHUS

EVERGREEN

Osmanthus heterophyllus

osmanthus (*O. heterophyllus,* sometimes sold as *O. aquifolium* or *O. ilicifolius)*. To cultivate them as background shrubs, pinch the tips of new growth on young plants to encourage bushiness and occasionally cut back any wayward branches on established plants. These shrubs also make fine informal or semiformal tall hedges. Sweet olive can be trained as an espalier.

Delavay osmanthus (*O. delavayi)* is an arching plant to about 6 feet high and a little wider. Given adequate room to branch, it needs little pruning—just remove any weak or dead branches.

PEROVSKIA
RUSSIAN SAGE
EVERGREEN
✂ BEFORE SPRING GROWTH FLUSH

Growing 3 to 4 feet high and wide, Russian sage produces flowers on the current season's growth. To encourage vigorous new shoots, cut the whole plant nearly to the ground each year before new spring growth begins. Trim off spent blossoms to extend the flowering period.

Russian sage acts as a perennial in cold-winter climates; prune it back to live wood in spring after frost danger is over.

PHILADELPHUS
MOCK ORANGE
DECIDUOUS
✂ AFTER BLOOM

Most kinds of mock orange have fountainlike growth and range in height from 3 to 10 feet or more. Give them plenty of

room to develop to full size naturally, because cutting them back to fit a limited space ruins their charm. They bear blooms in late spring on the previous year's wood, and so should be pruned after flowering.

Plants begin to send out many new shoots after the bloom period—some come from the ground, others from low on stems that have flowered. Young plants and lower-growing varieties usually need to keep most or all of this new growth. Prune the tips of stems that flowered, cutting them back to a pair of vigorous new shoots. Thin out the new shoots only if some are growing too close together.

In time, you will have to cut some of the oldest stems to the ground to give new stems room to grow; choose canes that are no longer producing strong new shoots. Do this more often on the extra-vigorous, tall-growing kinds than on the smaller types. Check annually to see if your plant needs thinning out. If you haven't kept up with the plant and it's become a mess, rejuvenate it by lopping all growth low to the ground—either after bloom or during the late dormant season.

Philadelphus coronarius

PHOTINIA
EVERGREEN AND DECIDUOUS
✂ LATE DORMANT SEASON OR
AFTER BLOOM

These medium to large shrubs are vigorous growers. Pinch new growth to encourage bushiness, particularly to pro-

Three of the four common species and their varieties are dense shrubs that can eventually reach tree size: *O. fortunei,* sweet olive (*O. fragrans),* and holly-leaf

mote branching low on the plant. Pinch a new shoot while it is 1 to 2 feet long; then pinch the resulting branches if they in turn become too long. Whenever plants become crowded, thin out some of the oldest, least vigorous growth and any dead wood in the plant's center. Either prune during the late dormant season or wait until after bloom if you want flowers.

Many photinias can be converted to small trees by limbing up, or they can be trained as trees from the beginning. They are also often used for hedging. Although redtip *(P. × fraseri)* is popular as a sheared hedge, its fairly large leaves look ragged when cut in that manner—try semiformal or informal training instead. Prune this particular hybrid after its red spring foliage turns green, in order to enjoy its best feature.

Pieris

PIERIS
EVERGREEN
✄ AFTER BLOOM

These medium-size, graceful, elegant plants need little pruning. They grow densely and fairly symmetrically; any irregularity of shape is usually attractive and should be maintained.

Plants will produce growth from leafless wood, but only a single shoot is likely to grow from a cut made there. To promote branching on an unbranched stem, head it back to a group of leaves. Remove dead wood and any poorly placed branches with thinning cuts.

Pinus mugo mugo

PINUS mugo
(P. montana)
SWISS MOUNTAIN PINE
CONIFEROUS EVERGREEN
✄ SPRING

This extremely variable pine may grow 15 to 20 feet tall, though its expanding new growth can be pinched back partially or completely in spring to keep the plant considerably smaller (see more about pines on page 42). The several dwarf varieties usually need no pruning at all; they include mugho pine *(P. m. mugo)*, a rock garden and border plant growing to about 4 feet tall.

PITTOSPORUM
EVERGREEN
✄ ANYTIME

Most pittosporums are large plants that can be grown as specimen shrubs, hedges, screens, or topiary (for the latter, hand shears produce the best effect). The popular *P. tobira* 'Wheeler's Dwarf' is the runt of the group, at only about 3 feet high. All pittosporums allowed to branch naturally need a little shaping from time to time: thin out weak and dead branches as well as any wayward shoots that detract from the plant's form.

You can grow *P. crassifolium, P. eugenioides, P. rhombifolium, P. tenuifolium,* and Victorian box *(P. undulatum)* as formal hedges, maintaining them almost indefinitely at any height over 5 feet. For a softer, more natural look train those same species, willow pittosporum

(P. phillyraeoides), or *P. viridiflorum* as tall informal or semiformal hedges. When an old hedge (or individual plant) becomes woody at the base or just too large, cut it back to a bare framework before the spring growth flush.

PLATYCLADUS orientalis
(Thuja orientalis)
ORIENTAL ARBORVITAE
CONIFEROUS EVERGREEN
✄ ANYTIME, BUT ESPECIALLY BEFORE SPRING GROWTH FLUSH

Though botanists bestow a distinct identity on this arborvitae, to most gardeners the species and its many named varieties are simply oriental versions of the American arborvitae. For pruning tips, therefore, see *Thuja occidentalis* on page 85.

PONCIRUS trifoliata
HARDY ORANGE, TRIFOLIATE ORANGE
DECIDUOUS
✄ LATE DORMANT SEASON

Though hardy orange grows naturally as a small tree, you can also use it as an impenetrable large semiformal or informal hedge. For a really unusual hedge, choose the 6-foot dwarf 'Flying Dragon': its contorted branches and long, curved thorns are a focal point in winter, when the plant is leafless. Prune only enough to maintain the hedge form, leaving intact as much of the branching as possible. Be sure to wear gloves while pruning: puncture wounds from these thorns can fester.

PRUNUS
EVERGREEN
✄ BEFORE SPRING GROWTH FLUSH

The growth habit of these evergreen shrubby relatives of cherry, peach, and plum trees can be summed up in one word: dense. The most common kinds are Carolina laurel cherry *(P. caroliniana),* hollyleaf cherry *(P. ilicifolia),*

English laurel (*P. laurocerasus*), Portugal laurel (*P. lusitanica*), and Catalina cherry (*P. lyonii*).

Left unpruned, they will become increasingly large shrubs until they reach tree size. You can also use them as medium or large semiformal and informal hedge plants. For lower hedges, use the dwarf varieties of English laurel. Though English laurel is often sheared, doing so mutilates its large leaves; for a better appearance, make selective cuts back within the plant. To maintain any of these plants as privacy screens, periodically cut back wayward branches. Zabel laurel (*P. laurocerasus* 'Zabeliana') is sometimes trained as an espalier.

Prunus laurocerasus 'Zabeliana'

PYRACANTHA
PYRACANTHA, FIRETHORN
EVERGREEN
✂ AFTER FRUITING

These plants, grown for their bright fall or winter berries, range from low ground covers to tall, upright, treelike shrubs. Some of the larger erect kinds can be trained as small trees from the start, or converted from shrubs by limbing up. Because pyracanthas can withstand severe pruning, you can train them as standards, formal espaliers, and sheared hedges and topiary. However, many gardeners think the plants look best (certainly they fruit more) when their natural, irregular form is maintained.

Blossoms and fruit appear on short branches all along the previous year's wood. On shrubs left unpruned, the berries will form farther and farther out on increasingly long branches that may droop or break under the weight of a heavy crop. Also, without attention a pyracantha can grow quite large. There are two ways to control a shrub's size without clipping it. You can pinch new growth to encourage branching and compactness, or you can cut out branches that have borne berries and thin excessively long branches to laterals growing in desirable directions.

Because of their dense, thorny growth, pyracanthas make fine barrier or hedgerow plants for your garden. In these configurations, just prune back any wayward branches.

Ground cover and low shrub varieties need pruning only to shape the plants. Cut off vertical stems on ground covers to maintain a uniform height. On low shrubs, cut back any wayward stems that detract from the overall appearance. Wear gloves as you work: thorn wounds can fester.

All but the ground cover and dwarf varieties are easy to train as formal or informal espaliers. For the tidiest look, cut back flowering branches (except those that form the main framework) to just above the first flower cluster. Make all cuts back to a side branch or cluster of leaves.

The bacterial disease fireblight may be a problem. If you detect any blackened growth, remove it according to the instructions on page 16.

RHAMNUS
DECIDUOUS AND EVERGREEN
✂ DORMANT SEASON

Generally, the various types of rhamnus need pruning only to direct or control their shape. If a branch gets too long and makes the plant lopsided, cut it back to a well-placed lateral. Keep low growers low by thinning out upward-growing branches or cutting them back to horizontal side branches.

Taller kinds can be limbed up into small trees or trained as tall formal, semiformal, or informal hedges. These include alder buckthorn (*R. frangula*), coffeeberry (*R. californica*), common buckthorn (*R. cathartica*), and Italian buckthorn (*R. alaternus*).

Tallhedge buckthorn (*R. frangula* 'Columnaris') is almost exclusively a tall hedge; naturally very slender (about 4 feet wide), it grows to about 15 feet tall but can be maintained as low as 4 feet by shearing.

Rhaphiolepis indica

RHAPHIOLEPIS
EVERGREEN
✂ AFTER BLOOM

Neat, dense, and malleable sum up the predominant qualities of these border, background, and informal hedge plants. Most are low growing; even the taller kinds rarely reach more than 5 or 6 feet.

They need little pruning. To encourage bushiness, pinch the branch tips at least once a year right after flowering, starting when the plants are young. To encourage spreading growth, pinch or head back upright branches. To make plants more upright, pinch or head back horizontal growth. Cut back overly long shoots to keep the plant compact. For a more open shape, allow plants to grow naturally, and thin out small and crowding branches from the interior.

If distinctively light green, soft leaves appear on stems close to the ground, your plant has been grafted onto a quince rootstock. Pull these shoots off whenever they appear.

RHODODENDRON
RHODODENDRON, AZALEA
EVERGREEN AND DECIDUOUS
✄ VARIES BY TYPE

Botanically speaking, all azaleas are rhododendrons, but obvious differences set most azaleas apart from most rhododendrons. These aren't limited to appearance—the growth patterns also differ, prompting variations in how the plants are pruned.

RHODODENDRONS

To prune properly, you must understand how these evergreen plants grow and how climate affects them. Also realize that they may take several years to become established in your garden before they bloom. In mild-winter climates, do any extensive pruning in winter or early spring, before the growth buds begin to sprout; in cold-winter regions, wait to prune until frost danger is past. You can do some shaping while the plants are in bloom, using the cut branches for indoor decoration.

HOW PLANTS GROW. Growth comes in flushes. In cold-winter areas there may be one growth spurt in spring, but in a milder climate two or even three per growing season. Each new shoot has a few leaves scattered along its length. When growth stops, leaves toward the shoot's end cluster together to form a whorl. At the tip of each shoot is either a growth bud or a flower bud: the former are slender and tapered, the latter shorter and rounder. Beneath both kinds of terminal buds lie several growth buds clustered at the base of the leaves in the whorl.

PINCHING. To encourage a bushier plant, pinch off the terminal growth bud in winter or early spring, before or just as the bud begins to grow. The next flush of growth will stimulate several buds in the whorl to sprout. The result will be that several branches will grow, making the plant bushier. (The growth buds of the whorl will sprout naturally after the bloom period if the terminal bud is a flower bud.)

Pinching off the terminal growth bud is particularly important on a young plant, where a shoot may elongate for several growth flushes without branching if the terminal bud remains intact. By pinching regularly, you can guide a young plant's form so that it will need little shaping in later years.

Rhododendron

CUTTING BACK. If plants need pruning to correct their shape, cut back to just above a leaf whorl; new shoots will grow from dormant buds just beneath the cut. If you have to cut back into bare wood, cut just above a band of faint rings on the bark that indicates where there was once a whorl of leaves; the small bumps under the bark are dormant growth buds. To remove branches entirely, make cuts back to joints with other limbs.

DEADHEADING. To prevent seed formation, which can reduce the next year's bloom, remove spent flower trusses, especially on younger plants. Be careful not to damage the growth buds at the base of each truss (see illustration on page 52).

REJUVENATING. To renew an old, overgrown, leggy rhododendron, cut back a third of the limbs to about 8 to 12 inches above the ground each year for 3 years. Try to cut just above a band of faint rings (see "Cutting Back," above); if you can't, cut back to about 12 inches and hope for regrowth.

Some rhododendrons won't take this sort of pruning. Members of the Fal-

coneri series and so-called tree rhododendrons in general will not produce new growth from bare wood. Rhododendrons in the Thomsonii series and smooth-barked species and hybrids likewise put out little or no growth from bare wood. Train these rhododendrons from youth by pinching.

AZALEAS

Unlike rhododendrons, azaleas include both deciduous and evergreen shrubs. Prune deciduous types while they are dormant and leafless (wait until frost danger has passed in cold climates). You can prune evergreen azaleas along with rhododendrons in winter or early spring, before the growth buds begin to sprout. Because of the way evergreen azaleas grow, you can also prune them anytime during the growing season.

HOW PLANTS GROW. Evergreen azaleas grow steadily throughout the growing season, whereas deciduous azaleas put out a strong but briefer growth spurt similar to that of rhododendrons. The new shoots of both types of azaleas produce leaves that are fairly evenly spaced along the branches. At the base of each leaf is a growth bud. This means that new growth will sprout from almost anywhere you make a cut—in either leafy or bare wood. Consequently, you needn't be quite so careful about pruning an azalea as you would a rhododendron. This close arrangement of buds likewise allows you to shear azaleas into formal hedges (they also make attractive semiformal and informal hedges).

PINCHING. The shoots of evergreen azaleas may grow long without branching, but you can counteract this tendency by pinching the tips. During the growing season, pinch as often as needed to develop the branching you want.

If necessary to give balance to a plant, you can pinch the growing tips of deciduous azaleas during the growing season.

ADDITIONAL PRUNING. Keep evergreen azalea plants compact by cutting back new growth after the flowers fade. You can either shear the plants or make selective cuts.

Deciduous azaleas may become woody and unproductive as they age. To keep them vigorous, remove old, weak stems during the dormant season.

ROSA

ROSE

DECIDUOUS

✂ VARIES BY TYPE

The gamut of roses available to today's gardeners includes modern hybrids, various "old-fashioned" types (known as old garden roses), old and new types of shrub roses, and species roses. On most of these plants, you'll be doing two kinds of pruning—minor pruning throughout the growing season to regulate growth, and major pruning in the late dormant season or after bloom to remove dead, damaged, or diseased wood, renew flowering shoots, and promote symmetry.

During the growing season, check the emerging new shoots to see what direction they're taking. Prune out any poorly located or unnecessary shoots. Rose fanciers often disbud their bushes: that is, they remove some of the flower buds so that the remaining ones will produce larger blooms.

After flowers fade, it's a good idea to remove spent blossoms on modern repeat-flowering roses—hybrid teas, grandifloras, floribundas, and miniatures—in order to thwart seed setting, which occurs at the expense of flowering. When doing so, cut stems as far down as necessary to keep the bush shapely; cut above an outward-facing bud over a five-leaflet leaf. On the other hand, newly planted roses and weak or small plants that you're trying to build up need all the leaves they produce. On such plants, just snap off the faded flowers but leave all of the foliage. You can deadhead repeat-flowering shrub roses as well, though their general vigor keeps them productive without this attention.

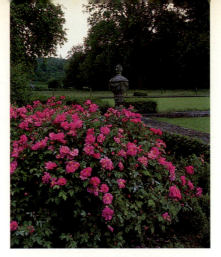

Rosa gallica 'Officinalis'

See the directions that follow for major pruning that should be done yearly—either in the late dormant season, when growth buds along the canes begin to swell (for repeat bloomers), or after bloom (for spring bloomers). Check with your local Cooperative Extension office for the recommended pruning dates in your area. Low (or "hard") pruning and high (or "light") pruning have both had their champions in the past. Current-

ly, rose experts hold the view that light to moderate pruning (when you have that option) produces the best possible garden plants and most abundant flowers.

HYBRID TEA, GRANDIFLORA, AND FLORIBUNDA ROSES. Regardless of where you live, you can apply the following guidelines to pruning these widely grown repeat-blooming modern roses. Make your cuts in the late dormant season.

Remove all dead wood and all weak, twiggy branches. If an older cane produced only weak growth that season, remove it at the bud union (the knobby area low on the trunk, where the desirable variety has been budded to the rootstock). Cut it out at ground level if the plant isn't budded but is growing on its own roots. On budded plants, pull off any suckers.

Open up the bush by removing all branches that cross through the center. This gives you a vase-shaped plant (a slen-

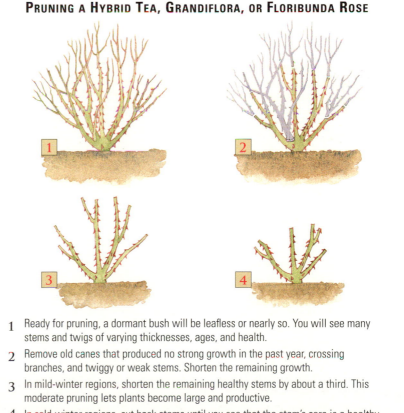

PRUNING A HYBRID TEA, GRANDIFLORA, OR FLORIBUNDA ROSE

1. Ready for pruning, a dormant bush will be leafless or nearly so. You will see many stems and twigs of varying thicknesses, ages, and health.
2. Remove old canes that produced no strong growth in the past year, crossing branches, and twiggy or weak stems. Shorten the remaining growth.
3. In mild-winter regions, shorten the remaining healthy stems by about a third. This moderate pruning lets plants become large and productive.
4. In cold-winter regions, cut back stems until you see that the stem's core is a healthy white. The bush's final size will depend on the severity of the winter.

der or fat vase, depending on the plant's natural habit) without a central tangle of twigs and leaves where insects and diseases could flourish. Rose growers in very hot climates often just shorten those branches, because their foliage shades the other canes from the scorching sun.

Remove up to one-third of the length of all new growth formed during the past year. To encourage really large bushes, some growers in the mildest-winter areas prune back the last year's growth only to pencil-thick stems. In cold-winter regions, where canes may be killed back to their mulch protection (or must be cut low to fit into a protective device), more than the usual one-third of the past year's growth must be cut away. Unless the bush has a very spreading growth habit, make all pruning cuts above a growth bud that points outward. Where rose cane borers are a problem, seal all pruning cuts made into stems that are pencil-thick or larger with ordinary white glue.

MINIATURE ROSES. Prune these repeat bloomers in the late dormant season. Cut out dead wood, remove canes that have made only twiggy growth during the year, and cut out spindly stems. Reduce the remaining growth by about half, pruning to outward-facing growth buds. The finished plant should have a symmetrical outline.

SHRUB AND OLD GARDEN ROSES. The growth habits of these roses vary from shrubby to nearly climbing. In fact, some produce long, arching canes that can be trained in the manner of climbers; these plants should be pruned according to whether they are spring-flowering or repeat-flowering (see page 100).

The majority in this category are vigorous plants that need a bit of annual shaping and thinning but relatively little cutting back. Because most are grown as specimen shrubs, pruning is done mainly to keep them shapely. Remove all dead growth and cut out canes that are old or weak and producing no strong new growth. When this is done, shape the bush if necessary: cut back wayward stems that skew the plant's overall shape.

Repeat-blooming shrubs should be pruned when you prune hybrid teas: in the late dormant season. Spring-flowering shrubs are traditionally pruned right after flowering has finished; strong new growth made after that bloom will bear the flowers for the following spring. However, many growers find it simpler to do some pruning on these plants during the dormant, leafless period before spring growth starts, when it is easiest to see all growth. At that time you can cut out dead stems and the old, unproductive stems and canes that would bear few flowers in spring. A postbloom touch-up pruning then concludes the year's pruning work.

SPECIES ROSES. Most of these roses flower only in spring and thus should be pruned as spring-flowering shrub roses are. Prune the repeat-flowering kinds as directed above for repeat-blooming shrub roses.

Rosmarinus officinalis 'Blue Spire'

ROSMARINUS officinalis
ROSEMARY
EVERGREEN
AFTER BLOOM

The basic species makes a dense, rounded shrub to about 3 or 4 feet high and a bit wider, with gracefully upward-sweeping branches. Unpruned, it and its varieties will grow larger, eventually becoming a dense tangle of leafy-tipped woody branches. Reducing the size of such a plant is a tricky undertaking, because the bare stems won't sprout new growth.

Avoid the problem by pruning the plant while it is still young. Pinch the growing tips each year or nip back new shoots to encourage branching. Cut back any leggy branches to a point where leaves are growing. Plants will take shearing into low formal hedges; they will also make good informal hedges.

Dwarf or prostrate rosemary ('Prostratus') produces horizontal stems and branches that may curve upward, then down, and then twist or curl. It may form a dense, rather wavy ground cover, cascade down a retaining wall, or grow up over a low wall. This form needs little pruning; just remove wayward stems. To keep it flat, pinch it back or shear it.

SALIX
WILLOW
DECIDUOUS
LATE DORMANT SEASON

The shrubby willows include rose-gold pussy willow (*S. gracilistyla*), purple osier (*S. purpurea*), dwarf purple osier (*S. p.* 'Gracilis'), and halberd willow (*S. hastata*). Prune them by thinning out the oldest stems and any crowded interior branches annually. If a plant begins to lose vigor or becomes too large for its space, lop it to the ground; vigorous new stems will renew the plant. Dwarf purple osier is sometimes trained as a formal hedge.

Larger shrubs that may grow into small trees include French pussy willow (*S. caprea*) and *S. discolor,* a plant referred to simply as pussy willow. To keep them shrubby, shorten the stems or

Salix hastata 'Wehrhahnii'

cut the whole plant to the ground whenever it gets too big. A simpler alternative is to grow the plants as shrubs during their early years, gradually allowing them to make the transition into small trees.

Redstem and yellowstem willows are varieties of the tree form *S. alba*. Keep them shrubby with hard pruning; they will become thickets of colorful stems in winter. When a young plant reaches 6 to 8 feet high, cut out all weak stems and head back the remaining ones to about a foot above the ground. These will send forth brushes of long, vigorous stems that will turn brilliant colors by the next winter. At winter's end, thin those out and head back the remaining stems to about two buds. Follow this procedure for several years, until the plant becomes too large or the stumps at the bottom look too ugly; at that point, cut the whole plant to the ground and start all over again.

Salvia leucantha

SALVIA

SAGE

EVERGREEN OR SEMIEVERGREEN

✂ BEFORE SPRING GROWTH FLUSH

For several of the shrubby sages, such as *S. clevelandii* and purple sage (*S. leucophylla),* pruning is more a matter of personal taste than of necessity. Without pruning, they develop into sprawling but attractive plants. To keep them compact, cut back the previous year's growth by as much as half and thin out any weak, crossing, or wayward stems.

You can let densely foliaged autumn sage (*S. greggii*) grow at will, but in time the plant may become floppy. For compactness, cut its most recent growth back

by as much as two-thirds. You can also grow the plant as a formal, semiformal, or informal hedge.

Mexican bush sage (*S. leucantha*) sends up many stems from the roots. In frost-free climates you must cut the older stems to the ground yearly to keep the plant from becoming woody and unattractive. Elsewhere it acts as a perennial, dying to the ground with the first frost and rebounding in spring.

SANTOLINA

EVERGREEN

✂ BEFORE SPRING GROWTH FLUSH AND
    AFTER BLOOM

Santolinas form low, dense, spreading, and mounded clumps of fine foliage. Except for the dwarf forms, unpruned plants will spread extensively, becoming sparse and woody in the center. Replace a plant if woodiness takes over.

Cut back the clump yearly, before the spring growth flush, to keep it compact. You can simply prune as needed around the edges (as though you were giving the plant a haircut), or you can cut the whole plant back to a few inches high (though this limits bloom). A lopped plant may die to the ground in the coldest part of its range but will come back from the roots. After the blooms fade, shear or clip off the flowering shoots. You can grow santolina as either an informal or a sheared hedge.

SARCOCOCCA

EVERGREEN

✂ ANYTIME

These clump-forming shrubs send up many stems from the ground. They can spread into sizable colonies, but they grow so slowly that you don't need to do much pruning. Occasionally cut old, weak, or overlong stems to the ground. You may want to do this after the tiny but intensely fragrant flowers finish blooming, in late winter or early spring. Rejuvenate an old, neglected plant by cutting it to the ground before the spring growth flush.

Sarcococca hookerana humilis

Planted against a vertical surface, *S. ruscifolia* and the similar *S. confusa* form natural espaliers.

SPIRAEA

DECIDUOUS

✂ VARIES BY SPECIES

Spiraeas fall into two broad categories: those pruned after bloom because they flower on the prior year's wood, and those pruned in the late dormant season because they bear on the current season's shoots.

AFTER BLOOM. Spiraeas that bear blossoms on the previous year's growth, early in the growing season, include *S. cantoniensis, S. prunifolia, S. thunbergii, S. trilobata,* and *S. vanhouttei.* Most carry their flowers on short, leafy shoots growing from last year's wood, though some bloom directly on the old wood. Prune after flowers fade (or do it during bloom and use the clippings for indoor decoration).

Annually remove a few of the oldest stems to the ground; you can also thin out some older branches. Keep in mind the natural habit of the plant so that you don't inadvertently alter it by pruning—some members of this group have arching branches, others a more erect habit. To confine those with a suckering habit, use a spade to sever unwanted stems on the outer edges of the clump.

These plants are often employed as hedges. The arching types are best suited for informal hedges, and the more upright types can be grown informally or semiformally. Continues >

LATE DORMANT SEASON. Spiraeas producing flowers on the current season's wood, later in the growing season, include *S. albiflora*, *S.* × *bumalda*, and *S. japonica*. Members of this group tend to be low-growing, shrubby types, usually with a suckering, spreading habit. They are used as specimen shrubs, border plants, and low semiformal or informal hedges.

Prune while the plant is still leafless, before spring growth begins. You can prune hard, cutting to the ground the oldest and weakest stems and shortening the remaining stems to as few as two buds. This will give you larger flower clusters and a smaller, neater plant. To get a larger plant with abundant but smaller blooms, just thin out the oldest stems. On low, dense shrublets, simply cut out old, twiggy stems.

If their spent flowers are removed, some members of this group will produce a second (but less lavish) bloom.

Syringa

LILAC
DECIDUOUS
✄ VARIES BY SPECIES

To most gardeners, the word *lilac* means one plant: common lilac (*S. vulgaris*). However, many other lilacs exist. Most, like the common species, produce their flowers on the prior year's wood, and thus are pruned after bloom. A few bear on new spring growth and are pruned in the late dormant season.

AFTER BLOOM. In addition to the common species and its many varieties and hybrids, others blooming early on last season's growth include Chinese lilac (*S. chinensis*), *S. meyeri*, *S. patula*, and Persian lilac (*S. persica*). The following pruning information applies specifically to common lilacs, though it can be adopted for the other early bloomers.

For several years while the plants are becoming established, they need no pruning: just pinch any stems that grow too long. When the young lilacs are old

Syringa meyeri

enough to bloom, remove their spent flower spikes just above the first leaves beneath the bloom clusters—the growth buds there will provide the next year's blossoms. Also prune out any wayward, crossing, or dead wood. To promote branching, you can cut back shoots that did not flower and that have a single terminal bud. (Shoots with two terminal buds are likely to produce flowers.)

As the plants mature, their main stems become thicker and woodier. They produce new growth progressively higher on increasingly bare stems. You can limb up these plants into small trees, or keep them bushy by cutting a few of the oldest stems to the ground each year. Lilacs produce enough basal shoots to easily replace those stems. Thin out excess basal shoots and remove weak and crowding stems. In the case of grafted varieties, remove any growth rising from the base.

If a plant is very overgrown and woody, remove a third of the oldest stems each year for 3 years. This method ensures that the shrub will always produce at least some spring flowers, and after 3 years you will essentially have a new plant.

LATE DORMANT SEASON. Types bearing flowers at the tips of new shoots, toward the end of the lilac season, include late lilac (*S. villosa*), Hungarian lilac (*S. josikaea*), nodding lilac (*S. reflexa*), *S.* × *swegiflexa*, and the group of extrahardy hybrids known as *S.* × *prestoniae*.

As you do with the early bloomers, allow these young plants to grow pretty much unhindered until they become established. Once they start blooming, prune them in the late dormant season.

Cut back the previous year's growth to varying lengths, so that blooms will appear throughout the shrub. On a mature plant, also cut out a few of the oldest stems yearly to encourage young shoots and to ensure flowering throughout the plant. As with the early bloomers, excise crowding, weak, or dead wood.

TAXUS

YEW
CONIFEROUS EVERGREEN
✄ ANYTIME, BUT ESPECIALLY BEFORE SPRING GROWTH FLUSH

Yews are slow-growing, long-lived, and random-branching conifers that will tolerate heavy pruning even though they need very little when allowed to grow naturally. Because they will sprout readily from bare wood, they are classic plants for shearing into topiary figures or formal hedges. The various yew types also make tidy knee-high to very tall informal and semiformal hedges.

The most commonly grown shrubby yews are varieties of English yew (*T. baccata*) and Japanese yew (*T. cuspidata*), as well as hybrids sold as varieties of *T.* × *media*. To cultivate a natural look, prune only wayward branches that depart from the plant's basic shape. Make cuts within the foliage, so that cut branch ends won't show. To renovate an old, overgrown plant, cut it back to a bare trunk or to within 1 to 2 feet of the ground before the spring growth flush—it will put out new growth.

On older columnar yews, such as Irish yew (*T. baccata* 'Stricta'), branches

Taxus baccata 'Repandens Aurea'

often spread outward. To counteract this tendency, head back outward-falling branches to sturdy vertical members. On very large, old plants you can tie branches together with rope or insulated wire. Join branches on opposite sides of the plant so that they counterbalance one another. This is a better solution than encircling the plant with wire (a method that is effective but very noticeable).

THUJA occidentalis
AMERICAN ARBORVITAE
CONIFEROUS EVERGREEN

✂ ANYTIME, BUT ESPECIALLY BEFORE SPRING GROWTH FLUSH

The basic species is a very large, dense, random-branching conifer that is seldom planted in gardens. Instead, nurseries offer many varieties that may be pyramidal, columnar, globular, or flat topped, and that range in height from 2 to 25 feet. These usually exhibit dense, neat growth that rarely needs shaping. But for a regular geometric shape or a formal hedge, shear new growth as often as required during the growing season. Dwarf varieties also make good low informal hedges.

When making selective cuts, prune within the foliage outline so that the cuts won't show. Never cut back into a bare branch where there's no indication of green growth; a leafless branch won't sprout new shoots. On all upright and medium to tall varieties, try to maintain a single central leader.

Oriental arborvitae (*Platycladus orientalis*), though often listed separately, is a similar plant that is pruned in the same manner as American arborvitae.

TSUGA
HEMLOCK
CONIFEROUS EVERGREEN

✂ SPRING AND SUMMER

These random-branching conifers will sprout new growth from bare wood, making them ideal candidates for formal hedges. A sheared hemlock hedge can be maintained at any height between 4 and 20 feet.

The few shrubby varieties require little or no pruning when allowed to branch naturally. If needed, make selective cuts well into the canopy so that overlapping foliage will hide them.

Viburnum davidii

VIBURNUM
DECIDUOUS AND EVERGREEN

✂ AFTER BLOOM FOR DECIDUOUS TYPES; LATE SPRING FOR EVERGREEN TYPES

Even though there are a great many kinds of viburnums, directions for pruning them are remarkably uniform.

When you plant a deciduous viburnum, thin out any obviously weak stems and shorten the remaining ones. During the first year, cut out any crossing branches and weak shoots. For the next several years, let the plant develop naturally, just removing any broken or dead wood. When the oldest main stems stop producing vigorous growth, cut them to the ground to encourage strong new shoots. Also cut out weak and twiggy wood in the plant's center.

Evergreen viburnums need no initial pruning unless a plant is noticeably lopsided. To correct this problem, cut back overly long stems to laterals to balance the plant's shape. As with deciduous viburnums, thin out dead and weak stems as well as any crowding branches in the plant's center. You can cut back any wayward stems to laterals, though you can also leave them and see if the rest of the plant catches up with them.

Both deciduous and evergreen viburnums make attractive informal hedges. You can transform large viburnums into multitrunked small trees by limbing up.

WEIGELA
DECIDUOUS

✂ AFTER BLOOM

The basic species is a vigorous plant up to 6 to 10 feet tall and arching even wider; many smaller varieties are also available. Row plantings make nice informal hedges. Plants flower mainly on short shoots growing from the previous year's branches, but also sporadically on the current season's growth. They tend to become rangy unless regularly pruned.

Each year after bloom, cut back branches that have bloomed to unflowered side branches. Leave only one or two of these laterals on each stem. Cut some of the oldest stems to the ground. Of the new shoots rising from the plant's base, retain only the strongest and best-placed ones, removing all others. As an alternative to this yearly procedure, you may opt to cut back the whole plant about halfway every other year (shorten the stems to different lengths, for a more pleasing effect).

You can thin out weak, broken, or dead branches anytime. In cold climates, prune out winter-damaged growth after all danger of frost is past. You can renew an old, ragged plant by cutting it to the ground in the late dormant season; retain only the sturdiest of the new shoots that emerge.

Weigela florida

V I N E S

Vines are among the most versatile plants in the landscape. They can be used to frame entryways, decorate bare walls, break up the monotony of long fences, mask unattractive sheds, dress up pillars, and produce masses of blooms in tight spots. A vine over an arbor or pergola can turn a bare, cold structure into an inviting leafy or floriferous outdoor room.

Though these multifaceted, flexible-stemmed plants are often referred to as climbers, they don't really climb, or even remain upright, on their own in the open. But given the proper support, most vines will ascend by means of twining stems, tendrils, or various clinging devices. A few vines have no means of holding on and must be secured in place.

The many commonly grown vines have a wide range of characteristics. They may be deciduous, semievergreen, or evergreen. Some are lightweight enough to scale a flimsy lath trellis without damaging it, whereas others attain hundreds of pounds and will crush all but the sturdiest supports. Some have a restrained growth habit; others are rampant, covering everything in their path. All vines can contribute immeasurably to a landscape if used wisely, with an eye to their mode of climbing and their ultimate size and weight. For specifics on training and pruning selected vines, consult the encyclopedia at the end of this chapter.

The clinging vine *Parthenocissus* lends character and color to this home.

The vining forms of winter creeper *(Euonymus fortunei),* including this one with variegated leaves, use aerial rootlets to climb both inanimate and living supports.

TYPES OF VINES

Rather than being grouped like trees or shrubs, as deciduous or evergreen, vines are often categorized by their climbing method. To grow vertically, a vine needs not only a support but also some way to hold onto it—otherwise, it will fall loose and sprawl or mound on the ground.

Most vines have a natural mechanism that allows them to grip the support as their stems elongate. A smaller number have no way of holding on and depend on you, the gardener, to secure them to the support. When you select a vine for a particular location or purpose, be sure to choose one whose mode of climbing suits the situation.

TWINING VINES. The new growth of these vines twists or spirals as it grows. It will coil around a support or around itself (and around nearby plants as well), requiring some guidance and thinning. Most twining vines have too small a turn circumference to encircle a large post on their own; an ideal support is a cord or wire that can be attached to a structure with eyescrews or bolts.

Some examples of twining vines are wisteria, honeysuckle *(Lonicera),* jasmine, silver lace vine *(Polygonum aubertii),* and Carolina jessamine *(Gelsemium sempervirens).*

VINES WITH TENDRILS. Specialized structures along the stems or at the ends of leaves reach out and wrap around whatever is handy—a wire or cord, another stem of the vine, or an adjoining plant. Tendrils grow out straight until they make contact, then reflexively contract into a spiral to grasp their host.

Vines that climb with the aid of tendrils include ampelopsis, passion vine *(Passiflora),* and violet trumpet vine *(Clytostoma callistegioides).*

CLINGING VINES. These vines adhere tightly to surfaces by means of specialized growths on their tendrils or along their stems. Boston ivy *(Parthenocissus tricuspidata)* and distictis are among the clinging vines that hold on by means of suction disks at the ends of tendrils. Cat's claw *(Macfadyena unguiscati)* derives its name from the clawlike hooks on its tendrils. Ivy *(Hedera)* and climbing hydrangea number among the vines with aerial rootlets, or small roots along their stems.

All of these clinging devices, collectively known as holdfasts, can damage brick, wood, concrete, and other building materials. Note that once a clinging tendril or stem is pulled free, it won't reattach itself.

VINES THAT REQUIRE TYING. Some vines have no means of attachment and will sprawl unless tied to a vertical support. Then they climb only in the sense that their stems will continue on a vertical path toward the sun if you periodically secure them to the support as they grow. A few of these plants—notably climbing roses and most types of bougainvillea—can hook themselves onto adjacent shrubs or trees with their thorns.

VINE ATTACHMENTS

Twining stems

Tendrils

Suction disks

Aerial rootlets

Needs tying

Unlike most other vines, climbing roses have no natural mechanism for scaling heights and will climb only if tied to a vertical support.

CHOOSING A SUPPORT

Vines can be grown on many structures, including fences, arbors, pergolas, trellises, and the walls of houses, garages, and garden sheds. In matching a vine with a support, you must take into account several factors: the vine's climbing method, the vine's ultimate size and weight, and the support's size and strength.

CLIMBING METHOD

If you want a twining vine to grow vertically, provide it with something slender that will accommodate its fairly small turn circumference. Most twiners can more easily climb a cord, wire, or bamboo pole than a large post or column. To get a twiner up a wall, attach the narrow support up to the height you intend the vine to grow. Ideally, position the support at least a foot away from the wall to give the vine room to spiral and to allow for air circulation. Use eyescrews, bolts, or other hardware to hold the supports securely in place.

A vine that climbs by means of tendrils also needs a slender support; if the tendrils can't get around the support, they may wrap around the plant stems instead, making a mess and causing the vine to flop loose rather than climb. Because tendril grabbers attach themselves to the support at discrete points instead of spiraling themselves around it as twiners do, they are ideal covers for open latticework such as chain-link fences, plastic netting, and lath trellises.

Vines that must be tied can be grown on all types of structures—even a smooth vertical one, if you can attach hardware to it to anchor the ties. Because you'll have to secure the vine at

USING OTHER PLANTS FOR SUPPORT

In the wild vines grow up and through other plants, "borrowing" them for their support. Instead of training your climber on an inanimate structure such as a fence or wall, you can copy nature by sending the vine scrambling through a living tree or large shrub. The ideal host plants are those with an airy, open habit and the ability to withstand competition for moisture and nutrients.

The best vines to train through other living plants are twining or rambling ones that won't outgrow the host plant or weigh it down. Many types of clematis (which twines its leaf stalks) and climbing roses are often used this way. Clinging vines can easily march up tree trunks. The aerial rootlets of types such as winter creeper (see photo on opposite page) can penetrate the bark, so be sure you choose healthy, robust host trees for such vines. Don't risk damaging a valuable shade tree by allowing a clinging vine to climb it.

You can train a vine up a dying or dead tree whose garden utility you'd like to extend. Just be sure that the tree is stable and in no danger of falling over or presenting some other hazard. Because you don't have to consider competition, you can choose a vigorous vine, even one that would strangle a healthy tree.

This spring-flowering *Clematis montana rubens* has twined its way through an oak tree. The vine would normally be pruned after bloom—if you could get to it.

Each of these twining vines is well suited to its support. At left, fairly lightweight potato vine *(Solanum jasmi-noides)* is trained on a flimsy rustic trellis. At right, the much heavier *Actinidia kolomikta* grows over a garden wall.

A single wisteria vine is vigorous enough to cover a sturdy arbor. This one's stem was handwrapped around one post and then allowed to twine on its own once it reached the arbor top.

various points along its length, be prepared to affix ties from a ladder. You can let vines that twine their stems or tendrils climb up out of your reach, though you probably will have to prune them from a ladder.

Because of holdfasts' potential to damage surfaces, be careful where you plant a clinging vine. The holdfasts can get under and lift wood siding; they will also trap moisture, causing wood to decay. On brick or concrete block the holdfasts may infiltrate the mortared joints, weakening them. Certainly, don't grow clinging vines on any surfaces that you intend to paint or stain in the future. And don't use them as temporary cover, either, because removing them completely is no easy task. After pulling off most of the vine, you still have to dislodge the unsightly remains of the holdfasts that stubbornly stick to the surface, often out of your reach.

MATCHING SIZE AND STRENGTH

The structure you choose to cover should be capable of supporting the vine's size and weight. Some vines remain on the small side, whereas others know no bounds. For example, many clematis varieties attain only 6 to 10 feet at maturity, but Virginia creeper *(Parthenocissus quinquefolia)* and the closely related Boston ivy are limited only by the size of the structure on which they grow. Despite the fact that neither Virginia creeper nor Boston ivy is a true ivy, their blanketing of entire buildings on college campuses in the eastern United States gave the name Ivy League to those schools.

Relatively small, lightweight plants such as potato vine and many clematis varieties don't require a very large or strong support. They are ideally suited to such structures as picket fences or thin wood or wire trellises.

Large, heavy vines like passion vine, trumpet creeper *(Campsis),* and wisteria need a sturdy support such as a big chain-link fence or a roomy arbor whose posts are anchored in concrete. These vines can weigh hundreds of pounds at maturity. Unless you plan to be vigilant about keeping a very rampant grower in check, be wary of training vines such as ivy on house walls, especially those of single-story homes; they can easily push up roof shingles and damage eaves, gutters, and downspouts. These monster vines can even work their way through small openings into a home's interior.

TRAINING YOUNG VINES

Vine training consists mainly of choosing the desired number of stems—pinch the terminal growth bud as needed to induce more branching—and guiding them onto the chosen support. Vines with no means of holding on will have to be secured by their stems as they grow. Vines that can hang on may be tied up at first as a temporary measure, or periodically as an adjunct to the vine's own holding mechanism.

The type of tie you use to secure a vine—whether temporarily or permanently—depends on the vine. Good choices for lightweight plants include soft twine, raffia, wide rubber bands, green plastic garden tape, or clear grafting or budding tape. For heavy vines, particularly those having no means of gripping the support, use heavier, durable materials such as rope, plastic-coated electrical wire, or strips of canvas or rubber.

Keep a clinging vine close to the support until the holdfasts can achieve good contact with the surface. You can do this by tying the vine in place or by tacking plastic mesh over the stems until you see evidence that the plant is supporting itself. Once clinging vines gain a foothold, even very heavy or vigorous species won't have to be fastened in any way.

CLIMBING ROSES

Left to its own devices, a climbing rose will produce long canes that keep growing upward, terminating in a relatively paltry flower display. This upward growth at the expense of flowering laterals is due to the plant's strong apical dominance—the suppression of lateral growth buds by a hormone in the terminal growth bud.

Bending the canes into arches will "break" the hormonal control and cause the many buds along the canes to develop into shoots, each one heading upward. Most of these shoots will grow 8 to 16 inches, depending on the rose variety and growing conditions, before terminating in blossoms. A few "growth laterals" will keep climbing unless they too are arched over (see illustration below).

If you have a house wall or high fence to cover, let the plants grow unhindered until they form long canes; this will usually take 2 or 3 years. Then bend the canes away from the vertical on either side of the plant's base. If the canes are fairly stiff, you may only be able to spread them into a fan shape. If they're limber enough, however, they can be angled outward more sharply. Tie the canes into position.

Some shorter, stiff-caned climbers (known as pillar-climbers, or pillar roses) will grow upright yet still produce flowering laterals, so they needn't be arched over. These more closely resemble floppy shrubs than climbers. Keep them erect by tying them to a pillar or other support.

Arching over the canes of this repeat-flowering climber has resulted in abundant blooms.

For information about pruning climbing roses, see page 100.

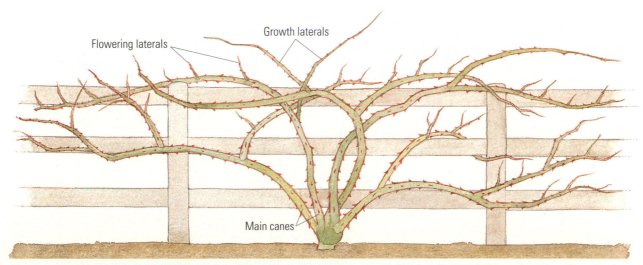

Flowering laterals

Growth laterals

Main canes

Arching over the main canes causes buds along their lengths to develop into shoots, most of which bear flowers. A few are long, flowerless growth laterals; arched over, they too will produce flowering laterals—either late in the season or in the next year.

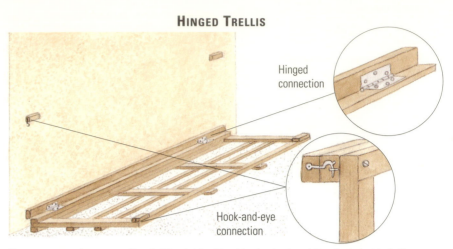

Hinged
connection

Hook-and-eye
connection

You can grow a vine on a wall and still paint it without having to rip out the plant. Just train the climber on a hinged trellis that you can lower to the ground. First attach 2-by-4s to the top and bottom of the trellis; then attach the reinforced trellis to additional 2-by-4s secured to the wall. Use hinges to make the connection at the bottom, hooks-and-eyes at the top. Once the structure is in place, plant the vine and begin training it.

Hardware to support a heavy vine can be attached directly to masonry; however, for a more initially attractive look—or for more flexible attachment—try the system shown here. This bougainvillea (below right) appears to be growing directly on a wood trellis mounted against a concrete block wall. The vine is actually trained on heavy-duty galvanized wires stretched between eyescrews inserted into the trellis (above). Some of the vine's thorns may hook onto the wires, but the stems must be tied in place for complete attachment.

Vines with a nonclinging method of climbing also need your help when beginning their ascent. As the stems and lateral shoots grow, guide them so that they will wrap their tendrils or twine themselves around the structure. Although some twining vines naturally wind clockwise and others counterclockwise, don't worry if you start them off in the wrong direction—they'll change course on their own. When necessary, tie the stems of twiners and tendril grabbers to keep them from falling away from their support. Getting a nonclinging vine to cover a support with large openings, such as a trellis or lattice-work fence, is a cinch—just weave the vine through the spaces.

Once they're started on their path, nonclinging climbers can make it up narrow posts on their own. They'll need more help getting up wide-diameter ones, such as those commonly used in sturdy pergolas and arbors. There are several ways to ease the ascent: spiral the vine by hand and tie it in place, or give the vine something to grasp by stringing galvanized wires or cord through eyescrews or bolts inserted into the post. Wire mesh wrapped around the post will provide tendril grabbers with a surface they can climb.

These same types of climbing aids can be affixed to a flat vertical surface such as a house wall, to create a suitable climbing surface. As an alternative, you can train a vine onto a hinged trellis that you can lower to the ground when you want to paint or otherwise maintain the wall surface (see illustration above). Don't choose too rampant a grower, though, because it will quickly outgrow the trellis.

When using a tree or large shrub as a support, plant the vine at least 18 inches away from its base. Provide a temporary support, such as chicken wire or plastic mesh, on the lower part of the tree to get the vine started; you can remove the support after a year or two. With shrubs, you can tie the vine to a low branch until it begins to twine or ramble on its own.

PRUNING ESTABLISHED VINES

Given enough space, clinging vines don't need much attention once they gain a foothold—and, in fact, pruning is problematic once the vine has attached itself to a surface. You can't just prune out a stem or an overlong shoot at its base—you must also yank loose all the holdfasts. You can, however, thin out shoots that are heading out of bounds and remove growth that juts out too far from the vine's main plane. If a rampant grower has been trained on the walls of your house or any outbuilding such as a garden shed, you will periodically have to cut away any growth that threatens to overrun the doors, windows, or eaves.

The stems of vigorous twiners like this evergreen *Clematis armandii* tend to become snarled. Often the best way to sort out the problem is just to snip through the tangles. Resultant dead growth will be easier to identify and remove later on.

Other types of vines—those that twine, hold on with tendrils, or must be tied—can more easily be pruned. Even when allocated sufficient space, most need regular pruning. If you don't actually prune your vines annually, at least assess them yearly to see if they need any work.

As you would with trees and shrubs, begin by removing the "three Ds": dead, damaged, and dysfunctional growth. Unlike other plants, however, vines tend to become tangled—so you may have to unsnarl stems before you can prune. Some growth may be so tangled that pruning it off is the most expedient way of dealing with it. Remember, thinning cuts will produce less regrowth than heading cuts—keep this in mind if your goal is to keep a vine from becoming too dense and overgrown.

Once you've removed undesirable or unwanted growth, consider whether the vine is leafy enough toward the bottom of the plant. If foliage is concentrated at the top, cut off some old stems to promote leafy young growth lower down. You can also make heading cuts toward the bottom of the vine to promote branching. Most vines respond well to pruning cuts made during the dormant season. If the vine is a rampant grower, prune in both the dormant season and the summer to restrain it.

On blooming plants, pruning out older stems will encourage flowers throughout the vine rather than in clusters near the top of the vine, where you can't readily enjoy them. This task is especially important to perform on vines that bloom late in the season on new growth, because the new growth will soon grow up and out of sight on unpruned plants. Prune such vines before spring growth begins. (You can prune vigorous types again after bloom to tame them.) Wait until after the spring flower display to prune a vine that bears on the previous year's shoots. For information on pruning twice-flowering clematis varieties, see page 96; for repeat-blooming climbing roses, see page 100.

Rampant clinging vines such as ivy will engulf doors, windows, and eaves if given the chance. Cut back any shoots that head in unwanted directions.

You may have to prune heavily to keep a vine in good order. You'll notice that some vines, such as wisteria, form a sturdy framework of woody stems and laterals; they can be pruned back to their basic framework. Others, such as jasmine, have weaker stems and no real structure to work with. Thin them to prevent their becoming too dense and unmanageable.

Sometimes a vine will be too far gone to rescue with maintenance pruning. If it has become a big tangled mess that you can't easily sort out, or is full of dead wood, try rejuvenating it before spring growth begins. If there are any young shoots near the base of the vine, leave those; otherwise, cut the whole vine low to the ground and retrain the new growth that emerges.

Actinidia kolomikta

Vines
A PRUNING GUIDE

The following pages contain instructions for pruning many popular vines, which are listed alphabetically by their botanical names. (If you know your plant only by a common name, check to see if it's listed, with a cross-reference to the botanical name, in the index at the back of this book.)

Below the botanical name you'll find any widely used common names, the type of vine (for example, "deciduous" or "evergreen"), its climbing method, and a symbol (✄) preceding the best time of year to prune it. Even if summer pruning isn't specified, remember that summer is a good time for additional pruning of rampant vines. Of course, you can remove damaged, diseased, or dead growth at any time.

Beneath the "at-a-glance" details you'll find information on how best to manage that specific vine.

ACTINIDIA

DECIDUOUS

TWINING

✄ LATE DORMANT SEASON

The following two ornamental vines—somewhat less vigorous relatives of the kiwi vines raised for their edible fruit (see page 125)—are grown for their colorful foliage rather than their small blooms. *A. kolomikta,* which spreads rapidly to 15 to 20 feet or more, has white- and pink-splashed green leaves. Silver vine *(A. polygama),* which may twine 15 feet, has silvery foliage. Give them a strong support, such as a sturdy trellis or arbor.

Annually thin out entangling growth, leaving a well-spaced framework of main branches from which new growth will sprout. To renovate the vine, cut back all growth to the framework before spring growth begins.

AKEBIA

EVERGREEN OR DECIDUOUS

TWINING

✄ LATE DORMANT SEASON
  OR AFTER BLOOM

Rampant and evergreen where winters are mild, these vines are deciduous and less vigorous in cold-winter regions. Under good growing conditions they create fast cover, growing 20 to 40 feet or even more. A plant can be trained on an arbor or other stout structure or allowed to scramble through a tree.

You can remove weak and entangling branches in the late dormant season or later, after flowers have faded. If you prune after bloom, also prune back the shoots that flowered. To renew an overgrown plant, prune more drastically before spring growth begins. Either cut stems back to five to nine buds or lop the whole plant to the ground; keep only two or three of the new stems that emerge if you want a more open vine.

AMPELOPSIS

DECIDUOUS AND SEMIEVERGREEN

TENDRILS

✄ LATE DORMANT SEASON AND SUMMER

Two commonly grown species are the deciduous porcelain berry *(A. brevipedunculata)* and the semievergreen peppervine *(A. arborea);* both grow rampantly to 20 feet or more. They have invasive root systems, so site them away from desirable plants or put them where their roots can be confined. Give them a wall, arbor, or other strong support.

Each year, thin and shorten selected stems to control plant form and size. Whenever necessary, cut back unwanted stems and dig out suckers. You can cut the vines to the ground in the late dormant season and still get a show of ornamental berries, because the plants bloom and fruit on new growth.

Ampelopsis brevipedunculata

ARISTOLOCHIA

DECIDUOUS

TWINING

✄ LATE DORMANT SEASON
  OR AFTER BLOOM

These vigorous vines, which twine 20 to 30 feet, can cover an arbor or pergola in a single season. Dutchman's pipe (*A. durior*) has been a traditional choice for screening front porches. California Dutchman's pipe (*A. californica*) is sometimes trained through trees.

Thin out unwanted growth in the late dormant season or wait until after bloom. If a plant becomes too thick and tangled for selective thinning, cut it to the ground before spring growth begins.

BIGNONIA capreolata
CROSSVINE, QUARTER VINE, TRUMPET FLOWER
EVERGREEN OR SEMIEVERGREEN
CLINGING
✂ BEFORE SPRING GROWTH FLUSH AND SUMMER

This vigorous vine can cover a large space, potentially 30 to 50 feet, holding on by means of suction disks at the end of tendrils. Blooms are produced on new shoots from late spring to fall. The vine is useful for covering masonry walls, outbuildings, and sturdy fences or poles.

Before spring growth begins, cut back the previous season's growth by two-thirds to encourage new growth. During the growing season, cut back stems that are heading out of bounds and eliminate any weak growth. Remove suckers whenever they appear. You can cut the plant to the ground to renovate it.

Bignonia capreolata

Bougainvillea

BOUGAINVILLEA
EVERGREEN
MUST BE TIED
✂ AFTER FROST DANGER AND AFTER BLOOM

The vigor and growth habits of these tropical shrubby vines differ by species and named variety. Most types can easily spread 25 feet high and wide, making them suitable subjects for walls or substantial trellises and arbors. (They can also be grown horizontally, as ground covers.) Their thorns may help them hook themselves up onto vertical supports, but they should be tied as well. These plants flower profusely on new growth during warm weather.

Don't be afraid to prune to shape, direct growth, or renew the plant. If you want the vine to cover the top of an arbor, limit it to one to three main trunks; top the trunks just above where you want branches. Otherwise, train as many stems as you desire.

After all danger of frost has passed, remove any weak growth and thin out crowded branches—eliminate some entirely, cutting others back to two or three buds. Prune after flowering to shape and thin out excess growth. Nip back long shoots then and as needed throughout that growing season to keep them in bounds and encourage more flowering wood. Rejuvenate an overgrown plant by cutting it back to its framework in early spring.

CAMPSIS
TRUMPET CREEPER, TRUMPET VINE
DECIDUOUS
CLINGING
✂ LATE DORMANT SEASON AND SUMMER

These shrubby vines, which cling by aerial rootlets, are rampant in mild-winter climates: they easily cover 30 to 50 feet, scrambling over any obstacles and spreading by suckering roots. In colder regions they are a little more restrained. These plants bloom on new growth.

Without pruning, a plant may eventually become top-heavy and pull away from the arbor, fence, or other support on which it is trained. After one or more permanent trunks develop, shorten some branches each dormant season to two or three buds; thin out others. Also remove any weak or dead wood at that time. You will have to pull the holdfasts loose to do this work. During the growing season, frequently pinch back shoot tips to keep the plant bushy and covered with leaves at the base. Pull suckers whenever they appear.

Plants respond well to severe pruning. If an old plant has become unmanageable, cut it to the ground before spring growth begins and train a few strong new stems.

Campsis radicans

CELASTRUS
BITTERSWEET
DECIDUOUS
TWINING
✂ DORMANT SEASON AND SUMMER

Grown for their ornamental autumn fruit appearing on new growth, these vigorous vines will become tangled masses of intertwining branches and engulf nearby plants unless pruned regularly. One particularly aggressive species, *C. orbiculatus,* has escaped gardens and become a weed in the northeastern United States. American bittersweet (*C. scandens*) will strangle shrubs or small trees if allowed to climb them. These vines, which may grow 30 to 40 feet if given a large surface to climb, are best used in wild gardens or rough areas, scrambling over tree stumps or fences.

Each dormant season, prune out all weak growth and branches that have fruited; cut back the previous year's growth by about a third. If a vine has become too dense, thin out old and crowded stems. During the growing season, pinch back or thin out overaggressive new growth, especially shoots that are invading desirable plantings. Dig out suckers whenever they appear.

Plants respond well to drastic pruning, and can be renovated by cutting to the ground in the late dormant season.

Celastrus scandens

CLEMATIS

DECIDUOUS AND EVERGREEN

TWINING LEAF STALKS

✂ VARIES BY TYPE

Grown for their abundant blossoms, clematis vines climb by twining their leaf stalks around anything that offers support: stretched string, wire mesh, other plants' branches, or their own stems. Smaller types of clematis grow only 6 to 10 feet and are suited to lightweight structures; larger types grow to about

Clematis 'Henryi' and *Rosa*

25 feet and require somewhat stronger supports. The early training you give a clematis vine depends on whether it is deciduous or evergreen.

Follow the same procedure to train all deciduous clematis. At planting time, cut back the stems of the dormant vine to two or three pairs of growth buds, or to 6 to 12 inches from the ground, whichever is lower. Late in the next dormant season, cut back the first year's growth to two or three pairs of buds. Train the emerging shoots as the vine begins to grow again during the second spring.

Don't prune evergreen vines at first; just start training them after planting.

How you prune an established vine depends on its bloom time and vigor.

SPRING-FLOWERING CLEMATIS. These plants bloom on the prior year's growth. Prune them after flowering is finished.

For extravigorous species, such as evergreen *C. armandii* and deciduous *C. montana,* remove shoots that have flowered and thin out any excess growth. During the growing season, you may need to do more thinning and pinching to keep the vine within bounds and prevent it from tangling. Cut back superfluous new growth on *C. armandii* to two or three pairs of buds, so that it doesn't shade the rest of the vine.

Less vigorous growers need less pruning. Cut back shoots that have flowered to about half their length. Thin out weak stems and remove entangling stems.

SUMMER- AND FALL-FLOWERING CLEMATIS. These produce blooms only on the current season's growth. Cut back the prior season's growth to about 12 inches in the late dormant season (or, in mild-winter regions, in late fall, when the plant has entered dormancy). Each year the vine will grow larger and denser.

TWICE-FLOWERING CLEMATIS. The popular large-flowered clematis hybrids mostly fall in this group. The first blooms come on shoots produced the previous year; later flowers form on shoots that grow after the spring bloom.

In late fall or the late dormant season, prune lightly just to thin out superfluous shoots or to untangle snarled stems. To ensure a good spring display, leave as much of the last season's growth as possible. After spring flowers fade, cut back spent flowering shoots so that plenty of healthy new shoots will develop for summer blossoms.

Clytostoma callistegioides

CLYTOSTOMA

callistegioides (Bignonia violacea, B. speciosa)

VIOLET TRUMPET VINE

EVERGREEN

TENDRILS

✂ AFTER BLOOM

A strong grower to about 35 feet high and 50 feet wide, violet trumpet vine requires a substantial support, such as a sturdy fence or arbor. The plant blooms profusely in spring and early summer on the prior year's growth. After bloom, thin out excess growth and head back overlong shoots. Untangle shoots as needed during the year.

DISTICTIS
EVERGREEN
CLINGING
ANYTIME

Three vines, which can climb 20 to 30 feet, range in the following order from restrained to rampant: vanilla trumpet vine *(D. laxiflora)*, blood-red trumpet vine *(D. buccinatoria)*, and royal trumpet vine *(D.* 'Rivers'). Clinging by means of suction disks at the end of tendrils, these plants are attractive on high walls and on strong arbors and fences. They all bloom during warmer months.

Thin and head back as needed to control growth; remember, you'll have to pull the holdfasts loose. Pinch back all new growth heading out of bounds.

EUONYMUS fortunei
WINTER CREEPER
EVERGREEN
CLINGING
ANYTIME

This plant has many named varieties that differ in leaf color and size. More important, they differ in form: vinelike or shrubby (see the latter on pages 70–71). Vinelike varieties will grow as a ground cover or, given a vertical surface to climb such as a masonry wall or large tree, will use aerial rootlets to form a tightly clinging vertical mat of foliage to 40 feet or even higher. Prune as you would ivy (see "Hedera" at right).

× FATSHEDERA lizei
EVERGREEN
MUST BE TIED
ANYTIME

This sprawling hybrid between Japanese aralia *(Fatsia japonica)* and English ivy

(Hedera helix) can be trained as either a shrub or a vine that will climb 10 to 15 feet. Its stems lack the aerial rootlets of its ivy parent and so must be secured in place. Choose a strong support, such as a sturdy trellis or heavy wire attached to a house wall, because the vine can become heavy.

About two or three times a year, guide and tie new stems before they become brittle. Note that even a well-grown vine is leafless at the base. If the plant becomes unmanageable, cut it to the ground; it will regrow quickly.

Gelsemium sempervirens

GELSEMIUM sempervirens
CAROLINA JESSAMINE
EVERGREEN
TWINING
AFTER BLOOM

Growing to about 20 feet, Carolina jessamine sends out long, twining stems that will wind around supports and one another. The plant is often trained on trellises and fences, over mailboxes, or along house eaves, from which its branches will cascade gracefully. Without support it grows naturally as a mounding ground cover. Profuse spring blossoms appear on the previous year's shoots.

Periodically clean up tangled stems and thin out excess growth. If the plant gets top-heavy, cut it back severely—it responds well to any amount of pruning.

Hardenbergia violacea

HARDENBERGIA
EVERGREEN
TWINING
AFTER BLOOM

These vines, which grow at a moderate rate to about 10 feet, are attractive trained on arbors, spilling over the tops of low walls and fences, or twining through large shrubs or small trees. Plants bloom in late winter or early spring on the previous year's shoots. After flowers fade, thin out old, weak stems to keep the plant from getting leggy. Prune out any tangled growth as needed.

HEDERA
IVY
EVERGREEN
CLINGING
ANYTIME

A single ivy planting can cover both the ground and just about any vertical surface it encounters. Ivy can climb about 90 feet, clinging with its aerial rootlets to house walls, poles, and other structures. It's best to keep ivy out of trees, because it can damage them.

Give an ivy vine plenty of room or you'll find yourself constantly cutting it back and trying to pry off the holdfast remnants. When growing it on a building, prune to maintain window and door margins and to keep growth away from gutters, eaves, and downspouts. If you want a neat, flat surface, use hedge shears two or three times a year to give the ivy a "haircut." Unpruned ivy high up tends to produce shrubby growth terminating in clusters of insignificant green flowers that develop into black berries. To rejuvenate a planting, cut it to the ground.

Hydrangea anomala petiolaris

HYDRANGEA
anomala petiolaris
CLIMBING HYDRANGEA

DECIDUOUS

CLINGING

🗶 LATE DORMANT SEASON

An especially beautiful vine that becomes quite woody with age, this plant climbs by means of aerial rootlets, covering 20 to 50 feet or more. It can ascend tall trees and blanket walls or other large supports (be sure they're sturdy), though it can be kept much smaller by pruning.

Don't prune much until the plant is well established and climbing. Then cut back overvigorous growth and shorten any shoots that project too far from the vertical surface. In addition to disciplining the vine, this will stimulate the new growth on which blossoms are borne. Cut back to the framework to rejuvenate.

JASMINUM
JASMINE

DECIDUOUS, SEMIEVERGREEN, AND EVERGREEN

TWINING; MUST BE TIED

🗶 AFTER BLOOM

Jasmines include both twining vines and vining shrubs whose long, flexible stems can be trained upward and tied to a structure. Both kinds are attractive trained on trellises or spilling over the tops of fences and garden walls. Most types can grow 10 to 20 feet and are fairly lightweight. The plants can also be trained horizontally, as ground covers. The various species bloom on the previous year's growth, so prune after flowers fade.

Thin out crowded or tangled stems and pinch the tips of new growth to encourage branching and compactness. On older plants with overcrowded stems, cut out the oldest stems and thin out weak, twiggy, and dead stems. Prune jasmines severely to rejuvenate them. Winter jasmine (*J. nudiflorum*) looks best when cut low to the ground every few years.

Jasminum polyanthum

LONICERA
HONEYSUCKLE

EVERGREEN, SEMIEVERGREEN, AND DECIDUOUS

TWINING

🗶 AFTER BLOOM

Honeysuckle vines include both moderate and rampant growers. As a general rule, these plants should be pruned after flowering.

Give more training than pruning to the moderate growers, which include the deciduous gold flame honeysuckle (*L.* × *heckrottii*) and trumpet honeysuckle (*L. sempervirens*), the evergreen to deciduous woodbine (*L. periclymenum*), and the evergreen giant Burmese honeysuckle (*L. hildebrandiana*). These are often grown on stout trellises, arbors, and fences or along eaves. Guide their growth in the direction you want it to go; cut back stems that grow out of bounds; cut out any branches that are headed in the

Lonicera

wrong direction or are unwanted. Occasionally thin out older stems to make way for new growth.

Extravigorous Japanese honeysuckle (*L. japonica*) and its varieties need considerable pruning or they can become weeds, smothering less vigorous plants. They may be evergreen, semievergreen, or deciduous, depending on the climate. Prune them severely (cut back almost to the framework) each year to prevent undergrowth from building up. These dead stems present a fire hazard in the arid West. Remove suckers whenever they appear.

To renovate any old, straggling honeysuckle vine, cut it back to the main stems or to the ground during the dormant season.

MACFADYENA unguis-cati
(Doxantha unguis-cati, Bignonia tweediana)
CAT'S CLAW, YELLOW TRUMPET VINE

DECIDUOUS OR SEMIEVERGREEN

CLINGING

🗶 AFTER BLOOM

This rampant vine climbs 25 to 40 feet by means of hooked, clawlike, forked tendrils. It is frequently trained on masonry walls, sturdy fences, and chain-link fences as well as into tall trees.

The plant tends to be sparsely foliaged at its base. After early spring bloom, cut back some stems nearly to the ground to stimulate leafy growth low

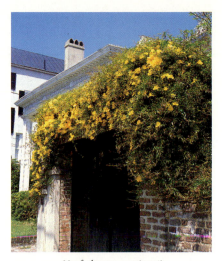

Macfadyena unguis-cati

down, and prune out any weak or old stems. As needed during the growing season, pinch back vigorous new shoots.

PARTHENOCISSUS

DECIDUOUS

CLINGING

DORMANT SEASON AND SUMMER

These large-scale foliage vines prized for their vivid fall color climb by means of tendrils with suction disks at their ends. Boston ivy *(P. tricuspidata)*, which is semievergreen in mild-winter regions, and Virginia creeper *(P. quinquefolia)* are often grown up masonry walls and

Parthenocissus quinquefolia

into tall trees. Though usually said to grow 50 to 60 feet, actually these vines are limited only by the size of the support. Silvervein creeper *(P. henryana)* is less vigorous, growing about 20 feet.

When vines reach the desired size, prune each dormant season to restrain their spread and—for those trained on buildings—to keep them away from doors, windows, and eaves. Cut out any wayward branches and any that have pulled away from their support, because the holdfasts will not reattach. You may not be able to do much more than this once a vine takes hold. During the growing season, do whatever trimming is needed to limit or direct growth.

PASSIFLORA

PASSION VINE

EVERGREEN, SEMIEVERGREEN, AND DECIDUOUS

TENDRILS

BEFORE SPRING GROWTH FLUSH
AND SUMMER

Without care these vigorous, heavy vines will become thickly tangled masses of stems and leaves. They can climb 20 to 30 feet by wrapping their wiry tendrils around anything they encounter, including their own stems. These plants are well suited to training on chain-link fences, large walls, and big, sturdy trellises. Most passion vines bloom on the current season's growth.

After a vine's second winter, give it at least one pruning annually. Remove some stems to keep the vine open and prevent a buildup of dead inner tangle. During the growing season, prune back excess and wayward growth.

In colder areas, winter freeze damage will mean you'll need to cut out dead and damaged stems. You'll still have to prune during the growing season in those regions to remove stems that are crowding others or heading where you don't want them. If a vine gets completely out of hand, cut it to the ground after all danger of frost is past and before spring growth begins.

POLYGONUM aubertii

SILVER LACE VINE

DECIDUOUS OR EVERGREEN

TWINING

LATE DORMANT SEASON
AND AFTER BLOOM

Evergreen in the warmer part of its range, this vigorous plant can be trained vertically as a quick screen on fences or arbors, or allowed to grow horizontally as a bank cover. It can extend as much as 35 feet, achieving nearly half that in one season. Blooms are borne on new growth.

Polygonum aubertii

Where silver lace vine freezes to the ground, cut the dead stems to their base in the late dormant season. The plant will regrow rapidly, though it will bloom later than usual that summer.

Where the plant doesn't freeze, before spring growth begins cut out some stems and head back the prior year's growth to stimulate flowering shoots. Thin out excess growth at the same time and again after bloom. As an alternative, treat the plant as if it had frozen, lopping it to the ground yearly in the late dormant season.

PYROSTEGIA venusta
(P. ignea, Bignonia venusta)

FLAME VINE

EVERGREEN

TENDRILS

AFTER BLOOM

Flame vine climbs quickly to 20 feet or more. Where well adapted, it grows rampantly and should be kept away from desirable plantings. In central Florida it is a popular vine for covering fences, pergolas, and small outbuildings and for climbing into undesirable trees. The plant blooms profusely in winter and early spring.

Prune right after flowering ends to restrain the vine. Cut back branches heading out of bounds, thin out excess growth, and remove dead and weak stems. To renovate the plant, cut all growth back to the framework before the spring growth flush.

Pyrostegia venusta

ROSA
CLIMBING ROSE
DECIDUOUS
MUST BE TIED
✂ VARIES BY TYPE

Various types of roses climb: true climbers, climbing sports of bush roses, and some shrub types that get carried away in mild climates. What they have in common is long, variably flexible canes that produce flowering shoots from growth buds along their lengths. The following will tell you how to prune climbers that produce several waves of blooms during the growing season as well as those that bloom only in spring; there are also directions for pruning the special category of rambler roses.

REPEAT-FLOWERING CLIMBERS. In this group are the most widely planted climbing roses: natural climbers (ranging from large flowered to miniature) and climbing sports of hybrid teas, grandifloras, floribundas, and miniatures.

Rosa 'Alexandre Girault'

After planting, let these roses grow unpruned for 2 or 3 years while they become established and build up strength to put out good climbing canes. During that time simply remove dead wood, weak growth, and spent flowers. Tie new canes into an arched position as they mature (see illustration on page 91). After this settling-in period, the plant will consist solely of long canes formed since planting; these will produce flower-bearing laterals. Climbing varieties differ in how they produce canes: some send up new canes from the ground each year, whereas others build up a more permanent woody structure and produce most of their long new growth from higher up on the plant.

In pruning these climbers, you want to foster the growth of flower-bearing laterals and to stimulate the emergence of new canes that will replace older ones as they become less productive. Each year, just before growth begins, prune out only the old and obviously unproductive wood—that is, stems that produced no strong growth the previous year. Next, cut back to two or three buds all of the laterals that bore flowers during the previous year. Avoid cutting back vigorous new, long canes unless lack of space compels you to do so; always try to train them into place first.

Prune pillar-climbers (sometimes called pillar roses), shorter climbers whose canes may reach about 10 feet tall,

in the same way as repeat-flowering climbers. Their canes needn't be arched over, but should be tied to a pillar or other support.

SPRING-FLOWERING CLIMBERS. As these plants bear blossoms on the previous season's wood, to get the most abundant bloom you should prune after flowering is over. However, you'll have an easier time sorting out the canes if you prune earlier, in the late dormant season—even though you'll lose some potential blossoms as a result. Whichever schedule you choose, prune out dead wood, remove any canes that produced only weak growth and few flowers, and thin the less vigorous of any tangled stems that remain. After plants finish blooming, they will produce new canes and laterals on which to carry next spring's flowers.

Removing spent flower clusters will tidy the plant, but you have more to gain in many cases by leaving the clusters in place. Some varieties may produce secondary blooms from the midst of or just below old flower clusters, and many develop a crop of decorative fruit, called hips, that lend winter interest.

RAMBLER ROSES. Included in this group are hybrids primarily of *R. wichuraiana*, though a few other species— *R. multiflora*, prairie rose *(R. setigera)*, and *R. sempervirens* in particular— have produced offspring that fit into this category. In late spring these climbers cover themselves with clusters of small blossoms; after bloom, they send out many long, limber canes from ground level and a lesser number of long laterals from growth that has flowered. The following spring's bloom will come on this new growth.

Prune ramblers after flowering has finished and new growth has started. Cut out canes that have just bloomed but show no sign of producing any long, vigorous new shoots. As the new canes and laterals lengthen and mature, train them into an arch.

SOLANDRA maxima
CUP-OF-GOLD VINE
EVERGREEN

MUST BE TIED

✂ BEFORE SPRING GROWTH FLUSH
AND SUMMER

A rampant grower to about 40 feet, cup-of-gold vine is often used on large walls and pergolas, along eaves, and as bank cover. Prune it regularly to promote branching, denseness, and more flowers (these are borne on new wood). Before spring growth begins, shorten long, vigorous shoots and cut out weak growth altogether. In summer cut back wayward or excess shoots as needed and occasionally pinch growing tips. (Plants sold as *S. guttata* are usually this species.)

Solanum wendlandii

SOLANUM
EVERGREEN OR SEMIEVERGREEN

TWINING

✂ BEFORE SPRING GROWTH FLUSH

Potato vine *(S. jasminoides)* and Costa Rican nightshade *(S. wendlandii)* are vigorous twiners to about 20 feet. Train them on arbors, pergolas, and trellises or along eaves—or let them scramble through large shrubs or trees. These vines are relatively lightweight.

Prune them (severely if needed) at the beginning of the growing season to limit their growth and promote new shoots, which will bear blossoms. Untangle stems, shorten overvigorous shoots, and thin out weak or excess growth. On potato vine, prune off rampant runners that grow along the ground.

Trachelospermum jasminoides

TRACHELOSPERMUM
jasminoides
STAR JASMINE, CONFEDERATE JASMINE
EVERGREEN

TWINING

✂ BEFORE SPRING GROWTH FLUSH

A shrubby plant that can be grown as a ground cover or vine, star jasmine blooms in spring and summer on short laterals produced on older wood. To train it as a vine (it can twine to about 25 feet), plant it next to a support—trellis, fence, or post. Let the stems grow without pinching; then tie them to the support. Try to select a plant that has not already been pinched to promote bushiness; if possible, purchase one that has been staked upright.

Cut back established vines by about a third each year to keep them from getting too woody or sparse. Remove dead wood and weak growth; also shorten long, vigorous shoots. You can head a plant back to its framework or even cut it to the ground to renovate it.

WISTERIA
DECIDUOUS

TWINING

✂ DORMANT SEASON AND SUMMER

These spectacular spring bloomers are extremely vigorous, capable of growing about 40 feet high and 100 feet wide. To avoid wrestling with tangled, overgrown vines, give them regular dormant-season pruning and follow-up attention during the growing season. Because the vines can attain considerable weight, make sure the arbor or other support structure is sturdy and durable; it's best not to use a tree as a support. Though the vines twine, they are so heavy that they should also be tied to the support.

EARLY TRAINING. You must train a newly planted vine to produce the branch framework you want—either single-trunked or multitrunked.

For a single-stemmed vine, encourage the growth of just one stem by limiting side growth. Pinch back all stems except the one you've chosen, so they don't become long streamers. In the dormant season, after the single stem has become tall enough, head it back at the desired height so that side branches will grow in spring.

For a multitrunked vine, select as many vigorous stems as you wish and let them grow. If the plant has just one stem initially, pinch it back to encourage several more to grow.

ANNUAL PRUNING. After a wisteria has developed a permanent framework, prune it regularly. Every dormant season, thin out excess growth. Cut back to two or three buds the flower-bearing laterals—you can easily recognize the short, fat-budded spurs that will carry the spring flowers. In summer, cut back the long, streamerlike stems before they twine and tangle in the main part of the vine. Save any stems that you want to use to extend the height or length of the vine, and tie them to a support. Pull suckers whenever they appear.

Wisteria floribunda

FRUITS, NUTS, AND BERRIES

More than any other category of plants, the various edible-crop trees, bushes, and vines depend on the art of pruning. Unpruned, they won't stop yielding (in fact, they may produce even more), but the fruit will be smaller and of poorer quality. That's because a thicket of twigs will shade the fruit and promote diseases. The center of the plant will die for lack of light, and weak limbs may break from the weight of even a moderate crop.

Early training is the key to success in growing such trees as apple, pear, cherry, and plum. On the following pages you'll learn how to develop a sturdy framework of branches well exposed to sunlight and air. Fruiting occurs best on well-angled branches, so you'll find out how to coax a branch into spreading wider than it does naturally. This chapter also explains how to prune mature trees to maintain their structure and renew fruiting wood; pruning instructions for the most commonly cultivated fruit and nut trees are included.

Pruning berry bushes and vines mainly consists of sorting out the canes to keep them from becoming jumbled, and removing all but the most fruitful wood. You'll find specifics here about managing some popular berry-producing plants so they keep you well supplied with their delectable bounty.

An old, seldom pruned apple tree is covered in springtime blossoms.

FRUIT AND NUT TREES

Some of the popular fruit and nut trees grown in home gardens demand little of your attention in return for supplying you with large, palatable crops. Others, however, need careful training while they are young, followed by attentive pruning in maturity if they are to yield good crops of easily harvested fruit year after year. Don't delay—provide the necessary care from the time you plant your tree. However much time you devote to training and pruning, you'll be rewarded many times over with the incomparable taste of home-grown produce.

TRAINING YOUNG FRUIT AND NUT TREES

Some fruit and nut trees need little more training than trees grown strictly as landscape ornaments (see pages 27–28), but most require special early attention to produce good harvests over the long term. Properly trained in youth, these trees will need far less corrective pruning once they begin bearing.

Your goal in the first several years is to develop a strong, well-balanced framework of branches capable of supporting the weight of bumper crops. The scaffold, or primary, branches should be well spaced along the trunk and radiating in different directions so they don't shade each other. For maximum fruit production all branches should be well exposed to sunlight and air, and their angles of attachment should be between 45° and 60° (see "Spreading the Branches" on page 107).

The permanent framework that you create will be your reference point later when you prune the mature tree. If the tree becomes overgrown for any reason, that original structure will serve as a blueprint for restoration.

You may want to start with a dwarf or semidwarf variety, if one is available; in maturity, its uppermost branches will be easier to reach for pruning and harvesting. But whether training a standard-size tree or one on a dwarfing rootstock, prune only enough initially to establish the desired framework. The reason for restraint is that pruning young trees delays fruiting.

The three main training methods are pruning to a central leader, to a modified central leader, and to an open center. In some cases, a particular method is recommended for a type of fruit or nut tree; in others, you'll have a choice. You will start the tree off in the same manner, regardless of the training method

you'll follow. In all cases, you want branches to start relatively low to the ground for easy picking.

If you're planting a 1-year-old unbranched tree (called a whip or a maiden), you'll have to force it to develop branches at the desired level. Heading back the trunk will stimulate lateral buds to grow; cutting back to 2 to 3 feet high is usually advised, but you can cut even lower if you want branches nearer the ground. The topmost shoot that develops will become the leader. Among the lateral shoots, you'll choose several to become scaffold branches. Note that shoots about 6 to 12 inches below a cut are less vigorous and thus easier to train into scaffolds than are shoots that develop closer to the cut.

A branched 2-year-old tree from the nursery may already have a satisfactory leader and scaffold limbs. But if the branching is poor, head back the tree as you would a whip and wait for new shoots to develop.

What you do with the central leader depends on which of the three training methods you choose: you can let it keep growing, cut it off after it gets to the ultimate height you want, or prune it off almost immediately.

CENTRAL LEADER

This method produces a straight-trunked, pyramidal tree. One tall trunk extends through the tree with tiers of branches radiating from it. Branches are progressively shorter toward the top of the tree, allowing light to penetrate to branches lower down. A central-leader tree is very strong; however, having only a single main stem increases its vulnerability should disease strike.

This central leader is bending under the weight of apples that have developed directly on it; they should have been removed at an early stage.

Many nut bearers grow naturally with a central leader; it doesn't matter if the trees become tall, because they generally need minimal pruning and their crops conveniently drop to the ground. With fruit trees, you're better off reserving this training technique for the dwarf and semidwarf varieties.

As the tree develops, you want to preserve a single upright leader. Pinch back any shoots that might compete with it. Don't let any fruit set directly on the leader, which might sway under the weight. Each dormant season for the first 3 or 4 years, choose a new, higher set of three to five scaffold branches; each set should spiral around the trunk with some vertical distance between each branch in the set. If a potential scaffold is in the right spot but meets the trunk at too narrow an angle, you can increase the angle with a limb spreader (see page 107). Each succeeding set of scaffolds should occupy an area about 18 to 30 inches above the previous set (less for the smallest dwarf trees). The open space between tiers is sometimes called a light slot, because it provides room for sunlight to penetrate to growth lower on the tree.

If branching doesn't occur where you want it to, again head back the central leader to just above buds that are in the desired location and allow side shoots to grow. The topmost bud should grow into an upright shoot that takes over the leader role; if it doesn't cooperate, tie it into an upright position until it straightens. Alternatively, instead of heading the leader you can try notching the bark just above a promising bud; this may cause a shoot to grow.

In the second dormant season, you can begin establishing lateral branches on the scaffolds. If lateral branches have already formed in desirable locations, remove any competitors. Otherwise, head back the scaffolds to force the laterals to branch.

To maintain the framework of a central-leader tree, keep its upper limbs shorter than its lower ones, as on a Christmas tree, and remove any undesirable growth—crossing and unwanted branches as well as water sprouts and suckers.

MODIFIED CENTRAL LEADER

The second training technique (see the illustration on page 106) is a compromise between the central-leader and open-center methods: it is suitable for trees that will grow too tall if you allow the leader to keep growing. You can plan on a modified leader from the beginning or switch to it later, from central-leader training, if you feel the upper branches of your tree will be too high.

Trained to a modified central leader, this apple tree has two tiers of scaffold branches.

Start out as you would in forming a central leader, but curtail the upright growth—usually after selecting two or three tiers of scaffold branches. Either remove the leader by cutting it back to a scaffold, or bend the leader over (and tie it down until it remains in place on its own), making it the topmost branch.

To maintain the framework, regularly remove undesirable growth as you would on a central-leader tree.

TRAINING TO A CENTRAL LEADER

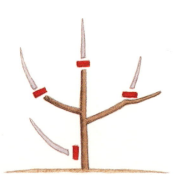

1 Choose the first set of three to five scaffold branches (only two are shown in these illustrations, for simplicity). Do this at planting if the tree is satisfactorily branched; otherwise, head back the trunk and wait until the first dormant season. Shorten or remove any shoots competing with the leader. Head back the leader to get a second tier of branches 18 to 30 inches above the first.

2 The next dormant season, choose a higher set of scaffolds. Remove ill-placed branches and head back the leader, if necessary, to get branching at the proper distance above the previous tier. Head back the scaffolds to force branching.

3 For good light penetration, maintain some open space between tiers and keep the limbs toward the top of the tree shorter than those toward the bottom. Don't allow fruit to set on the leader and bend it over.

1 Train as for a central leader (see pages 104–105) but stop upright growth, usually after two or three tiers of scaffold branches. Cut the leader back to a scaffold.

2 As an alternative, bend the leader over so that it becomes a scaffold. Tie it down until it remains in place on its own. Head it back to force branching.

OPEN CENTER

An open-center tree is also called bowl shaped or vase shaped—giving you a clue to what the tree should look like. There is no central leader; instead, several major limbs angle outward from the top portion of a short trunk. A tree trained to an open center can be kept shorter than it would be if trained to a central leader or modified central leader. Though an open-center tree is structurally weaker than the other types, its several main limbs give it a better chance of survival in the event of disease.

If you plant a branched tree, you'll probably want to head it back as you would a whip to get strong branches in just the right places. During the first dormant season after planting, choose three to five scaffold limbs to form the tree's superstructure. These should form a spiral around the trunk, each branch at least 6 inches higher than the last. Choose well-angled branches; if necessary, spread them (see opposite page). Head back any long scaffold limbs to 2 to 3 feet from the trunk. When doing so, cut back to an outward-facing bud if the branch is swooping upward, to an upward-pointing bud if the branch is spreading too wide.

On this open-center apple tree, scaffold limbs arise from an abbreviated trunk.

During the following summer, head back all scaffold branches that have become too long. To promote lateral branching cut back (to 2 or 3 feet) any limbs that weren't long enough to head during your winter pruning.

The next dormant season, select two strong lateral branches on each scaffold limb to become part of the permanent framework. Cut back each scaffold limb to the outermost lateral branch you've chosen. Then cut back the laterals to 2 to 3 feet if they exceed that; otherwise, pinch back the leafy tips the following summer.

As the tree develops, shorten any overly long limbs and keep the center open by removing water sprouts and crossing, poorly placed, or crowded stems. Be sure to pull out any suckers before they gain a foothold.

TRAINING TO AN OPEN CENTER

1 At planting, head back the trunk to 2 to 3 feet high (or even lower, if desired). Remove all other shoots.

2 In the first dormant season, choose three to five scaffold branches spiraling around the trunk and having at least 6 inches of vertical space between them. Head back the branches to 2 to 3 feet in length.

3 In the second dormant season, choose two strong lateral branches on each scaffold and cut back the scaffolds to the outermost lateral. Head back the laterals to 2 to 3 feet, to force additional branching.

SPREADING THE BRANCHES

As you select scaffold and lateral branches on your developing tree, you may find that some otherwise promising limbs are too narrowly angled. Ideally each branch should meet the trunk or parent branch at an angle of between 45° and 60°. Such well-angled branches are the most fruitful, and they begin bearing their crops sooner. Limbs with narrower angles tend to be more upright, producing vigorous tip growth instead of flowers and fruit. Too wide an angle isn't good, either: the closer to the horizontal (90° angle) a branch is, the more upright shoots it will produce (unless it has been moved gradually into that position, as is done with horizontal espalier patterns).

Luckily, you can train a branch to assume a more desirable angle if you do so while it is young and pliable. You simply bend the branch to the desired position and keep it there with a limb spreader (a device to hold the branch in place). At the end of the growing season, check to see if the branch stays there on its own. If it doesn't, keep the limb spreader in place awhile longer.

Some suppliers catering to professionals sell prefabricated limb spreaders, but you can easily make your own from common household materials. The following list suggests various ways to

SEVERAL TYPES OF LIMB SPREADERS

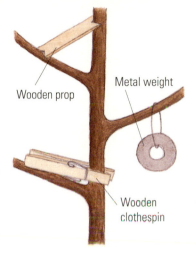

Wooden prop

Metal weight

Wooden clothespin

widen the angle—either by propping something in the branch crotch or by weighing down the branch. (In the less likely situation of having to decrease the angle of attachment, you can force the young branch up and anchor it to a higher branch with string.)

∽ Clip a spring-type wooden clothespin to the parent branch just above the fork. The legs of the pin should be roughly parallel to the limb you're spreading.

∽ Prop a lath strip or other small piece of wood (notch the ends to fit around the limbs) in the branch angle. Some gardeners who grow a lot of fruit trees keep a ready supply of wooden props cut to various lengths. You may have to replace props with longer ones as the limbs grow.

∽ Insert a toothpick tightly between the two limbs. Wait to do this until the shoots have stiffened somewhat, or the toothpick may pierce the tissue.

∽ Weigh down the branch so that it will bend at the desired angle. For example, you can drape a heavy plastic bag filled with gravel over the branch, or hang fishing sinkers or washers from it.

∽ Tie the branch to a stake anchored in the ground.

PRUNING MATURE FRUIT AND NUT TREES

Some fruit and nut trees produce bountiful crops with little pruning, but most benefit from regular sessions with shears or saws. The major reasons for pruning are to renew fruiting wood, keep fruiting sites throughout the tree well exposed to sunlight and air (because an overly dense canopy results in a smaller, poorer-quality crop), and maintain plant vigor. But be careful: excessive pruning can drastically reduce your harvest and weaken the tree.

Evergreen trees can be pruned anytime in mild climates, anytime other than fall or winter in frost-prone areas. You can prune deciduous trees during the dormant season, while they are leafless (wait until late in the dormant season in cold-winter climates); during spring, when the trees begin to grow and bloom; or in summer. During the dormant season, you can more easily see the shape of the tree, distinguish new wood from old, and identify fruiting spurs and buds. In many regions, especially those east of the Rockies, waiting until spring growth begins is recommended for stone fruits (apricot, cherry, plum, prune, peach, nectarine) as a disease deterrent. In all regions where the

climate permits it, you may want to prune some trees in summer to improve the quality of their fruit or to remove unwanted growth; see "Summer Pruning" on page 109. Remember, if you're playing catch-up because you (or your predecessors) postponed pruning for a long time, spread the job out over 2 or 3 years, or even longer.

Regardless of the special needs of a particular type of fruit or nut tree, you start out in the same way by removing the three Ds: dead, damaged, and dysfunctional growth (see page 14). Be sure to eliminate suckers (if allowed to grow, they may overtake the desirable variety on a grafted tree) and water sprouts; removing these vigorous shoots in summer makes them less likely to reappear. After this, you prune to maximize fruit production. That means renewing fruiting wood as required by the tree species, thinning out any large limbs that shade other fruit-producing branches, and removing unproductive wood such as small, shaded branches growing from the lower surface of larger branches.

It's essential to know at what points your tree bears so that you don't accidentally eliminate more fruiting sites than you intended. Observe your trees closely at harvest time. Apple, pear,

TOP: This open-center Japanese plum tree has well-placed scaffold limbs, but it is cluttered with twiggy growth that accumulated over several years when it was unpruned.

MIDDLE: Pruning begins with the removal of the smallest-diameter shoots in the tree's center. Other excess growth is thinned out and the outer branches shortened to form a rounded crown.

BOTTOM: The finished tree shows a much more open center, with considerably more light and air between branches.

plum, cherry, apricot, and almond trees all bear on knobby or twiggy protrusions called fruit spurs (see opposite page). Peach and nectarine trees produce on 1-year-old wood, as do filberts and hazelnuts. Avocado, citrus, pecan, persimmon, and walnut trees are tip bearers, producing fruit at the ends of the current season's growth. Tip bearers produce a lot of fruit whether they're pruned or not; however, extensive cutting back of these trees after spring growth has occurred will obviously reduce the harvest. In ideal climates figs produce two crops yearly, the first on 1-year-old wood and the second on the tips of new growth. In frosty climates only the second crop is produced, whereas in cool-summer areas only the first has time to ripen.

When removing superfluous limbs, be sure to thin rather than head them, to avoid stimulating a lot of new growth in that area. As you thin, remember to cut outside of the branch collar, taking care not to slice into it or the branch bark ridge (see page 26). Some fruiting trees such as peach and nectarine are an exception to the rule about making mostly thinning cuts. On those trees, you'll make a lot of heading cuts to encourage new fruiting wood. When doing so, head back to outward-facing buds rather than ones that point toward the interior of the tree.

Some species of fruit trees set more fruit than they can mature to a good size; these will benefit from fruit thinning. This will also help even out annual production, so that you don't get a heavy crop one year and a light one the next. Many trees naturally drop much of their fruit while it is still small (a phenomenon called June drop, though it can occur anytime from late spring into midsummer, depending on the fruit type and climate). Wait until after this natural drop to thin the developing fruit further.

RESTORING A NEGLECTED TREE

Often people who buy older homes end up inheriting at least one large, overgrown fruit tree on the property. Renewal is certainly worthwhile if the subject is an apple, pear, or other long-lived tree. You probably wouldn't want to bother with a peach or nectarine tree: by the time it's old enough to become a neglected mess, it's likely on its last legs.

Examine the tree before you make any cuts. If you detect a basic structure (central leader, modified central leader, or open center), your goal will be to get back to that form by removing superfluous wood. If it's unstructured, you'll have to create some kind of framework by choosing scaffold and lateral branches. If the tree is too big for your purposes, plan to reduce its size gradually (see "Crown Reduction" on pages 32 and 33).

You can remove harmful growth at once—dead, dying, broken, and rubbing branches—but spread the other pruning over several years. Thin out some of the crowded stems each year to open up the tree and let in sunlight and air. Also thin out poorly angled limbs and excess branches, but limit your removal of big branches to one or two annually. Shorten overly long limbs

FLOWER BUDS AND FRUIT SPURS

Distinguishing buds that produce leafy shoots from those producing fruit can be crucial when pruning fruit and nut trees. If you are heading back growth to a bud in order to stimulate branching, for instance, you should cut just above a leaf bud rather than a flower bud. (A fruit is the ripened ovary of a flower, so all fruit begins as flower buds.) It takes some practice to distinguish the two, but flower buds tend to be plumper than leaf buds. Some types of trees have compound buds—for example, on peach and nectarine trees, two flower buds flank a leaf bud.

On some fruit and nut trees, flower buds grow in clusters called fruit spurs; each year the spurs put out blos-

Apple spurs

soms, form fruit, and lengthen just a little. Depending on the species, these spurs may look like short shoots or stubby twigs. How long a spur remains productive also depends on the species; all are fruitful for at least several years and some are very long lived. Apples, pears, cherries, plums, apricots, and almonds all bear on spurs.

Fruit and nut trees are much more productive when their flower buds are exposed to sunshine—that's why we prune to keep the interior of a tree open. If the light level reaching a flower bud is too low, the bud will wither before it can bloom or produce any fruit.

Thinning out crowded spurs

---

to a side branch to keep them from breaking under a heavy crop load. The large cuts you make will give rise to water sprouts; remove them in summer while they're still small. In fact, you may want to do much of the pruning during the summer if your growing season is long enough and early frost damage isn't a factor; otherwise, make major cuts during the dormant season.

SUMMER PRUNING

You may associate pruning fruit trees with the winter dormant season, but additional pruning in summer can be beneficial—as long as it's done on healthy trees in a suitable climate. Where frosts come very early, summer pruning is risky. If you're uncertain about the effect in your climate, prune just a little and no later than a month before the first fall frost date, and see what happens.

Pruning solely in the dormant season has an invigorating effect on a tree, but if you also prune in summer, you'll induce less new shoot growth. This two-season pruning approach will keep dwarf and semidwarf trees in check, benefiting gardeners with small spaces and making the fruit easier to harvest. The stunting effect diminishes on more vigorous standard-size trees.

A welcome by-product of summer pruning is the better fruit color you get when the developing fruit is exposed to more sunlight. Don't remove too much leafy cover in intensely sunny areas, however, or the branches and fruit will become sunburned.

The best time to summer-prune is when new growth appears to be slowing down; the shoot tip should be succulent and the base starting to turn woody. This may happen anytime from June until August, depending on your climate. You can limit summer pruning to new growth, or you can also remove old wood if you want to drastically reduce tree size. Prune out any new shoots that develop below the cuts: do so in early fall in mild-winter climates, but wait until normal pruning time in colder climates.

If your goal is to stimulate lots of vigorous shoot growth, you're better off pruning in the dormant season or just as growth is beginning. That's the case with peach and nectarine trees, whose fruiting wood must be renewed yearly. However, even on those trees you can remove some leafy cover in summer to expose the fruit to more sunlight and air.

TOP LEFT: The ideal time to prune new growth on this apple tree is when the shoot tip is succulent but the base is beginning to turn woody.

TOP RIGHT: Starting at the shoot base, count up two or three leaves above the basal whorl of leaves; cut off the shoot just above the leaf.

LEFT: Pruning side shoots throughout the tree during summer exposes fruit to more sunlight, thus allowing it to develop better color. A year later, the pruned shoot will produce a spur with an apple, instead of just foliage.

Managing some common fruit and nut trees

On the following pages you'll find tips for training and pruning the fruit and nut trees most typically grown in home gardens. Each listing begins with the type of plant (deciduous or evergreen), the recommended training methods or common forms for it, and the best times of year to prune it. For basic information about the various training methods, refer to pages 104–106. Although summer pruning is not necessarily specified, you may do at least some pruning—or even most of it—at that time if your climate is suitable.

Almond

DECIDUOUS
OPEN CENTER
✂ DORMANT SEASON

Almond trees grow 20 to 30 feet high; they are erect when young, spreading and dome shaped in maturity. The trees, which are grafted, typically live about 50 years. The nut crop is harvested from late summer into fall.

Like their close relatives the peaches, almond trees are best trained to an open center. Once a tree has attained its basic shape, most pruning is done for wood renewal to ensure steady crops. The nuts are borne on spurs containing lateral clusters of buds; they are productive for about 5 years. During each dormant season, remove about a fifth of the oldest fruiting wood; at the same time, cut out dead wood and any crossing or crowded branches.

A young almond tree grows vigorously and may put all its energy into vegetative growth at the expense of the fruit-bearing spurs. If this happens, withhold fertilizer and stop pruning for a season or two to slow excess growth.

Apple

DECIDUOUS
CENTRAL LEADER; MODIFIED CENTRAL LEADER; OPEN CENTER; ESPALIER
✂ LATE DORMANT SEASON

Most apple varieties form broadly upright trees; their mature size depends on the rootstock on which the variety is grafted. Those most commonly planted in home gardens are semidwarf and dwarf trees, ranging from somewhat to much smaller than the 20- to 30-foot height of a standard-size tree. The apples are borne on knobby spurs with fuzzy buds at the end. These spurs may produce for up to 20 years, but they tend to weaken after about 3 years. Fruit ripens from July to early November, depending on the variety.

As long as knobby spurs are productive, retain them—they will bear more apples next year.

The preferred training methods for apple trees are central leader (ideal for smaller and medium-size trees) and modified central leader (to keep larger trees within easy

TOP: An orchard with rows of open-center almond trees in bloom.

BOTTOM: The almond husk, which resembles an undersized leathery green peach, splits to reveal the edible nut.

reach). Open-center training is sometimes used on wide-spreading varieties such as 'Golden Delicious'. Apples are also ideally suited to formal espaliers.

Prune as little as possible during the first 5 or 6 years—the following are the few essential tasks. Keep narrow-angled limbs from developing, especially on naturally upright varieties (see "Spreading the Branches" on page 107). Don't let side branches outgrow the leader or secondary branches outgrow the primary branches. If fruit sets on the leader, pick it off before it causes the stem to bend.

Mature apple trees need only moderate pruning: removing weak, dead, or poorly placed branches and twigs, especially those growing toward the center of the tree. Keeping the center open will encourage the development of strong new wood with new fruiting spurs; it will also discourage mildew. Note that excessive fruit set will reduce flower bud formation for the following year. To prevent this, thin the developing fruit to 4 to 6 inches apart when each is about the size of a nickel.

Spur varieties, types of apple trees with small shoots every few inches along the branches, usually need less pruning than other apple varieties because they're naturally more open. Even easier to maintain is the colonnade apple, which develops a single spirelike trunk to 8 feet tall. Because fruiting spurs form directly on the trunk or on very short branchlets, this tree's total width does not exceed 2 feet.

Where fireblight disease is a problem on apple trees, remove any blackened growth promptly, cutting back to healthy tissue (see "Removing Diseased Growth" on page 16).

Most apple trees, like this antique variety, 'Sierra Beauty', have a broad, upright shape. This one is trained to a modified central leader.

APRICOT

DECIDUOUS

OPEN CENTER; MODIFIED CENTRAL LEADER; ESPALIER

DORMANT SEASON OR SPRING

Apricots are good dual-purpose fruit and shade trees growing to about 15 feet high and wide. They can also be trained as espaliers, but the pattern shouldn't be too rigid. The plants, which are grafted, generally live 20 to 30 years. They bear fruit on spurs (with buds arranged laterally) that form on the previous year's wood and remain fruitful for about 4 years. Most varieties ripen their fruit from late spring into summer.

Because apricot trees tend to form too dense a canopy, open-center training is usually recommended. In cold-winter areas, hardy apricot varieties are sometimes trained to a modified central leader.

Apricot trees tend to form a dense crown; eliminate excess growth with thinning cuts.

Fruit-bearing spurs of apricot trees are productive for about 4 years.

Trees need only moderate pruning each year in winter or, to minimize their vulnerability to disease, just as growth begins anew in spring. Remove dead, diseased, or broken branches and any that cross through the tree's center or crowd major limbs. To promote the growth of new fruiting spurs, remove older, unproductive branches with their exhausted spurs; cut back to vigorous young branches bearing good fruiting spurs or to new branches that will send out spurs as they grow. To avoid increasing the canopy's density, make thinning rather than heading cuts.

To get bigger apricots, do this: after the fruit has set, remove the smallest ones, leaving about 4 inches between them.

AVOCADO

EVERGREEN

ALLOW TREE TO ASSUME NATURAL FORM

AFTER HARVEST

Avocado trees are budded to a rootstock. Most types grow to about 40 feet tall; their forms range from upright to spreading and from symmetrical to irregular, according to the variety. The trees bloom in winter; the fruit, which forms at the tips of the current season's growth, ripens from summer into winter, depending on the variety.

Train young avocado trees as you would any landscape tree (see pages 27–28). After that, let the tree assume its natural form. You can promote lower branching and shape trees to some extent by pinching terminal shoots.

Mature avocado trees usually need very little pruning; just remove any dead or damaged branches. Continual dieback of interior branches is normal; usually they simply fall off. If tall trees are in danger of being uprooted by windstorms, reduce their height (see "Crown Reduction" on pages 32 and 33). Avocado bark is sensitive to sunscald; if the removal of a branch exposes a previously shaded trunk to strong sunlight, coat the newly exposed bark with whitewash or flat latex paint (white or light brown).

Avocado trees often suffer freeze damage. If only part of the tree is affected, wait until regrowth begins before cutting back to live tissue. If the tree is killed to the ground, it will usually resprout. Therefore, growers in freeze-prone regions often take precautions to ensure that the grafted variety—rather than the less desirable rootstock—will be the one to grow back. They graft the variety very low on the rootstock, plant deeply so that the graft union is at or below ground level, and then mound soil around the trunk as it grows.

ABOVE: Some avocado varieties are upright, others spreading.

RIGHT: Fruit is borne at the tips of new shoots.

CHERRY

DECIDUOUS

CENTRAL LEADER; MODIFIED CENTRAL LEADER; OPEN CENTER; ESPALIER

DORMANT SEASON OR SPRING

Two main types of cherries are grown for their fruit: sweet cherry and sour cherry (the latter is also known as tart cherry or pie cherry). Trees live about 30 years. Standard-size trees grow on their own roots, but gardeners with limited space can also find varieties grown on dwarfing rootstocks. Fruit ripens from late spring to early summer.

Standard-size sweet cherry trees grow 20 to 35 feet tall; some varieties are equally broad. Sour cherry trees are shorter (topping out at about 20 feet), wider spreading, and more irregular in shape than their sweet counterparts. Either can be trained to a central leader, modified central leader, or open center. They can also be espaliered; a Belgian arch or a fairly upright pattern such as a fan shape work best.

Prune during the dormant season, or wait until spring—pruning as growth begins is advised as a disease deterrent in many areas, especially east of the Rockies.

During your initial training, be especially careful when choosing scaffold limbs on sweet cherry trees; most varieties tend to form narrow-angled branches. Select wide-angled limbs and use limb spreaders (see page 107) where necessary to force branching at the desired angle. Remove any branches growing upright against the trunk.

ABOVE: This sweet cherry tree (guarded by a scarecrow) has an open center.

RIGHT: Fruit is borne on long-lived spurs.

Corrective pruning of cherry trees during the first 5 or 6 years should consist of removing suckers, water sprouts, and stems that rub against permanent branches. If branches fork (that is, if branches of equal size arise from the same point), either remove one of the limbs or cut it back severely.

Once properly trained, mature cherry trees need only light pruning. Because the fruit is borne on long-lived spurs containing a whorl of buds, the trees don't have to be pruned specifically for fruit production. Aside from removing weak or damaged branches, prune cherries only to maintain their shape and eliminate undesirable growth. In cold-winter areas, pruning may not be needed year after year. If a tree's center becomes too crowded as it matures, thin lightly. Don't remove too much leaf cover in hot-summer areas, though, because the bark is sensitive to sunburn.

CITRUS

EVERGREEN

ALLOW TREE TO ASSUME NATURAL FORM; ESPALIER

ANYTIME (BUT NOT DURING FALL AND WINTER IN FREEZE-PRONE AREAS)

Citrus includes oranges, mandarins, pummelos, grapefruit, lemons, limes, kumquats, calamondin, citrons, and assorted hybrids. Most citrus trees sold in nurseries are budded onto a rootstock. Depending on the citrus species and variety, plants range from 6 to 30 feet tall (dwarfs and semidwarfs are one-half to two-thirds of the standard size). Shapes include upright, spreading, and irregular. Just about any type of citrus can be espaliered, though varieties with vining branches or an open growth habit are especially suitable. Some kinds can be planted close together and pruned as hedges; lemons, sour oranges, and calamondin are the best candidates for this treatment.

Most types of citrus set a single crop that ripens in fall or winter; everbearing types (lemons, limes, citrons, calamondin) can set fruit throughout the year, though they do so most heavily in spring. The fruit is borne at the tips of the current season's growth. You can prune citrus anytime in frost-free regions, but avoid pruning during fall and winter in areas subject to freezes.

Traditional training methods don't really apply to citrus. You can follow the lead of commercial growers, who nip back wild growth on young trees and then prune later mainly to remove twiggy growth, weak branches, and suckers. They often leave branches on the trunk right down to the ground, because production is heaviest on lower branches. The leafy skirt protects the sensitive bark in intensely sunny climates; if bark is exposed, protect it with whitewash or flat latex paint (white or light brown). In humid regions, remove the lower branches to deter disease: the extra open space will improve air circulation and minimize the splashing of fungus spores from soil to tree.

Lemon trees often grow long, pendulous branches carrying foliage and fruits at the very ends. You can cut back these long branches severely to encourage fruiting closer to the tree's center.

To preserve flowers and fruit on a citrus hedge, don't shear it. Instead, grow it as an informal or semiformal hedge and use hand pruners to remove growth selectively.

To rejuvenate an old citrus tree, begin by thinning out dead wood and twiggy stems to let more sunlight and air into the tree and force healthy new growth. That may do the job. If not, you can cut back branches severely, as citrus wood has many dormant buds along it that will produce new growth.

If citrus plants have been frozen, give them a chance to recover before pruning. After new growth appears in late winter or early spring, wait for any dieback to show up; then cut back to live wood in midsummer.

A citrus tree can be grown either with its branches to the ground or with its lower limbs removed. The 'Valencia' orange trees above illustrate the two options.

This fig tree, shown during dormancy, displays the typical low-branching, wide-spreading vase shape.

FIG

DECIDUOUS

OPEN-CENTER TREE; SHRUB; ESPALIER

DORMANT SEASON AND SUMMER

Fairly fast growing to between 15 and 30 feet high, a fig tree is typically low branched and spreading. These fruiters are grown on their own roots and can live 100 years or more. Where hard freezes are common, the wood freezes back severely and the plant turns into a big shrub. In some colder areas, the plant will die to the ground each winter but will send up new shoots in spring. A fig can be trained as a formal or informal espalier.

Under the most favorable growing conditions, most fig varieties produce two crops a year. In early summer, the first crop comes on wood formed the previous year. The second crop appears in late summer, borne at the ends of new growth that formed while

In ideal climates, fig trees produce two crops yearly.

the first crop of figs was maturing. In colder climates, only the second crop is produced. In cool-summer areas, only the first crop ripens.

A fig is somewhat indifferent to pruning: it can take quite a bit yet still bear an ample crop—but it will also bear with no pruning at all. In climates where the plant freezes, any pruning consists mainly of removing damaged stems after growth resumes in the spring. You have more options in terms of training and pruning in mild-winter regions. For maximum beauty and shade you can let the plant grow naturally, only pruning off unattractive or poorly placed limbs and dead, weak, or crossing branches. Or, to increase your harvest, you can train the tree to an open center, keeping the main scaffold limbs close to the ground. After a main framework has formed, prune to encourage new wood and to remove crowded stems in the center. As needed, limit the tree's spread or height by thinning branches back to laterals closer to the center.

Do any major pruning during the dormant season; pinch back runaway shoots in summer. If you get two crops, avoid cutting back heavily between them, as it can seriously reduce the size of the second crop and remove growth that will carry the next year's first crop.

FILBERT AND HAZELNUT

DECIDUOUS

OPEN-CENTER TREE; SHRUB; HEDGEROW

DORMANT SEASON AND SUMMER

You can train a filbert or hazelnut to a single-trunked small tree with an open center. However, most types are shrubby, growing 10 to 18 feet with multiple trunks, and it's easier to let them assume their natural habit. The plants, which grow on their own roots, tend to produce many suckers that will spread into thickets unless cleared out three or four times a year. For a boundary hedgerow (a thick hedge), plant mixed varieties in a row 4 feet apart and let the suckers grow. If you're growing the plants as individual trees, remove the suckers in summer.

ABOVE: An orchard of European filbert trees.

RIGHT: Nuts are borne on the previous season's wood.

Nuts ripen by the end of August and drop in early fall; they are produced on 1-year-old wood. Prune bearing plants moderately each dormant season to encourage new growth on which the following year's nuts will form.

PEACH AND NECTARINE

DECIDUOUS

OPEN CENTER; ESPALIER

DORMANT SEASON OR SPRING

A standard-size fruiting peach or nectarine can grow rapidly to 25 feet tall and wide, but well-pruned trees are usually kept at 10 to 12 feet. The trees can also be espaliered; a fan shape, Belgian fence, or informal pattern works best. In most regions, fruit ripens between June and September, depending on the variety. The trees, which are grafted, are quite short lived—about 15 to 20 years.

The plants are highly susceptible to perennial canker, caused by a fungus that infects open wounds in cool weather. In

Both peaches and nectarines are produced on the prior year's growth.

areas where this disease is a problem (mainly east of the Rockies), pruning at blossom time reduces the chance of infection. In the West the trees are usually pruned during the dormant season.

Peaches and nectarines don't make good central-leader trees; they are best trained to an open center. Typically, three to five scaffold branches are established. Branched nursery trees often have shoots that are too weak or poorly placed to make good scaffolds; if this is the case, cut back the trunk and select three of the best shoots to grow thereafter. If the nursery tree has one or two good branches, cut back the trunk above them and select additional shoots. To form a low and spreading tree, cut the scaffolds back to outward-growing lateral branches after the first and second years' growth. During the next couple of dormant seasons prune only to remove broken, diseased, or low-hanging stems.

Mature peach and nectarine trees, which produce on 1-year-old branches, need more pruning than other fruit trees. Severe annual pruning does more than renew the fruiting wood—it renews wood throughout the tree. Without this pruning, a tree will bear its fruit farther and farther away from the center, resulting in sagging branches that can easily break.

Each dormant season, remove about two-thirds of the previous year's growth. The best way to do this is to prune out any

Peach and nectarine trees are best suited to open-center training.

weak and crowding new growth; then head back the remaining branches to staggered lengths, so that fruit will form throughout the crown. Cut back some one-third of the way, others two-thirds, and the remainder nearly all the way. Keep the center open by removing any vigorous shoots growing through the middle (summer is a good time to do this), but leave the small shoots—these will bear fruit. During the growing season, thin the developing fruit to 4 to 8 inches apart.

Genetic dwarf peaches and nectarines form shrubs 5 to 6 feet tall that look like shaggy green mops. You must prune to keep the center of the shrub open; otherwise, it becomes crowded and often diseased. Thinning will encourage fruit of good size and color by allowing light to reach the innermost flower buds.

Listing continues >

This dwarf peach, 'Sensation', is thinned to keep its center open to sunlight.

ESPALIER:
TWO-DIMENSIONAL TRAINING

The art of espalier—training a plant to grow in a two-dimensional, or flat, plane—began hundreds of years ago inside the walled gardens of medieval Europe. Trained against the walls, fruiting trees were cleverly protected from animals, thieves, cold, and wind, yet absorbed extra warmth from the wall whenever the sun shone. An espaliered fruit tree yields large, easy-to-harvest crops for the small amount of space occupied—and the fruit is of high quality, as each branch is fully exposed to sunlight and air. A long line of such trees is not only productive but highly ornamental. Espaliers take some effort, though, not only in training the plants but in maintaining the flat design: be prepared to prune at least several times a year.

These peach trees form a Belgian fence pattern.

An informal espalier—one without a precise pattern—requires the least amount of work. You just plant the tree in front of a structure, allow it to branch naturally, and then remove any growth that juts out too far into the wrong plane.

A formal espalier demands more attention and patience to train the plants into a definite pattern. Some of the most popular patterns for fruit trees are cordon, fan, and Belgian fence (see the opposite page for illustrations of these and other patterns). If none of the standard designs appeals to you, develop one of your own. In all cases you manipulate the limbs by tying them to the support. Plastic nursery ties, raffia, bits of string, and clear grafting or budding tape all work well as ties. To maintain the motif, you prune out excess growth. Don't expect the full design to become clear immediately; it may take several years of diligent training.

Semidwarf and dwarf apple and pear trees are the best candidates for precise geometric patterns. Less rigid designs, such as a Belgian arch, are best for apricots, cherries, and plums. Figs can be grown formally or informally. Japanese persimmon trees are best treated informally, and citrus produces more fruit if grown that way. Peach and nectarine trees can be espaliered informally or in a Belgian fence or fan shape, but they will need just as much heavy pruning as they do when grown as normal trees.

For fruit trees that need cross-pollination, remember to plant at least two compatible varieties to get fruit set. You can combine them in the espalier if their habits are similar, or you can espalier a single variety and have the other growing as a tree nearby.

HORIZONTAL CORDON

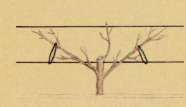  

1 At planting, select two branches for the first tier; remove all other shoots and head back the leader to just above the wire. Bend branches at a 45° angle and secure them to the wire.

2 In the first growing season, gradually lower the branches until they are horizontal by season's end. Keep the newly sprouted leader erect and tie it to the second-tier wire.

3 In the first dormant season, head the leader close to the second wire. Select two branches for a second tier and remove competing shoots. Prune the laterals on first-tier branches to three buds.

ESPALIER PATTERNS

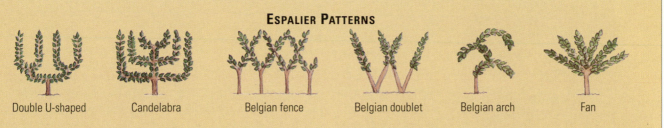

Double U-shaped   Candelabra   Belgian fence   Belgian doublet   Belgian arch   Fan

TRAINING AN ESPALIER

Espaliers can be either freestanding or supported against vertical surfaces. The simplest approach to the latter method is to tie an espaliered tree directly to a lath trellis set in the ground parallel to a wall or fence. If you want a more transparent look, insert eyescrews or bolts in the vertical structure and thread 12- to 14-gauge galvanized wires between them. For adequate air circulation, fix the wires at a distance of 8 to 12 inches from the structure. To create a freestanding espalier, stretch wires between 4-by-4 posts sunk well in the ground. For both types of espalier, leave about 18 inches of vertical space between rows or tiers of wires.

Choose a full-sun location; in hot-summer areas, however, avoid planting against a light-colored, south-facing wall or you'll cook your fruit. For a row, set trees at least 6 feet apart for very horizontal patterns, 2 to 4 feet apart for narrower ones. Don't neglect to allow ample room for trunk expansion when planting in front of a structure. Then proceed to begin forming the pattern of your choice.

HORIZONTAL PATTERNS. Head back an unbranched whip at or just above the lowest support wire, retaining two buds facing in opposite directions—and, if the design calls for the trunk to continue upward, a third bud to grow vertically. If you planted a branched tree, select the two best branches below the first wire to form the first horizontal tier.

During successive seasons you'll need to train the tree according to your chosen design. For a horizontal cordon, for example, follow the steps shown in the illustrations below. To prevent one branch in a pair from outstripping the other in growth, you can adjust the branch angles—raising them to increase vigor (and hence growth rate), lowering them to reduce it. When lateral growth on these branches reaches 12 to 14 inches, prune it back to three buds.

DIAGONAL PATTERNS. If the diagonal pattern begins at the first wire, as in the Belgian fence, head back the leader at planting time; choose two buds to form the diagonal arms. For a diagonal pattern that begins at ground level, such as the Belgian doublet, plant two trees at 60° angles; don't head the trees, but rather prune off any branches.

PRUNING AN ESTABLISHED ESPALIER

Obviously, one goal of routine pruning is to maintain the espalier's pattern. But you also want to stimulate the formation of flower buds (and thus fruiting) and to keep fruiting sites well exposed to sunlight and air. Where the growing season is long enough and early frosts aren't a concern, the best time to prune an espalier is in summer (see page 109). Formal patterns will probably need pruning every few weeks. In intensely sunny climates, maintain good leaf cover or the branches will be scorched.

4   In the second growing season, gradually bring the second-tier branches to a horizontal position. Keep the leader upright and tie it to the third-tier wire.

5   Repeat the process for additional cordons. Continue to prune wayward growth after the espalier is established.

This apple tree is trained in a horizontal cordon.

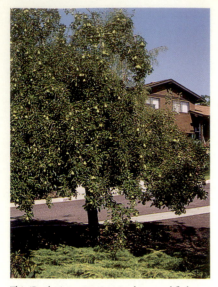

This 'Bartlett' pear tree is trained to a modified central leader.

Train grafted pecan trees to a single, upright trunk.

PEAR

DECIDUOUS

CENTRAL LEADER; MODIFIED CENTRAL LEADER; OPEN CENTER; ESPALIER

DORMANT SEASON

Pears naturally grow upright—that is, taller than wide—and develop many branches that are vertical or nearly so. They are long lived, lasting as long as a century. Standard-size trees can reach 30 to 40 feet or even taller. Dwarf and semidwarf trees range from about one-half to three-quarters of that size, depending on the rootstock. All types can be trained as espaliers. Pear trees produce fruit on knobby spurs that remain productive for up to 5 years. Depending on the variety, the crop ripens from July to late October.

European pears, hanging from knobby spurs, seldom need thinning.

Like apple trees, pears can be trained to a central leader or modified central leader (the former is best confined to dwarfs, as fruit will be out of reach on larger trees trained that way). Pears also respond well to open-center training—and there's a good reason to opt for this where the bacterial disease fireblight is a serious problem. With several main limbs, the tree has a better chance of survival if seriously infected. Whichever training method you choose, use limb spreaders to widen pears' typically narrow branch angles (see page 107).

Once the framework is established, prune lightly each year to maintain good form and to thin out weak, broken, or crowding branches. Remove upright stems growing through the interior of the tree. To avoid heavy new growth, and the resultant risk of fireblight, do not prune severely in any one season. If you see any blackened, burnt-looking growth (fireblight can cause entire branches to die back quickly), promptly cut back to healthy tissue (see "Removing Diseased Growth" on page 16).

Thinning the fruit of European pear varieties is seldom necessary. Thin Asian pears to one per fruiting spur.

PECAN

DECIDUOUS

CENTRAL LEADER

DORMANT SEASON OR DURING NUT DROP

Nuts are borne at the ends of the current season's growth.

Most pecans grown for nut production are grafted varieties; they should be trained to a single trunk with strong, wide-angled branches. Left to their own devices, the grafted trees tend to develop multiple trunks having narrow, weak forks. Trees growing on their own roots usually form a central leader with little or no training; they can grow 70 to 100 feet or taller, with a broadly oval canopy. Pecans will produce for about 75 years.

On a grafted tree, prune off all but one vertical trunk. Develop permanent scaffold branches starting at about 6 feet; however, keep temporary branches (shortened to about 6 inches) on the lower trunk for 2 or 3 years to protect the tree from wind and sunscald.

During the formative years, eliminate extra branches where two or more limbs arise from closely spaced buds.

Pecan trees bear nuts at the tips of the current season's growth; the mature nuts drop in autumn. Established trees need little pruning—mainly just to remove suckers from below the graft union and dead, broken, or poorly placed limbs.

PERSIMMON

DECIDUOUS

CENTRAL LEADER; MODIFIED CENTRAL LEADER; ESPALIER

DORMANT SEASON

Two types of persimmon trees are grown: the native American persimmon, which grows on its own roots and has an upright habit to about 60 feet tall; and the Japanese or Oriental persimmon, which is grafted and grows about 30 feet high with a wider-spreading shape. The Japanese species makes a good informal espalier, and in some areas is pruned heavily and grown as an informal or semiformal hedge or screen. Both types of

persimmons are long lived—at least 60 years (and some Japanese persimmon trees in Asia are several hundred years old). They are tip bearers, producing fruit at the end of the current season's growth. Harvest time is late fall into winter.

Persimmon trees are usually trained to a central leader or modified central leader. The goal of pruning in the early years is to establish a strong framework, because the wood is brittle. Limbs on the Japanese species, which bears larger fruit than the native species, can easily snap under the weight of a heavy crop.

On mature persimmon trees, remove the usual undesirable growth—dead, damaged, diseased, or crowded branches. Also pull out suckers; you

'Fuyu' (above) and other persimmons grow at the ends of new shoots.

A native American persimmon tree (top) is typically taller and more upright than a Japanese or Oriental persimmon tree (bottom).

won't have to do this to the native species if you let it follow its predilection to form a thicket. It's not necessary to renew fruiting wood on the American persimmon, because it tends to shed small branches on its own. But do shorten the branch ends of the Japanese species, both to keep them strong enough to carry a heavy crop and to stimulate new growth. If the branches are straining under an unusually big crop, remove some of the fruit to relieve the weight.

PLUM AND PRUNE

DECIDUOUS

CENTRAL LEADER; MODIFIED CENTRAL LEADER; OPEN CENTER; ESPALIER

DORMANT SEASON OR SPRING

European and Japanese varieties, the main types grown for fruit, are grafted onto another rootstock. Standard-size trees will grow to 30 feet but can be kept to 15 with pruning. Varieties grown on dwarfing rootstocks attain about 8 to 10 feet; these lend themselves to informal espaliers or to simple formal ones, such as a Belgian arch. Plum and prune trees live approximately 20 to 50 years.

All types bear fruit on spurs that are productive for up to 5 years; these appear as whorls of buds flush with the stems or as stubby protrusions from the stems. Japanese

Japanese plums are carried on spurs and on year-old wood.

This 'Satsuma' Japanese plum tree is trained to a modified central leader.

plums bear on 1-year-old wood as well as on spurs. The fruit ripens from June into September, depending on the variety. Prune all plums and prunes during the dormant season, or—as a disease deterrent in some areas east of the Rockies—as growth begins in spring.

Trees can be trained to a central leader (this is most practical for types on dwarfing rootstocks), to a modified central leader, or to an open center. Select strong, wide-angled branches for the scaffold. Japanese plums will offer many more potential scaffolds than do European varieties. Avoid the formation of tight crotches where lateral branches meet the scaffolds; if necessary, force branches to the desired angle with limb spreaders (see page 107).

On established trees remove water sprouts, suckers, and any dead, damaged, diseased, or crossing stems. European plums, Damson plum, and all prunes are only moderately vigorous, so they need little additional pruning beyond thinning out some of the annual shoot growth.

Japanese plums (and some Japanese-American hybrids) are much more vigorous, producing many long new shoots each year. An unpruned tree will become large and floppy, and its limbs may break under the weight of a heavy crop. Each year, therefore, prune overly long shoots: head them back to laterals or remove them with thinning cuts if they are badly placed or crowding. These trees also tend to produce excess upright growth; shorten the vertical shoots to outside branchlets. Japanese plums tend to overbear as well, so you'll want to thin the fruit to 4 to 5 inches apart.

To reduce exposure to the bacterial canker prevalent on these trees in the South, don't leave stubs when pruning and remove dead or broken branches right away.

The scaffold branches on this young English walnut tree grew from unnecked buds.

WALNUT

DECIDUOUS

CENTRAL LEADER; MODIFIED CENTRAL LEADER

DORMANT SEASON OR DURING NUT DROP

The various types of walnuts grown for nuts—English walnut (including Carpathian and Hardy Persian varieties), black walnut, and butternut—are large trees that lead double lives as landscape ornaments and nut producers. Both grafted plants and seedlings are grown. The trees typically grow 50 to 75 feet tall in home gardens and may live for 100 years. They produce nuts at the tips of the current season's growth; nut drop occurs in late summer or early fall.

Walnuts, encased in greenish husks, are carried at the ends of new growth.

Walnut trees can be trained to a central leader or modified central leader, with the first permanent scaffolds 6 to 8 feet off the ground. Note that some buds on walnut trees are necked—that is, they sit on a short stem. Don't allow scaffold branches to develop from necked buds; rub off these buds and allow your permanent limbs to grow from more ordinary-looking buds without the little stem. Leave some shortened shoots along the lower trunk during the tree's developing years, to protect the trunk from sunburn.

Once the basic framework has been established, walnuts need little pruning other than removing broken or diseased branches. But you should cut back to laterals any branches that are excessively long, and prune out stems that form a very narrow angle with the trunk.

BERRY BUSHES AND VINES

When allowed to grow unsupervised, berry-producing bushes and vines become more of a liability than an asset to a garden. They tend to colonize large areas, sprawling over other plants and concealing much of their fruit in a tangle of canes or branches. Tamed, however, they will keep to their allotted spaces and produce luscious, easy-to-pick crops. Proper training and pruning is the secret to managing these plants.

TOP: Untrained, untamed grapevines clamber into neighboring fruit trees.

BOTTOM: Raspberry canes are arched over and woven through wire to neaten them.

TRAINING AND PRUNING BERRY BUSHES AND VINES

Berry bushes and vines need a firm hand from the time they're planted if they are to produce good-quality fruit and not make a mess of your garden.

The fruit bushes discussed here—blackberries, blueberries, currants, gooseberries, and raspberries—send up new stems from the ground yearly. More than training, blueberry, currant, and gooseberry bushes need attentive pruning, as described on the following pages, to encourage a continuing supply of fruitful stems and eliminate played-out ones.

All types of blackberries and raspberries (known collectively as brambles) need training as well as regular pruning. The stems of some bramble varieties are self-supporting yet can easily become jumbled unless organized in some way. Other varieties have trailing stems that definitely become tangled if not trained to a structure. The purpose of training is to sort out the canes that will bear fruit in this year—and that should thereafter be removed or cut back—from those that will produce next year. Trellises of various designs are commonly used for this. In a home garden, the simplest structure would be a set of posts with galvanized wire strung tightly between them. If you string a pair of parallel horizontal wires, you can train this year's fruiters to

A simple, sturdy raspberry trellis consists of double rows of strong wires strung through 4-by-4 posts.

the top wire and next year's to the lower—or let next year's pile up on the ground. To restrain sprawlers, you may want to grow the plants in rows and confine them by stringing pairs of parallel wires at different levels on either side of the rows.

By their very nature berry vines, like other vines, need support. That is especially true for grapes and kiwi, two rampant growers discussed on the following pages. Training is also critical for organizing their stems: both grapes and kiwi bear fruit only on new shoots produced from last season's growth. Proper training will expose these fruiting branches to sunlight and air. The vines are typically trained to a permanent framework consisting of a trunk and fruiting arms. Suitable training structures include trellises, arbors, fences, and the same type of post-and-wire arrangement as described at left for brambles. Subsequent yearly pruning removes stems that have fruited and encourages new fruiting wood.

BLACKBERRY

DECIDUOUS

✄ MIDSUMMER AND DORMANT SEASON

Blackberry varieties from the midwestern and eastern states are typically stiff caned and upright to about 4 to 6 feet. Types grown in the West tend to be trailing (some are so distinctive that they have separate names, such as

Blackberries are borne on second-year canes.

'Arapaho', a thornless erect blackberry, is trained in hedgerows contained by wires strung between crossbars.

Prune blueberry bushes during dormancy (left); plants bear large crops of berries on the prior year's growth (right).

boysenberry, loganberry, marionberry, and ollallieberry). In the South, trailing types known as dewberries are often grown. Crosses between upright and trailing types are called semierect.

All blackberries bear fruit in the summertime. Though their roots are perennial, their canes are biennial: they develop and grow one year, flower and fruit the next. Hence the need to distinguish the two types of canes when training and pruning.

Though they don't need support, erect types can be tied to wire to help organize and harvest the canes. During the first year, cut back the canes to 2 to 2½ feet in midsummer to encourage side branching; cut the resultant side branches to 12 to 15 inches long late in the dormant season. After these branched canes bear fruit in the second year, cut them to the ground. Meanwhile, new canes will be growing from the ground; start the whole process over again.

Trailing and semierect types are best grown on some kind of trellis, even though semierect canes often become more upright as plants mature. In the first year, let the canes grow without pruning or training. When growth begins in the second year, train the 1-year-old canes onto the structure; thin to the desired number of canes and prune them back to 6 to 8 feet, spreading them fanwise. After harvesting, cut to the ground all canes that fruited. Now train the current season's canes onto the structure.

BLUEBERRY

DECIDUOUS (SOME ARE SEMIEVERGREEN)
✂ LATE DORMANT SEASON

Lowbush blueberry plants grow from a few inches tall to 2 feet high, spreading by underground roots to cover large areas. Most highbush varieties grow upright to 6 feet or more; a few are sprawling and less than 5 feet tall. Rabbiteye plants are often taller than highbush plants. All produce their summer fruit on 1-year-old growth.

Most highbush and rabbiteye varieties are handsome plants suitable for shrub borders or informal hedges. They will shape themselves, but they often produce so many fruit buds that their berries are undersized. This habit also slows the overall growth of the plants; therefore, you prune them to prevent overbearing. It's a good idea to keep first-year plants from bearing at all by stripping off their flowers. On older plants, cut back twig ends to a point where flower buds are widely spaced. Or simply remove some of the oldest branches (those more than 1 inch in diameter) each year. While you're at it, eliminate any weak shoots.

Remove flowers from first-year lowbush plants as well. Keep mature plants productive by cutting back all growth to 1 to 2 inches from the ground every few years. A plant won't produce any fruit in the season following such drastic pruning, so cut back only a third of your plants yearly to maintain a constant fruit supply.

ERECT BLACKBERRIES

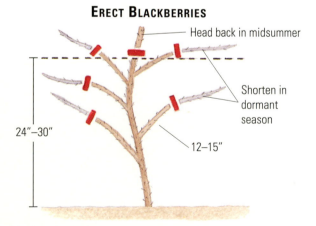

Head back in midsummer

Shorten in dormant season

24"–30"

12–15"

Head back each cane in midsummer to encourage branching; then shorten the resulting laterals during the dormant season. After a branched cane produces fruit in the second year, cut it to the ground.

SEMIERECT AND TRAILING BLACKBERRIES

Year-old canes

24"

36"

New canes

Cut to the ground after harvest

After canes grow for a year, train them onto the wires. After they produce fruit in their second year, cut them to the ground. Then train the new canes onto the wires.

CURRANT AND GOOSEBERRY

DECIDUOUS

✂ LATE DORMANT SEASON

These many-stemmed shrubs, growing 3 to 5 feet high and requiring no support, are closely related. Currants are thornless, whereas gooseberry varieties range from thorny to nearly spineless. The fruit is harvested in late spring to summer.

Currant bushes are thornless, making pruning a little easier.

Gooseberry bushes, like the red currants at top right, don't fruit on wood more than 3 years old.

Red and white currants bear most of their fruit on spurs of 2- and 3-year-old growth; gooseberries also produce at those sites, as well as along the sides of 1-year-old shoots. These plants are pruned similarly. After the first growing season, keep six to eight of the strongest stems. The next year, retain three or four stems each of 1- and 2-year-old growth. The following year and thereafter, remove all but three or four canes each of 1-, 2-, and 3-year-old growth. No bush should contain canes more than 3 years old (you'll notice that canes darken and peel more as they age). Shorten any overly long branches as needed during each dormant season.

Black currants fruit best on spurs of 1-year-old shoots. After the first growing season, keep six to eight canes. Each dormant season thereafter, leave three or four 2-year-old canes and six 1-year-old canes (you can keep more if the plant is very vigorous). Don't cut back the tips of black currant branches.

This red currant bush is thinned (top), leaving several canes each of 1-, 2-, and 3-year-old wood (bottom).

GRAPE

DECIDUOUS

✂ DORMANT SEASON

If all you want from a grapevine is leafy cover for an arbor or patio, you need only train a strong vine up and over its support and thin out the tangled growth each year. For good fruit production, however, you must follow more careful pruning procedures to ensure that the vine doesn't produce too much fruit—and that the fruit it does bear is of good quality. Depending on the variety and climate, the fruit ripens from early summer into fall. Prune during the dormant season; if you wait until late in the season, be sure to prune before the buds swell.

Fruit is borne on the current season's shoots, arising from growth that formed the previous season. The 1-year-old growth has smooth bark; older branches have rough, shaggy bark.

Several pruning methods are popular for grapes. The two most widely used are spur pruning and cane pruning. Muscadine grapes, grown in the South, are spur pruned. Generally, American varieties and French-American hybrids are cane pruned and European varieties spur pruned; there are exceptions, so use the method recommended for your variety. Regardless of the method chosen, the initial process of creating a framework is the same. See the training and pruning directions on the next page.

Continues >

Cane pruning is the method recommended for 'Buffalo', an American grape variety.

This grapevine, trained over a garden fence, is both fruitful and decorative.

PLANTING Set the bare-root grapevine before a post at the same depth as it grew in the nursery, and cut the stem back to two buds. (In some areas, planting deeper and cutting to one bud is recommended; check locally.)

FIRST SUMMER Let the vine grow unchecked; don't try to train its growth. The more leaves, the better the root development.

FIRST WINTER Select the sturdiest shoot for the trunk and remove all other shoots at their base. Tie the trunk to the post; then shorten the trunk to the three or four lowest buds.

TWO-WIRE TRELLIS Set stout posts in the ground 15 to 20 feet apart (farther apart for the more vigorous grapes, such as muscadines) so that their tops are 5 feet above the ground. String sturdy galvanized wire across the post tops and also at the 2½-foot level.

SECOND SPRING From the vigorous new shoots choose the strongest upright one for the continuation of the trunk; tie it to the post. Select two strong lower shoots for arms and tie them to the first wire. (If you don't have branching where you want it, pinch the trunk as needed to let new shoots develop.) Cut off all other shoots.

SECOND SUMMER When the trunk reaches the top wire, pinch it back to force branching. Train the two strongest shoots along the top wire; remove any others. Tie the lower arms along the lower wire; pinch back any lateral shoots developing from those arms to about 10 inches.

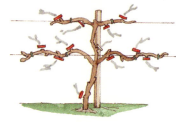

SECOND WINTER Cut back all growth on the trunk and arms; make sure both sets of arms are loosely tied to the wire. Don't prune yet for fruit production; vines are too immature.

THIRD SUMMER Allow the vine to grow, but remove any shoots sprouting on the trunk. Cane pruning and spur pruning differ from here on.

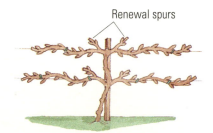

Renewal spurs

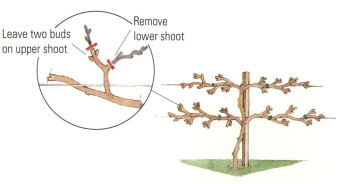

Leave two buds on upper shoot

Remove lower shoot

CANE PRUNING FROM THIRD WINTER Cut back each arm to 12 buds; these will bear fruit the next summer. Select two strong lateral shoots near the trunk and cut each to two buds; these are the renewal spurs. During next winter and every winter thereafter, remove the fruiting canes at their base. The renewal spurs will have produced several new shoots from which new fruiting canes can be selected. Choose the two longest and strongest shoots and cut each to 12 buds; tie these shoots to the wire. Select the two next best shoots as renewal spurs and cut each to two buds.

SPUR PRUNING FROM THIRD WINTER Remove weak side shoots from the arms. Leave the strongest shoots (spurs) spaced 6 to 10 in. apart, and cut each to two buds. Each spur will produce two fruit-bearing shoots during the next growing season. During next winter and every winter thereafter, remove the lower shoot on each spur and cut the upper stem to two buds. Those buds will develop into stems that bear fruit the following summer.

KIWI

DECIDUOUS

DORMANT SEASON AND SUMMER

Kiwi vines are rampant growers that are more easily managed if trained onto a structure such as a sturdy T-bar trellis (see illustration). Most ways of trellising grapes are also suitable for kiwi. Limit the plant to one strong, upright trunk and several main horizontal branches; these will be the vine's permanent framework.

Just as grapes do, kiwi vines bear fruit on new shoots from growth formed the previous summer. For greatest fruit production, prune a kiwi vine as you would a cane-pruned grapevine (see opposite page). Remove weak, damaged, and tangled growth. On old vines, cut off a few of the oldest fruiting shoots each year. Newer fruiting shoots will replace them. You will probably have to do additional pruning in summer to restrain a kiwi vine—cut out snarled stems and shorten overly long shoots. The fruit may be harvested in fall.

Unless you have a self-fruiting variety, you will need to grow a male plant to pollinate the female, fruit-bearing plant. Because the male plant's sole purpose is flower production, you can prune it back drastically after bloom.

KIWI VINE TRAINED ON A T-BAR TRELLIS

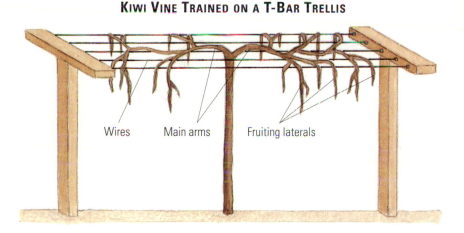

Wires   Main arms   Fruiting laterals

TOP: Kiwi fruit is carried on new side shoots growing from the prior year's wood.

BOTTOM: Prune twice yearly to tame rampant kiwi vines.

RASPBERRY

DECIDUOUS

AFTER FRUITING AND LATE DORMANT SEASON

Red raspberries, the sorts most commonly grown, include two types: summer-bearing raspberries, which fruit annually in summer on second-year canes; and everbearing (also called fall-bearing) raspberries, which produce twice on each cane, in the fall of the first year and again in the summer of the second year.

Raspberry plants are erect, with long, straight canes; they can be grown as free-standing shrubs and staked, but they're tidier and easier to manage if trained on a trellis or confined to a hedgerow (pairs of parallel wires strung 3 and 5 feet above the ground along either side of a row of plants). After planting cut back the cane, leaving just enough (about 6 inches) to serve as a marker.

Summer-bearing varieties should produce three to five canes in the first year. Tie these to the trellis when they get tall enough (or confine them to the hedgerow). To keep rows neat, dig or pull out any canes that grow more than 1 foot away from the trellis (or outside of the hedgerow). In the late dormant season cut the canes back to 5 or

How you prune a red raspberry bush depends on whether it is summer bearing or everbearing.

5½ feet (to 4 feet for a hedgerow). When growth recommences, new canes will appear all around the parent plant and even between the rows. After the original canes bear fruit, cut them to the ground. Tie the best 5 to 12 new canes to the trellis (or confine them to the hedgerow); they will bear next summer. Cut the remainder to the ground.

Everbearing raspberries fruit in their first fall on the top third of the cane and again in their second summer on lateral branches on the lower two-thirds of the cane. Cut off the upper portion after it has fruited, leaving the lower portion to bear next year. Cut out the cane entirely once it has fruited along its whole length.

As an alternative, you can follow the example of growers who cut everbearing canes to the ground yearly in fall after fruiting is finished (wait until the late dormant season in cold-winter regions). You'll sacrifice one of the annual crops in return for easy maintenance and a prolonged crop in summer. Use a powerful rotary mower in a large berry patch.

Black raspberries (blackcaps) are clump-forming plants with arching canes. No support is necessary. In summer, head back new canes at 1½ to 2 feet to force branching. At the end of the growing season, cut out all weak canes and remove those that fruited during the current season. In the late dormant season, cut back the remaining branches to about 10 inches. Fruit will be borne on side shoots from these branches. If you prefer trellising, head back new canes at 2 or 3 feet.

All raspberries are vulnerable to cane borers. Prune out and destroy any damaged canes below the entry points (look for pinhead-size holes in canes at or near ground level).

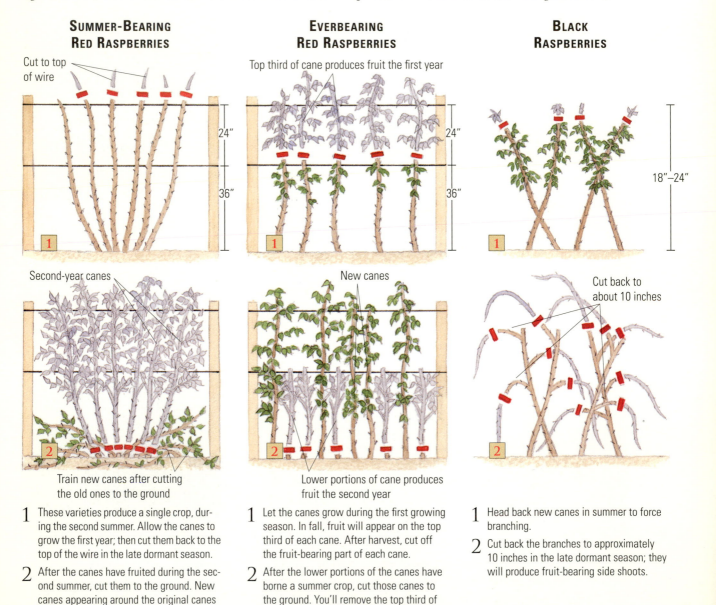

SUMMER-BEARING RED RASPBERRIES

Cut to top of wire

24"

36"

1

Second-year canes

Train new canes after cutting the old ones to the ground

2

1 These varieties produce a single crop, during the second summer. Allow the canes to grow the first year; then cut them back to the top of the wire in the late dormant season.

2 After the canes have fruited during the second summer, cut them to the ground. New canes appearing around the original canes will bear next summer.

EVERBEARING RED RASPBERRIES

Top third of cane produces fruit the first year

24"

36"

1

New canes

Lower portions of cane produces fruit the second year

2

1 Let the canes grow during the first growing season. In fall, fruit will appear on the top third of each cane. After harvest, cut off the fruit-bearing part of each cane.

2 After the lower portions of the canes have borne a summer crop, cut those canes to the ground. You'll remove the top third of new canes after they produce fall berries.

BLACK RASPBERRIES

18"–24"

1

Cut back to about 10 inches

2

1 Head back new canes in summer to force branching.

2 Cut back the branches to approximately 10 inches in the late dormant season; they will produce fruit-bearing side shoots.

INDEX

Page numbers in **boldface** indicate a main entry in one of the plant-by-plant pruning guides.